W9-ABG-814

The City as Catalyst

Other books by Diana Festa-McCormick:

Les Nouvelles de Balzac
Balzac

The City as Catalyst____

A Study of Ten Novels

Diana Festa-McCormick

Rutherford • Madison • Teaneck
Fairleigh Dickinson University Press
London: Associated University Press

© 1979 by Associated University Presses, Inc.

Associated University Presses, Inc.
Cranbury, New Jersey 08512

Associated University Presses
69 Fleet Street
London EC4Y 1EU, England

Associated University Presses
Toronto, Ontario, Canada M5E 1A7

First Printing 1979
Second Printing 1980

First paperback edition 1980

Library of Congress Cataloging in Publication Data

Festa-McCormick, Diana
    The City as Catalyst.

    Bibliography: p.
    Includes index
    1. Fiction—History and criticism. 2. Cities and towns in literature.
I. Title.
PN3352.C5F4   809.3'3   77-85595

ISBN 0-8386-2156-2 (cloth)
ISBN 0-8386-3081-2 (paper)

PRINTED IN THE UNITED STATES OF AMERICA

To Sergio, Marco, and Carlo
And to Henri
  "Vous me prêtâtes une ouie
  Fameuse et le temple; si du
  Soir la pompe est évanouie
  En voici l'humble résidu."

Contents

Introduction: The City

Upon entering the last quarter of the twentieth centruy, man seems to be obsessed, in fascination or in horrified contemplation with the theme of the city. Courses in urban studies are proliferating at all levels in our colleges. Volumes on the sociology of city life appear every month. The architecture of cities is severely scrutinized by art critics, aestheticians, champions of improved environment, politicians. The boldest of innovators among the architects have more than once indulged in what Frank Lloyd Wright in his autobiography called "an angry prophecy and a preachment," denouncing the city as "only a temporal hangover from the infancy of the race, to be outgrown as the performance of humanity grows," asserting that "civilizations died of cities" and that "those civilizations that built the greatest cities invariably died with them."[1]

Never perhaps since the erection of cathedrals following the year 1000, or since the flowering of medieval cities in Italy and the Low Countries in the centuries that followed, has mankind enjoyed such an opportunity to rebuild or to build urban centers, parks, roads, airfields, and waterways, as it has in the era ushered in by the cataclysmic destructions of World War II in Europe and in Asia. Elsewhere, in Venezuela and in Brazil, in Iran, in the newly independent countries of Africa and Oceania, cities have been mushrooming; administrative, shopping, and recreational centers have been erected; spacious parkways have been provided. Nevertheless, instead of deriving pride from these accomplishments—far superior, qualitatively and otherwise, to that of the nineteenth century, which had proved incapable of creating a viable style until a few bold spirits evolved one in Chicago (notably Richardson and Sullivan)—it seems that our age feels oppressed by what has repeatedly been termed "the shame of our cities."

Literature is, according to a hackneyed but not altogether inappropriate phrase, a criticism of life. It has indeed, with the nineteenth-century novel, provided the most cogent form of social criticism. Cities were not spared by Balzac, Dickens, and Zola, who alternately knelt in adoration at the altars of Paris and London (their dens of vice and prostitution, their jails, their markets, the wily contrivances of their lawyers) and inveighed against their diabolical power to corrupt. That twofold attitude toward the magnetic appeal of cities was assumed from the earliest antiquity, probably as soon as nomadic tribes encountered sedentary villages, plundered them, and ended in being assimilated by their cultures. The gardens of Babylon, the famed Sumerian and Egyptian capitals, the Athenian city in which Pericles took such pride, Republican Rome, and the metropolis boldly founded by Alexander to succeed Athens as the focus of Hellenism—all were extolled to the skies by statesmen, chroniclers, and poets. But they were also very soon assailed by moralists and by satirists for their venality and debauchery, for their pageants, for their organized games, and for the luxury of their art, which served only as decoys to draw the thoughts of people away from the monotony of work and from the urge to rebel against their rulers. Medieval Rome, the Florence of Dante and Savonarola, Avignon during its papal greatness, likewise aroused more denunciatory anathemas than eulogies in the Middle Ages. Even Venice, always expert at fomenting a myth around its uniqueness, seldom enjoyed the benefits of a literature portraying its seductiveness while its painters never ceased being fascinated with its canals, its galleys, and its palaces. The classical authors of seventeenth-century France often dealt harshly with Paris: one of the most genuinely Parisian among them, Boileau, composed a satire against its noise, traffic jams, pollution, and rampant crime. He was, of course, borrowing a classical topos from the Roman satirists. Horace in particular had, in a well-known satire (book 2, satire 6) contrasted the din of the cities with the peace of agrarian existence, for which he had yearned: "Hoc erat in votis." The English writer Raymond Williams treated many instances of British poets and prose writers praising pastoral life and lamenting the desertion of villages (see bibliography). The British writers at the time of John Gay and of the coffee houses of Addison and Steele proved, for a time, more entranced by the charms of urban life than their French contemporaries. The latter, most conspicuously Marivaux in his novels and Rétif de la Bretonne, enjoyed depicting country girls and peasants whose morals became corrupted (and their fortune easily made as a compensation) when they flocked to Paris to seek employment and sophistication.

With Rousseau, with the nostalgia for country churchyards and Cumberland lakes, the mourning for deserted villages, the idylls of Swiss poets and the pastoral miniature epic of *Hermann und Dorothea*, poets and novelists felt little urge to place city life at the core of their creation. The growth of industrialism in the nineteenth century, and the economic necessities that drew people to the city, brought about a new mood reflected in the literature of the time. The country more and more stood for integrity and wholesomeness, where urban centers appeared as forces of evil and corruption. Dickens's *Bleak House* is a good example of this double image, in which the serenity of nature in village life is contrasted to the suffocating air of London. Raymond Williams points out that "emigration to the colonies was seized as a solution to the poverty and overcrowding of the cities." Escape into distant regions became the dominant dream of peace. *Wuthering Heights, Great Expectations,* and *Alton Locke* are illustrations of "the way out from the struggle within English society to distant lands."[2]

The Romantics of England often focused their dreams around Scotland, the Alps, and Italy. Those of France remained attached to the one city where the king, the salons, and the Academy bestowed prestige and honors. Vigny wrote in 1831 a somber, apocalyptic poem on Paris doomed by revolutionary mobs and by the curse of hyperdeveloped civilization. Hugo usually reserved his evocations of old and of modern Paris for his novels. He remains, with Balzac and Zola, one of the three greatest portrayers of Paris in French fiction. His vision of the capital has been studied by his admirers and detractors alike. Baudelaire, in part inspired or feeling challenged by the towering poet then in exile in Guernsey, strikingly rendered the poetry of the city in a section of his *Fleurs du Mal*, which was added to the second edition of the volume. He also formulated a theory of modernity in literature and art that was to inspire painters in the age of Impressionism. In Russia, both Moscow and St. Petersburg served as settings for novels of Tolstoi and

Dostoevski, from *Anna Karenina* to *Crime and Punishment*, "The Death of Ivan Ilych" and "White Nights," or *The Eternal Husband*.

The poets of the twentieth century have evinced scant inclination to follow in the footsteps of Baudelaire's "Tableaux parisiens" or of Verhaerern's impassioned verse rhetoric on "tentacular cities." The venture into the creation of modern epics on Paterson, New Jersey, or on the Brooklyn Bridge, was reserved to the American successors of Walt Whitman, William Carlos Williams and Hart Crane. Around 1908-10, a group of French writers, inspired by both Whitman and the theories of sociologists such as Durkheim and Tarde, evolved a whole ideological structure that they designated by the name of Unanimism. Their achievement in the realm of poetry amounted to little. Their technique was contrived and hampered by their insistence on the message they were determined to put across; and they were lacking in imaginative force. But one of them at least, who assumed the pen name of Jules Romains, was endowed with a clear and comprehensive intellect and with a dogged persistence in the demonstration of his views through both argument and practice. Other attempts at creating the "Unanimist" novel, even if without the ambitious label, in languages other than French are not fully satisfying as works of art: Waldo Frank's *City Block* or Alfred Döblin's *Alexanderplatz*. They are, however, to be hailed as among the very few attempts made in this century to break away from the complacent submissiveness with which the craft of fiction has consented to stay within its traditional and somewhat narrow precincts. Poetry, drama, and the essay have ceased even to try to portray the collective life of modern cities. It is up to the cinema and to fiction to respond to the challenge. The writer of fiction, more or less forced to retain the curiosity of his readers through a fairly continuous and cumulative plot, cannot avail himself of the ubiquitous mobility of the camera. Some novelists, however, John Dos Passos notably more successfully than Jules Romains and, more recently in France, Le Clézio, have borrowed the camera eye of the moviemaker, at the risk of harming credibility for the reader who likes to cling to characters in their steady process of development.

Of the many ways in which the city may become the central theme, or even the protagonist, in modern fiction, the most appealing one is to resort to it as a backdrop for the reveries, wanderings, thoughts, feelings, and deeds of the characters. In an age when the pantheistic ecstasies provoked by nature seem to have lost the appeal they once held for our romantic forefathers—at the very time when city dwellers have fled to suburban residences and attractive summer camps—the poetry of the city is often rendered in prose either by foreigners who have long and fondly dreamt of the picturesque place they would one day visit (Proust dreaming of Venice, for instance, Larbaud of London, Rilke of Paris) or by men from the provinces (D'Annunzio or Mauriac discovering the capital of their country with a sense of elation). Those poetical moments may occur as the all-knowing novelist describes the setting in which his characters evolve; they may assume the form of vignettes perceived by the heroes when a passionate mood in them enables them to seize the seductive aspects of streets, trees, and swarming life around them. The same novelists who have cursed the French capital as an arena for ferocious ambitions, Balzac for instance, are also those who have felt and conveyed, in a rich palette of adjectives and images, the alluring beauty of Paris: *The Girl with the Golden Eyes*, that strange tale of lesbian love, is also a most sumptuous display of colors in *The Human Comedy*. Zola, who in *L'Assommoir* and in three or four other volumes, did not recoil from exposing the sordidness of Paris in its workmen's districts—petty bourgeois dwellings and prostitutes' haunts —included in his long saga one volume at least, *Une Page d'Amour*, which contains the most delicate and rapturous tributes to the poetry of Paris. Iris Murdoch can intersperse her tortuous stories of wretched and self-tormenting couples with the most graphic and the most suggestive evocations of London streets, churches, and pubs (in *Under the Net* and several other novels).

It is to be expected that corruption, decay, and vice would provide more fertile material for modern novelists than the eventless social life of the rich and the snobs or the business districts where robbery takes on airs of respectability. Dickens had not flinched from the bitter and ugly reality of London, in *Bleak House* and elsewhere, even as he sentimentalized upon the misfortunes of martyred children. Bely treated St. Petersburg in the manner of an apocalyptic prophet who loved the very boulevards and quays and the gigantic statue that he doomed to annihilation. Dos Passos saw

New York as an inhuman force that grinded the lives of all ill-starred immigrants who arrived to its shores. He envisaged for the cruel city the same fate of Nineveh and Babylon, and of all capitals whose existence rested on the exploitation of nameless masses. He conformed in this to views expressed by the historian-sociologist-philosopher Lewis Mumford, for whom the expansion of small centers in what he calls the "megalopolis" produces a germ of evil and destruction. "This metropolitan civilization contains within itself the explosive forces that will wipe out all traces of its existence," he wrote, expressing a belief in a kind of fatality inherent in the very notion of large establishments, at the expense of the individual.[3] The Chicago novelists, Nelson Algren and James Farrell among the most vocal, have likewise been both fascinated and repelled by the splendor, the vitality, and the crass vulgarity of their city. All of them, the Americans more determinedly than the Europeans, appear to be convinced that a curse hangs upon the tentacular grip of the metropolis. Cruelly, devilishly, they mock all the utopian dreams of the nation that had once accepted it as a civic duty to pursue happiness, immune from the malediction that doomed the older continent. Like the somber James Thomson wandering in his Dantesque *City of the Dreadful Night* a century ago, they found no solace in the metropolis, only the wreckage of

> The joys, the peace, the life-hope, the abortions
> Of all things good which should have been our portions,
> But have been strangled by the City's curse.
> (section 9, ll. 18-21)

In the chapters that follow, allusions will occasionally be made to the poetical transfiguration of a city (Venice or London or Paris) by the imagination of a writer who eventually wends his way toward it like a pilgrim, to watch his dream be fulfilled or collapse. It would hardly be possible to eliminate altogether the role of the city as background and to divorce its parks and alleys and bridges from the moods of the characters who live and love and struggle there. After all, objects cannot but be seen through given sets of eyes, and the perspective varies with each viewer.[4]

My aim, however, is not to confront the novelist's vision with reality and to appraise the degree of objectivity of the images, but to look rather for the reverse procedure, whereby the object itself will direct or influence vision. There are writers who have seen in cities forces all of their own; they envisaged them not as elements of poetic reflection, but as dynamic energy incessantly in motion, reshaping man's destiny. For such authors, the city exists well beyond the negligible individual or even beyond the masses. It lives on, unconcerned and removed, while the inhabitants trudge their labyrinthine ways. In those novels, the city often is a catalyst, or a springboard, from which visions emerge that delve into existences unimaginable elsewhere. The city there acts as a force in man's universe; it is a constant element, immutable in its way while constantly renewing itself. It serves as a repository for miseries, hardships, and frustrations, but also for ever-renascent hopes. It holds up a mirror to man's folly; it derides his futility against a background of eternity. My attempt is through a very few novelists of several countries, to characterize the city as a protagonist in fiction, projecting visions and molding individuals.

Examples other than those chosen would have served as well— Farrell's Chicago; Döblin's Berlin; Joyce's Dublin; the London of Dickens, Virginia Woolf, Iris Murdoch, and Valéry Larbaud; the Vienna of Broch, Musil, and von Doderer. An exhaustive study of the city in literature, even if limited to nineteenth- or twentieth-century authors, would require many volumes, and perhaps the concerted efforts of many minds. My choices have been made more in keeping with personal preferences, with little aim at establishing principles of continuity in order either to justify sociological theories or to emphasize selected aspects of the city in literature. Rather, I have wanted to be an observer of the dramas contained within, so that from them might emerge the varied, contradictory, mutable, pervasive image, which is that of the city itself.

NOTES TO INTRODUCTION

1. Frank Lloyd Wright, *An Autobiography* (New York: Dell, Sloan and Pearce, 1943), p. 317.
2. See Raymond Williams's *The Country and the City* (New York: Oxford University Press, 1973), p. 281. Students of Dickens also have often shown how obsessed he was with London, as a living reality and as a metaphor, in most of his novels. Overcrowding, disease, poverty, injustice, the constant threat of prison for debtors, and the omnipresence of death were among the evils that his fiction denounced. A monograph, by Alex

Welsh, *The City of Dickens* (Oxford: Clarendon Press, 1971), treats in some detail that aspect of Dickens's fiction.

3.   See Lewis Mumford's *The City in History* (New York: Harcourt, Brace and World, 1961), p. 525.

4.   One of the most admired modern architects and town planners, Le Corbusier, never ceased advising his often unbelieving contemporaries that poetry, in the broader sense of the word, should rank high among the aims pursued by the science of "urbanisme." In a series of manifestos published in French as *Urbanisme* in 1929 and in America as *The City of To—Morrow* (Cambridge, Mass.: MIT Press, 1971) he asked "Why should not the town be, even today, a source of poetry?" (p.xxi). He warned those in charge of reconstructing Europe soon after World War II that "Hygiene and moral health depend upon the layout of cities. Without hygiene and moral health, the social cell becomes atrophied" (p. xxvii). Le Corbusier, Frank Lloyd Wright, and other architects who denounced the perils of intensive urbanization had been preceded by sociologists of the Chicago School, early in the twentieth century, and by Joseph Lincoln Steffens, who vituperated against urbanization in *The Shame of Our Cities* (New York: McClure and Phillips, 1904). The great German sociologist Georg Simmel, also early in the twentieth century, wrote an epochal essay, "Die grossstädte und das Geistesleben," which appeared in a collection entitled *Die Grossstadt, Vorträge und Aufsätze zur Städeausstellung*, edited by K. Bücher and others (Dresden: Von Zahn and Jaensch, 1903), pp. 185-206. It is translated by another eminent American sociologist, Edward A. Shils, as "The Metropolis and Mental Life," in *Syllabus and Selected Reading* (Chicago: University of Chicago Bookstore, 1936). Among the many books by Lewis Mumford, *The City in History* (see n. 3) has attained the status of a classic. In France a three-day symposium was held (April 29 - May 1, 1973) on the eighteenth-century city, at Aix-en-Provence, and the volume that came out of the discussions appeared in 1975, edited by Henri Coulet and published by Edisud, *La Ville au XVIIIe siècle*. A veteran champion of old streets and historical places in France, Georges Pillement, published a severe criticism of the wanton destruction of Paris: *Paris Poubelle* (Paris: Pauvert, 1974). In England modern historians have echoed, with somewhat less sanctimonious sternness, the prophecies of doom of the Victorian foes of the city: Carlyle, Ruskin, Arnold, and Morris. Among those historians are Donald I. Olsen (*The Growth of Victorian London* [London: Batsford, 1976]) and Derek Fraser (*Urban Politics in Victorian England* [Leicester: University Press, 1976]).

The City as Catalyst

1

Balzac's *Girl with the Golden Eyes:* Parisian Masks, Not Faces

Honoré de Balzac (1799-1850), who was bent on capturing all aspects of unrecorded history in his work, so as to show life's contradictions and the varied shapes of society, found in Paris an endless source of inspiration. Most stories from his collection of *Scenes from Private Lives* reflect the many-layered patterns of Parisian society. The well-known *Père Goriot* emphasizes the molding power of the big capital and the alternating flickers of success contrasted to the vast number of failures it imposes upon its inhabitants. *Louis Lambert, The Ass's Skin, Ferragus, The Duchess of Langeais, Lost Illusions, the Nucingen House,* even *Beatrix* or *Z. Marcas*, and others are part of the panoramic view of Paris to be found in *The Human Comedy*, that large number of volumes whose protagonists, men and women from all walks of life, form a lasting portrait of nineteenth-century France.

Balzac's main philosophical axioms pointed to the inseparable aspects of the physiological and psychological natures in man and to the roles of passion and will, both in defiance and affirmation of human limitations. The short novel I have chosen to examine is not among his best known. Critics seem mostly to have shied away from it, due perhaps to the delicacy of the subject matter and to the strong sexual overtones. Yet *The Girl with the Golden Eyes* is among the most curious in Balzac's literary production and, within its brevity, illustrates the author's inventiveness, daring, and the underlying premises of the destructiveness of all passions—be they those concerning ideas, or a search, or, as in this case, the urge to reign alone upon the heart and life of a loved one. Balzac has often shown in his works that all ideas that take possession of man, all desires for domination and exclusiveness, lead inevitably to doom.

The role of the city in *The Girl with the Golden Eyes* is indirect. Yet, through the author's initial presentation, it is all the more striking, insinuated in the events rather than forcefully projected in them. Paris is here both the theater and the main actor in the drama; it is the backdrop for action and the central focus upon which all action converges. The narrative was composed in 1834, early in Balzac's career when most of his shorter works were written. The language is evocatively rich and pictorial, influenced perhaps by the wealth of colors and contrasts the author had observed in Delacroix's canvases. The plot is complex and almost fantastic, but Balzac has often shown a predilection for the inexplicable, for random choices and alliances made through intuition and related to man's mystical nature. The title was to have been, initially, *The Woman with Red Eyes*, no doubt before the author's interest had switched from the strangeness of human relations to the manipulative force of the city. The emphasis, from the passionate "red" of the woman's eyes, then became subtly blended with the golden aura of Parisian life. The actual title connotes both the equivocal nature of the story and its brilliant coloring.

The introduction, or the opening pages, of *The Girl with the Golden Eyes*[1] has often been seen as a discordant note with little or no relation to the rest of the story.[2] The fact that Balzac published the work piecemeal, beginning it in 1834 and completing it the following year,[3] has lent more credibility to the assumption of discontinuity, of afterthought or change of intention, for those long passages on Paris and Parisian society. I tend to agree, however, with the view that the initial pages, far from being a mere setting that could easily be replaced with another, without thereby altering the balance of the story, are essential not only to the development but to the understanding of the work.[4]

The introductory pages do not, in fact, bear discernibly upon the events that are later unfolded. But it is here that the setting is presented in minute detail, and it is through this presentation that the story acquires a larger context and meaning than the mere plot might indicate. It is on the very first page also that one of the subtler themes woven throughout the composition is introduced—that of masks and the role they play in an unstable and compressed society. Masks are instruments that both dissemble and reveal, or rather they are the devious means to arrive at a truth buried within the conscience of man, in the act itself of masking that truth. Georges Buraud's definition is appropriate here: "A mask is the semblance of a face put upon a body to which it does not appear to belong and which nevertheless is born of it and circuitously expresses its mystery."[5] *The Girl with the Golden Eyes* deals precisely with a set of screens, interdependent and polymorphic in relation with the central force, Paris, itself a mask and a revealing stage. Upon that stage people hide and display themselves simultaneously, as they cloak themselves with the transparent Parisian veil. As the story opens, what is visible upon the countenance of the people is the very curtain behind which they are sheltered; that curtain is composed of nothing less than the streets of Paris, a cloak of anonymity that protects them and bares their faces.

> One of those sights in which most horror is to be encountered is, surely, the general aspect of the Parisian populace—a people fearful to behold, gaunt, yellow, tawny. Is not Paris a vast field in perpetual turmoil from a storm of interests beneath which are whirled along a crop of human beings, who are, more often than not, reaped by death, only to be born again as pinched as ever, men whose twisted and contorted faces give out at every pore the instinct, the desire, the poisons with which their brains are pregnant. . .? [P. 281]

The nakedness on people's features is the protective varnish put on when one is subject to external scrutiny. It is the removal of all expression so that inner turmoils remain invisible and buried within. Hence the pallor, the deathlike inpenetrability of countenances divested of vitality. Yet the baring of a face only removes the outer layer, the coloring of emotions and the hues of feelings. What remains beneath are the scars of desires and the force of passions; these, deprived of raiment, now barren and exposed, bend and reshape the very bones to which they cling. The nakedness is indeed a mask meant to protect the individual from the threatening presence of others, yet it ends by adhering to one's skin, and thus reveals a more intimate nature and all the contortions of inner struggles.

> Not faces so much as masks; masks of weakness, masks of strength, masks of misery, masks of joy, masks of hypocrisy; all alike worn and stamped with the indelible signs of a panting cupidity? What is it they want? Gold or pleasure? [P. 281]

The emphasis on the negative, "not" faces, establishes the circular movement that, begun with "one of those sights" of the opening lines, closes upon itself, with a questioning note that is not an interrogation and an assertion denying its very premises. Are not, in fact, the "masks of weakness" a mirror to man's inner defenselessness, or the "masks of misery, . . .of joy, . . .of hypocrisy" the reverse side of a conscience painted on the surface, the solftly woven cloth, transparent and porous, put upon the passions of men? The horrifying hollowness of spectral figures along the streets is thus, interchangeably, the core and the varnish of the Paris in which the people reside. It is also a mirror of the "cruel miasmas" (p. 203) of poverty and filth, and the vanity that scars the gilded halls of the rich.[6] Gold reigns here, through ephemeral pleasure or the oppressiveness of its absence, glittering or dull, in the rituals that it imposes upon the satanic Parisian temple. Gold is the mask itself that clings to the heart of people and dictates their actions:

> In no other country has life ever been more ardent or acute. The social nature, even in fusion, seems to say after each completed work: "Pass on to another!" just as Nature says herself. Like Nature herself, this social nature is busied with insects and flowers of a day—ephemeral trifles, and so, too, it throws up fire and flame from its eternal crater. [P. 282]

The comparison of Parisian life with nature implies cyclical renewal in which single facets of existence become absorbed within an expanded context. The characters in the story suggest the same pattern, each of them a mere segment of human nature, vital and yet incomplete, each essential in his own element but negligible within the complexity of a larger entity and scope. Together, they are a microcosm within the macrocosm of the city; separate, they deliver their lines and act out their brief span of life before they fade away, replaced by other events and other people in the ever-renewing scale of Parisian society.

The movement in the story projects a character, who leads onto another, introduces yet another, before closing upon a new figure that draws the final line and closes the circle of events. Each of the characters is a reality that hides behind a screen and a pretense that is a truth. Each wears a mask and acts a role, and truth oscillates between the image and the act, in keeping with the dictates of a law that binds them and defies their individual will. That law emanates from Paris, which has molded them and shaped their desires. The plot is complex. It involves a lesbian love, a heterosexual passion, covetous and calculating interests in the background, and, finally, bloody vengeance. The story closes on a note of emptiness, of remorse, and of irremediable loss. What is left is a sense of continuity in which passions, lost innocence, and vices are the constant pawns in an endless game of greed and domination.

The story, perhaps a little baroque and somewhat incredible, involves a young man, Henri de Marsay, who one day on the streets of Paris catches a glimpse of an extraordinary girl in a passing carriage. She spies him too, but the presence of an old woman guardian prevents an immediate encounter. It will come later, arranged by the girl, accompanied by all the accoutrements of romantic intrigue, including blindfolds and the risk of death. Marsay is taken to the abode of the girl and becomes her lover. The mystery increases, however, for behind the obvious candor and virginity of the girl, there is a consummate mistress in the art of love. At the culmination of her passionate surrender, Paquita murmurs a name, "Margarita." Feeling betrayed, Marsay organizes his vengeance and steals unexpectedly back into the house. When he reaches the innermost chamber and sanctuary of love, he finds Paquita dead in a sea of blood and, beside her, a woman standing in passionate and vindictive frenzy. They look in horror at each other, and in a flash recognize their alliance of blood: they are brother and sister, and the dead girl had loved their androgynous unity and surrendered to one love alone. The old mother who had bartered Paquita's freedom for gold, is paid again for her silence and tacit acquiescence. Beyond the violent triangle of desire and vengeance in which the roles are often tenuous and interchangeable, stands the greed of the old woman, who symbolizes Paris' manipulative force, and the facelessness of passions condemned to yield to the city's ascendency.

The first image to emerge in the story is that of a strikingly beautiful young man with purity of lines in features and grace in his demeanor. He is Henri de Marsay, son of Lord Dudley.[7] Young de Marsay, who never knew either his real or adoptive father, has the physical appearance of one, the name of the other, and the vices of both. With him emerges the first of the set of masks in the story. He is an ephebe whose delicate head would sit proudly upon the body of a woman; his "maleness" is thus tinged with a touch of femininity, suggesting at once male and female qualities, and hence a sort of incompleteness and, at the same time, a potential for realization in both. If sexual ambiguity lies at the core of the story's thematic structure, however, its importance should be measured against a backdrop of larger ambiguities. Sexuality is in essence a means more than an end, whereby all reality appears in turn diminished and enlarged in the face of a challenge. Just as Henri de Marsay's innocent appearance enhances his ability to harm, so does the graceful perfection of his beauty expose him to equivocal ties. It is important to notice in this conjunction that this conquering Don Juan who is conscious of his power upon both men and women is, in a way, as easily conquered as he is alluring. He had been thinking, for instance, "of nothing at all" (p. 307)—and had thus been far from organizing the eventual success of his enterprise—when he had been attracted by a young beauty looking at him in passionate recognition. Fatuously, he accepts the role of seducer, while he pursues the girl who had first spied him. It is known, of course, that Balzac had intended a more aggressive role for de Marsay when he first conceived *The Girl with the Golden Eyes* (See Castex, *Histoire de Treize*, in notes for a full genesis of the work). The implied passivity or frustration that later came to characterize the young man—from his first encounter with Paquita to the end, when he is reduced to witness the result of a vengeance he had intended to execute himself—could hardly have been accidental or meant to have little bearing upon the general context of the story. One tends to believe instead, that it must have been a device that should emphasize both the fallaciousness of all appearances—and hence what inevitably transpires behind all screens— and the subordinate nature of all actions and "initiatives" to the ruling force that emanates from the city. A more marked "manliness" and a clearer idea of his role would have made of de Marsay the main protagonist; but the title of the work itself implies that the central role is to be found elsewhere. The Girl with the Golden Eyes is obviously Paquita. But in a story subtly interwoven with the motif of masks, what is obvious is often deceptive.

The image of Paris in the story does not come out so much through a particular atmosphere or a section of town—although the story takes place in a precise location, between St. Lazare, Rue de Castiglione, and the Tuileries. Places themselves, such as streets and even Paquita's opulent and seragliolike apartment, do not reflect tastes or stations of life so much as they mirror a peculiar aspect of the city's energy. Paris' pervading force is gold. Although the initial pages of the story aim at embracing all facets of the power of gold, including that which is manifested through its absence and negation, the events in the story concentrate on the very sheen of the metal as it forms a kind of veil and magic transparency over the city's existence. Gold is not merely Paris' source of energy, it is also its protective covering through which the ugliness of corruption and bartering is not immediately visible. But at the heart of Parisian life there is gold, and the four protagonists of the story are all tacitly linked within its dominion.

Henry de Marsay, who is introduced as a "love-child" (p. 297) or a child of love, should more properly be called a gold child. If he was conceived in love, of love he retains merely the image, while the letters of his name remain spelled in the gold that bought them. Old de Marsay whose name he inherited never knew his adoptive child, and had only accepted him in exchange for money, thus conferring on Lord Dudley's love-child a gilded name. As for Paquita, her eyes are of a striking "golden yellow that gleams" (p. 308). Gold is, however, the girl's mask, a kind of adornment that glitters and enjoins attention and homage, but behind which there is a vulnerable face at the mercy of a passionate thirst. Paquita's eyes, transparent, catlike, and brilliantly spangled, both reflect and deflect the image of Paris. They magnetize and conjure visions of abandon and possession; but where the force of the city is kept hidden, Paquita seems to display it in a burst of fire and passion. Yet, precisely in the juxtaposition of the roles here, true strength rests: real, where it is veiled, illusory, where it seems patent.

Paquita's initial daring, when she discovers and approaches the young man who caught her attention, is soon put to a test. She cannot decipher the love letter de Marsay manages to get to her; in spite of her apparent emancipation, she can in fact neither read nor write. She must rely on Cristenio, the black man "who worships" her (p. 329), to have the letter interpreted. Paquita's only strength lies in the love and devotion she is able to inspire—a dependent sort of strength, therefore, subject to the vagaries and manifestations of all passions. She knows English, yet she is not English. Presumably, she knows Spanish, too, for that is her mother tongue. But the language of Paris escapes her. The words she utters are supposedly English, but the reader of course sees them transcribed in French, and never a word of English is in fact uttered in the conversations. The result is somewhat ambiguous: English, which is indeed French, and French which is supposed to be English. Both languages thus hold a measure of fiction and are a mask subordinate to the one they endeavor to hide, which is the language of the heart. Symbolically, more than the strict meaning of words escapes Paquita in the city where she has come to live, and she remains to the end an outsider. She is a stranger in a more complex way than that of mere nationality and diction. She watches the power play of gold and the games of love, subjugated by the first and entranced with the second. She knows that she must embrace a totality of life, but her links with truth are only sought in the realm of love. "The Balzacian character realizes that the poetry of the heart must integrate itself, unless it be doomed, into a social prose which *is* man's destiny," writes Michel Zeraffa.[8] "Prose" indeed escapes Paquita, and she only goes through the motions of grasping the demands of a society that she does not understand. What appears as a gleam of gold in her eyes does not come from the powerful influence of the precious metal. It is rather the muted reflection of her unappeasable yearning for love, and hence is a mask, the imitation of strength and dominance, which submits to the dictates of passion.

The power play that emanates from Paris, the tension that is established among all human beings who come within its sphere and that oscillates in whimsical motion between conquerors and conquered, is composed of an endless chain of gold. Within that chain, Paquita too has her link—not through her "golden eyes," which are a mere decoy, but through a force that has branded her life and against which she fights in vain. She is the child of a "slave bought in Georgia for her rare beauty" (p. 326), who had in turn sold her daughter for money. The old mother appears only briefly in the story, but her sphinxlike presence stands as a symbol of the city's mastery over the Parisian crowd through its gold. Her impenetrable face shows the barrenness of the unquenchable passion that bequeathed a double slavery to her daughter. Having herself been trapped through an exchange of gold, her physical freedom was curtailed; her taste for gambling has subjugated her spirit. Paquita's movements, too, are strictly supervised, and her spiritual bondage originates from her impossible yearning for unity in love. Mother and daughter have both ended in the Parisian maze, drawn and fastened within its glittering rays.

What Paquita shares also with de Marsay, in a deeper sense by far than the obvious attraction of the senses, is the common lineage that bartered their identity for the price of gold. Contingent on this heritage of personalities, which have eventually been assumed in defiance perhaps of their respective natures, the two share a certain ambiguity of behavior, or they violate at least some of the traditional social patterns. De Marsay's personality, in spite of his courage and dexterity, does suggest certain "feminine" qualities, while that of Paquita, her delicate beauty notwithstanding, is at times more in keeping with customary male comportment. Henri de Marsay had sensed from the first that she "must have downy threads on the third phalanx of her fingers" (p. 308), more like a tiger than a compliant girl. Their behavior when they meet in the love nest lined in purple and gold confirms these impressions. The young man arrives blindfolded, having been taken in great secrecy in a fast-drawn carriage, more like an abducted maiden than the conquering cavalier he is supposed to be. As he enters, Paquita "pushed him on to a divan" (p. 333) and, a little later, as he feels "with an indescribable intoxication the voluptuous pressure of this girl," she unties "with a gesture of wonderful sweetness the young man's scarf" (p. 335). Clearly, the roles are somewhat reversed, but ambiguity is here another facet of the theme of masks, which does not in itself suggest false premises but, rather, dimly defined boundaries. It is as if, at each turn, every character in the story could acquire a different personality without betraying the old one—as if both Paquita and de Marsay could, at will, be at least partially fulfilled in the role of woman or that of man, as a master or as a slave. "If I am a slave, I am a queen too" (p. 336), Paquita candidly admits, instinctively knowing that each role is limited, disguised and displayed at once, and subject to the unstable demands of the world in which she lives. "Give me a feast such as men give when they love," she entreats, "intoxicate me, then kill me" (p. 336). The lesson is clear, all has a price, and all conquest has a flaw; all is fluid and interchangeable, easily accessible and withdrawn at once. Paquita dresses her lover in "a robe of red velvet," "a woman's bonnet," and finally wraps him in a shawl before she surrenders to him (p. 337). Her supreme abandon is thus to a masked man, whose mask is transparent and enticing: a womanlike man whose embrace is both new and old for the virgin girl without purity. Their union will be for each the extension of the other, or another dimension of the self, each being, through a portion of the other, an androgynous totality: the young man, becoming partially woman, joined to the girl whose lesbian love has afforded her access to the domain of the male.

Literary masks are as insidious a presence as that of mirrors, which reflect reality and, at the same time, substitute an image in its place. Thus the reflected image often suggests a certain complexity of values, since features that would otherwise remain unnoticed without the presence of mirrors retain nevertheless a reality outside of them. But if both mirrors and masks are necessary for the discernment of truth, it follows that, with their removal, reality is no longer visible. It is, in a way, in order to see him better that Paquita decks Henri in a red robe and has him wear a woman's bonnet; and it is also through this disguise, one must assume, that she is able to discover fully her lover's maleness. "She discovers man with delight," says Félicien Marceau,[9] and with this discovery her femaleness is finally realized. But having seen beyond the mask, she now means, in a way, to shatter the mirror and behold her lover in sensuous and ecstatic surrender. "Be what you are" (p. 346), she tells him the next time she meets him, as he automatically reaches for the red robe. Masks are no longer needed, she thinks, and the nearness of their bodies will convey the truth. Ironically, however, if it is through masks that reality is better revealed, unfeigned reality reverts to masks. As she passionately holds her lover and looks rapturously at his undisguised features, Paquita now cries out, in recognition, the name of a woman—"Margarita." With that cry she reasserts the force of the mask as inseparable from naked reality. At the same time the cry points to the duality contained in the respective female-male identity of de Marsay and of her own, beyond all protective screens. The mask is itself a truth that cloaks truth, congruent with the notion that reality is a lie that shields equivocation. The power that brings them together in the story and makes of the two elements a single and compelling new reality, is Paris itself. Suffused in an invisible curtain of gold, the city is the underlying motif that molds and re-creates at each turn entities of blended truths and amalgamated lies.

A woman's name escaping a woman's lips at the very moment of supreme recognition of her lover's maleness, reestablishes abruptly the ascendency that the absent Margarita holds over Paquita and, implicitly, the force of the gold that had bought her. Margarita Euphémia Porrabéril of San Real had paid in gold for her most cherished possession and had thus conveyed to her beautiful slave a legacy of ambiguity embedded in the luminosity of the precious metal. The fact that the marquise is absent, however, during the developments of the story serves two purposes: first, it makes possible the lovers' meetings and keeps them, for the time being, undetected; second, it underlines the marquise's own dependency on the city's manipulative force for an unchallenged power over the girl. As long as she is in London, her blood-scribbled letters are a mere echo of her jealous domination, and Paquita can oppose to them her own resourcefulness and the strength of her desire for a man's love.[10] But when Margarita returns to Paris she becomes the city's own instrument, claiming in blood the life she had molded in gold. Since it was already clear at this point in the story that Paquita's absent lover and master is a woman, and that her physical resemblance with de Marsay is striking and instrumental in the girl's surrender, one cannot simply assume that Margarita's bloody vengeance and subsequent confrontation with her unknown brother have the only purpose of a dramatic denouement. The denouement could in fact have been equally dramatic, if less equivocal, had de Marsay himself been able to carry out his own intended vengeance against the girl and punished her for having enticed him to "open his heart" (p. 348), only to find that her heart was still contaminated by the presence of another. But this would have underlined the theme of jealousy and assumed rights, rather than the city's empire through gold masks.

While there are no doubts that Henri "had sworn Paquita's death" (p. 352), however, and that the girl in unquestionably doomed, the whole structure of the story points to the necessity of the girl's death through the same power that had shaped her life. When de Marsay steals back into the house in order to execute his own dismal designs, the victim has already been claimed by the marquise. The young man's subordinate role and, implicitly, his more feminine characteristics come once more to light here; they will retreat at the end only in order to establish an androgynous integration with his female counterpart, the marquise of San Real. "The woman has robbed me even of my revenge!" he exclaims; but he still believes he will have the last word by appealing to the law against the yet unkown "woman." Not until he enters the love chamber now splattered in blood[11] will he have sensed how ephemeral human will is and how vain are its desires. In a frenzy, Margarita stands over her now expired mistress and screams the last words of her short-lived triumph: "For the blood you gave him you owe me all your own! Die, die, suffer a thousand deaths!" (p. 355). The penalty for Paquita's transgression against her ambiguous sexual ties branded in gold, is blood; the loss of her virginity and her claim to identity beyond the dominion of masks entail death. But the story cannot simply end here, for this then would be the marquise's tragic vengeance and not the city's. Only when Margarita discovers Henri is she fully defeated, when she realizes that the girl had not truly betrayed her but that she had, rather, loved another aspect of the same person. "Forgive me, Paquita" (p. 356), she now utters, understanding finally that there are no masters and slaves, but only master-slaves, in a world of deceptive masks ruled by gold. Her last gesture of bitter acquiescence is to pay in gold the silence of Paquita's mother, as the events come finally full circle where the story began: in the realm of gold and masks introduced in the initial pages. The same power that had ruled over Paquita's life now buys the tacit approval of her death, while a golden mask figuratively covers the lime pit where her body is to be buried.

Thus the story ends on a note of total defeat for all. What remains is a set of screens that reveals more than it conceals the vulnerability of men. Gold changes hands, buys, sells in turn, and remains the only constant feature in the shifting world of Paris. The long descriptions of the restless Parisian crowds in the first portion of the story find an ironic coincidence in the concluding pages. The former presents larger and more impersonal crowds, and the latter show Henri de Marsay casually strolling in the same Tuileries where his adventure started. In both images, framed against a background of fermenting streets and the sudden mesmerizing calm of the park, the unseen force is that of the city. Paris is the only constant power in the story and the invisible thread that holds together a whole society, lending it "masks of weakness, of strength, of misery, of joy, of hypocrisy," only to expose the transient nature of a humanity caught in the magical reflection of its gold.

Notes to Chapter 1

1. The title is coined from the text itself. The story belongs to a series of three novels entitled *History of the Thirteen*, together with *The Duchess of Langeais* and *Ferragus*. The "Thirteen" are a group of young men who have formed an alliance based on daring exploits, sort of social conquerors and outlaws at the same time. To this group belongs Henri de Marsay of *The Girl with the Golden Eyes*. His reference to the difficulty of breaking some mysterious ties he has in Paris, when Paquita asks him to go away with her, is to the alliance itself. Also, when he returns to the girl's house with murderous intentions at the end, he is accompanied by four young men who belong to the famous "Thirteen." For a relation between the young adventurers and their troubled times, see Maurice Bardèche, *Une Lecture de Balzac* (Paris: Les Sept Couleurs, 1964), pp. 153-63. The English translation I have used for the quotations is that of Ernest Dowson: Honoré de Balzac, *The Thirteen and Other Stories* (New York: Croscup and Sterling Company, 1901), pp. 281-357.
2. See Genevieve Delattre's article, "De Séraphita à 'La Fille aux Yeux d'Or,'" in the 1970 edition of *L'Année Balzacienne*. Also, Pierre Barbéris's introduction to *La Fille aux Yeux d'Or* in the Livre de Poche (Paris) edition, 1972.
3. See Castex, *Histoire des Treize* (Paris: Garnier Frères, 1966), p. 355.
4. In this context, see Nicole Mozet, "Les Prolétaires dans *La Fille aux Yeux d'Or*," *L'Année Balzacienne* (1974), pp. 91-119, in which she sees in Paris the main "actant" in the multiple triangles of relationships.
5. Georges Buraud, *Les Masques* (Paris: Edition du Seuil, 1948), p. 13. The translation is my own.

6. See in this connection Léon Emery, *Balzac en sa Création* (Lyon: Audin Editeur, 1947), pp. 78-79. Paris appears as an organic edifice in Mr. Emery's interpretation, and from it springs a poetry of urbanism composed not only of granite and large buildings but of a forceful and sinister vitality.

7. For the role of Lord Dudley and that of other British "blood" in Balzac's work, see Pierre Reboul, "Les Anglais de Balzac," *Revue des Sciences Humaines*, facs. 57-58 (January-June 1950):70-93.

8. Michel Zéraffa, *Personne et Personnage* (Paris: Edition Klincksieck, 1969), p. 40. The translation is my own.

9. Félicien Marceau, *Balzac et son Monde* (Paris: Gallimard, 1955), p. 273 ("Elle découvre l'homme avec ravissement").

10. Albert Béguin, *Balzac Visionnaire* (Geneva: Edition Albert Skira, 1946), p. 114, points out in this connection that Paquita's curiosity for the love of a man is the equivalent of a desire for possession. Implicitly, then, it would amount to the same thirst for gold of which Balzac speaks in his introductory pages of the story.

11. In the history that P. Castex traces of the genesis of *The Girl with the Golden Eyes* (see n. 3), he mentions that Balzac had recently visited Delacroix's studio when he was working on the story, and this may account for the strong play of colors and contrasts of lights and shadows that appear in the text. The novel is dedicated to Delacroix.

2

Zola's *L'Assommoir:* **Paris's Stranglehold on the Lives of the Poor**

Balzac had reached the peak of his career when Emile Zola was born in Paris in 1840 (d. 1902). Twice an "emigrant"—from Paris to Aix-en-Provence when he was very young, back to Paris later as a student and in financial difficulties—he shares with the older master a fascination for the reality of city life and the complexities hidden within it. Both writers walked the indifferent streets of the capital in loneliness, facing an uncertain future and the anguished weight of the present. Both came to the full realization of their creative talent slowly and painfully in the shadow of the large capital, keenly aware of its mysterious force. For each of them literature became the vehicle through which the fermenting life of their times would find lasting contours. The visions that emerge from *The Human Comedy*—and the intricate patterns of lives that reappear volume after volume, of names that contain echoes, of faces that evoke memories—are presented on a different scale in Zola's large undertaking of the Rougon-Macquart cycle.

When Zola's father died quite suddenly in Aix, the future writer was only seven, and the financial changes brought about by the disappearance of the family's breadwinner created an early trauma and left lasting impressions on his life. He went from Aix to Paris in 1858, with meager resources and indefinite plans. Fortunately for future generations of readers, he failed his "baccalaureat" examination twice, thus avoiding perhaps a stifling career as a professor. He found employment at the customs office, and eventually became head of advertising at Hachette's. At odds with the drudgery of his daily task, he found comfort in writing. His first publication came in 1864, *Tales to Ninon*, followed the next year by a more imortant work, *The Confession of Claude*. It is, however, only after the appearance of *Therese Raquin* in 1867 that Zola envisaged the creation of the Rougon-Macquart cycle, meant to illustrate the influence of heredity and environment on the lives of his characters. In total agreement with Hippolyte Taine's theories and the belief that all human beings are essentially the result of three elements—heredity, environment, and time ("la race, le milieu et le moment")—he set about showing the infallibility of these laws. The result, not always faithful to the original design, is one of the greatest contributions in literary creation. If it neglected occasionally to lay the intended emphasis on the hereditary and deterministic factor of existence, Zola's work has by contrast exposed man's helplessness within an uncaring and exploitative society.

Zola's death on September 29, 1902, was due to an accident of toxic fumes escaping from a defective chimney. His end was thus an ironic illustration of human impasse in the face of elements beyond its control and outside its awareness.

Late in the nineteenth century the concept of literature as a faithful mirror of verifiable realities gradually gained strength. With Zola, it reached its summit, for he took it as an axiom and made it the basis for a whole literary movement. The Rougon-Macquart series of twenty large volumes was conceived as an illustration of fundamental precepts dealing with perceivable truths greater in principle than man's thoughts and his will. Such truths are to be found in the inevitability of character and moral traits inherited through bloodlines and fomented in family upbringing. Parents, children, cousins go through life in preordained fashion, victims of deterministic elements against which they struggle in vain. But these truths, basic as they are to the school of Naturalism, cannot be called self-evident or verifiable, except in relation to the elements and stories illustrated by the authors. Zola's tentacular family may even be considered arbitrarily rather than scientifically directed, in keeping with assumed notions and not with unquestionable truths. What is more striking in these novels, and surely more valuable, is the unmistakable reality of the atmosphere depicted, of objects and scenes, through which streets, houses, and stairways seem to emerge and become alive. These are the truths that make such masterpieces as *La Debacle, L'Oeuvre,* and *Germinal* haunting and challenging, and force the reader to face an enraged crowd, the eerie portrait of a dead child, or the slow descent into the dark recesses of a coal mine.

Several of the volumes in the Rougon-Macquart cycle deal with the pervasive power of Paris, and present various sections of the city with the differing social strata, the implied relationship between the physical aspects of streets and houses, and the moral behavior of the protagonists. They fulfill in a way the author's promise to reveal to the naked eye what is often concealed in the workings of the many-faceted city. In 1884, in his letter-preface to the manuscript of *A Love Story,* Zola explained the role of Paris in his work. What he says there is valid also for *L'Assommoir* and for the other novels in which the city plays a dominant role. "During the wretched days of my youth," he wrote,

> I have lived in garrets in the outskirts, from which all of Paris could be seen. That large Paris, motionless and indifferent, always there, within the frame of my window, appeared to me as the tragic sharer in my joys and my sadness. I have been hungry and I have wept in front of it; and, in front of it, I have loved, I have known my most intense moments of happiness. Well, from my twentieth year on, I had dreams of writing a novel in which Paris, with the ocean of its roofs, would be a character, something akin to the ancient choir. What I needed was an intimate drama, three or four human beings in a little room and then the immense city at the horizon, always present, watching the laughter and the tears of its children with its stony gaze.[1]

La Curée, Savage Paris, L'Assommoir, A Love Story, Nana, Pot-Bouille, Ladies' Delight, The Masterpiece, and *Money,* all present the magnetic force of a town sprawling beyond the slender hold of its people, taking over from them, pushing or clutching, fastening men and women to its streets and the contamination of its atmosphere. This Paris of Zola—an embryonic version of the motorized twentieth-century city now in existence, and still echoing in its "quartiers" the suggestive quality of some villages—is never a backdrop of intrigues, or sheer decor, or an arena even, a theater, in which actions are severed from the place where they evolved. It is, rather, a living presence, constantly asserting its power, directing fortunes and knitting all events with destiny.

L'Assommoir, published in 1877 and the seventh in the Rougon-Macquart series, stands as one of Zola's masterpieces and among the important novels of all times. Compact in characterization and development, visual, compelling, it depicts the uneventful life of an uncomplicated being, a washerwoman named Gervaise. What is relevant here is not so much the curve of Gervaise's fortune—mildly ascending before starting on the downslope, to end in a gradual plunge toward dissipation and, finally, death—but the forces that brought about the collapse of her simple dreams and of her obstinate efforts to hold on to a modicum of dignity. Those forces are all embedded in the city; for, although it was important for Zola to trace the hereditary factors driving Gervaise and her family toward the fatality of alcoholism, those factors are not crucial or distinctly manifest in the development of the story. What is conspicuous is the complexity of exterior forces at work, the dusky streets in which Gervaise comes to live and where the main attraction is the corner bar, the cramped tenement that is her home early in the novel and in which people swarm antlike, her life held in the throes of lingering poverty and in contact with dissolution in a remote section of the indifferent city. Readers are aware that, withdrawn but always present, Paris is the mold here, expanding and contracting, where resides a forgotten humanity of which Gervaise is a simple heroine and a victim.

The story, with the exception of the wedding-party exploration of Paris all the way to Place Vendôme and to the Louvre, takes place mostly in the same section of town and, for the greater part, in the same street and the same building. Yet there is a marked sense of movement and physical displacement, the impression of motion and change. What does change, in effect, is the perspective, which assimilates the characters' inner workings and their spiritual-moral oscillations with the objects around them. Streets and houses are thus seen in turn as images with color and shape, shadows, light, and also as receptacles, the holding grounds of people's lives, swaying with their presence and their fortunes. Each street, the apartment building, the rooms in which Gervaise lives, become themselves living mechanisms with hidden contrivances dictating motion and direction, and working in unison, fusing, with the rhythm and actions of the people they hold. It is in this blending of purpose and resolve, of people and objects, that Paris takes shape and assumes a reality greater than both people and objects while removed from both.

L'Assommoir contains, of course, a variety of personages: Gervaise's lover, Lantier; her husband, Coupeau; her sisters-in-law; acquaintances; and friends. Yet the novel essentially explores only her character, and it is only she who comes alive fully and fully reveals the inner workings of her mind and soul. The others are simply her world, quantities with various degrees of importance in the unfolding of her life and of the events that lead her to her brief triumph and final defeat. But the presentation of a single character does not limit the story either in horizons or in applicability, for each person embodies a whole class of beings, and Gervaise leads the way in conferring upon them depth and understanding. The narrow circle of her acquaintances, noticeable above all for its greed and vindictiveness, for weakness in temptation and ostentatiousness in celebrations, suggests a whole mass of other people from the same class, men and women who spend their days shaping metal and bricks, washing clothes or painting walls, all the unrecorded years of their uneventful lives. What emerges is the picture of a society, a segment of Paris that is not Paris but is shaped by it. It has only peripheral contacts with the rest of the city, yet it is a fundamental and visceral part of its existence.

The novel opens in a cheap hotel facing what is now the corner of Boulevard Barbès and Boulevard Rochechouart, but overlooking at the time the outer gates (Barrière Poissonnière) that led from the poorer sections of La Chapelle and Montmartre to the center of Paris. Gervaise, shivering, has been waiting through the night for the return of her lover, Lantier. The room is barren, the window opens onto a cold street, spectral at night and gradually coming alive with the bustling of workpeople going to their appointed tasks.

She looked to the right towards the Boulevard de Rochechouart, where butchers in blood-stained aprons were standing about in groups in front of the slaughterhouses, and now and again the fresh breeze wafted an acrid stench of slaughtered animals. To the left her eyes ran along a stretch of avenue and stopped almost opposite at the white mass of the Lariboisière hospital, then being built. She let her gaze travel slowly along the octroi wall from one horizon to the other; behind that wall she sometimes heard in the night the scream of men being done to death. And now she stared into secluded angles and dark corners, black with damp and refuse, terrified of discovering Lantier's body lying there dead with its belly stabbed through and through. When she looked up and beyond the unending grey wall which girdled the city like a belt of desolation, she saw a great light, the golden dust of sunrise filled already with the morning roar of Paris.[2]

Weaving in and out of Gervaise's apprehensions and anguished wait, Paris is introduced, drenched in the smell of blood, with cries suspended in the air, and dark recesses where fear and death stand watch. The lurid wall by the city is a barrier against sunshine and hope; there is only the "acrid stench of slaughtered animals" there, and "the scream of men being done to death." The suggestive quality of this often-quoted passage fuses the reality of both man and animal through sensory perception—those of hearing and of smelling, to be sure, but also that of seeing. It is Gervaise's eyes—and the reader's—that behold the vast boulevards, the butchers' splattered aprons, the forbidding wall, and the luminous rays behind it. The inner reality of dread finds a monster at every step; it is in turn echoed and nourished through the bitter smells in the air and the gloomy images all around. Objectivity does not mean removal from emotions here, nor does it mean the presentation of scientific reality divorced from man's passions and his thoughts. It is rather the blending of the two, and from this blending man and beast are joined in the powerful presence of poverty in a distant corner of the city.

With Paris, this first chapter introduces one day in the life of Gervaise. It is a day that begins when dusk has long receded into night and morning is still engulfed in darkness, a day arisen in tears and ending in dismay, bringing a renewed sense of loneliness in the face of betrayal, but also a certain determination and the shadow, at least, of a passing victory. Its importance is real and symbolic at the same time, for it brings change without suggesting renewal, and the act of chastising a rival is devoid both of triumph and of joy. The reader notices also that it is in this chapter, when the city is not yet in control of Gervaise's life, that occurs the scene at the washing house; the cleansing water—and the beating of Virginie's bare bottom, fiercer even than that administered to the soiled clothes—have a quality of redress, the enjoyment of order and propriety, in a place that tramples virtue and rewards expediency. Gradually, as the story advances and Gervaise settles more and more in the slums of Paris, cleanliness will give way to slovenliness, rectitude to impurity and profligacy. Hell lies in wait outside along the sidewalks, biding time but assured of victory.

> Hearing the laughter of Claude and Etienne who were at the window and quite happy again, she went over and put her arms round them, then lost herself in a dream as she stared at the grey road where that very morning she had seen the people stir themselves from sleep and face the gigantic daily toil of Paris. But now the labours of the day made the very paving-stones throw up a heat-haze over the city behind the octroi wall. And it was into this street, into this blazing heat that she was now thrown with her little ones, and she cast her eyes up and down the outer boulevards to left and right, stopping at each end with a dull terror as if life itself from now on was going to live itself out in this place, between a slaughterhouse and a hospital. [P. 49]

The "blazing heat" of the street has a smoldering quality, through which energy and courage will gradually diminish, along with the will to survive; the city-hell watches, symbolically, "between a slaughterhouse and a hospital," exuding the smell of illness and death, while Gervaise fearfully leans by the window in unconscious contemplation of her last days of innocence.

What follows is predictable. After a respite and a brief period of contentment, the downward movement begins unremittingly, and Gervaise's short-lived peace is shattered. Financial difficulties become the visible reason for the relaxing of moral fiber, but the causes for the eventual downfall are complex and lie much deeper than in the mere arithmetic of money. Gervaise is on her ascending curve when the reader first meets her; she is endowed with courage and the determination to be a responsible mother to her children; when Lantier abandons her with the two young sons to her charge in the miserable room of the Hotel Boncoeur, she is of course dismayed. Yet she soon pulls herself together and brings order to her life; she remains, for a time, pleasant, serene, hard-working, and painfully aware of the dangers of giving in to the temptations the city offers and of losing control over her life. Coupeau convinces her that he is just as well-intentioned, and she accepts him as a husband. The hard-working couple thus embarks on a fruitful and peaceful bourgeois existence, which only serves, however, to lull them into false security, a kind of sleep where dangers are ill-defined and seem remote. After four years during which dreams almost become reality, Coupeau suddenly falls and breaks his leg; the forced idleness gradually veers him toward Papa Colombe's corner bar and a distaste for work. Here is the tragedy in a nutshell; but Coupeau's accident and the disappearance of their savings are only catalysts in the ruin that ensues, one that had already been present in the first images that the city had offered.

The fact that the heroine of the story is not a Parisian is surely by design. Had Gervaise been brought up in the city slums and been accustomed to the tenacious fever for gain all around, and the games of spite and dominance, presumably she might have been a less likable person but one endowed with greater resistance against the stifling atmosphere and against the temptation of compassion for those who are less privileged. Her models would have been all the Lorilleux and the Boche who inhabit the crowded sections of town, those who have vile smiles in times of abundance but who refuse to open their doors to their old mothers in need; she might have been less tempted to keep her husband home when he broke his leg, and she would not have administered him such loving care as to sacrifice, with hardly a word of complaint, her hard-earned money. Coupeau would have gone to the hopsital to try to get well, and he might even have benefited from this and remained, perhaps, unspoiled. But Gervaise is from Plassans, in the South of France, where life is less harried and inimical, where ''it smelt better than it does here'' (p. 35) and where even greedy Lantier ''used to be quite all right'' to her (p. 36). Her life had been fully exposed to her share of suffering in the hands of a drunken father and a brutalized mother, but not to the dehumanizing effects of a mechanized world that leaves no room for sentiment. Perhaps her very meekness, which calls upon her the wrath of the rapacious Parisian world, might have preserved her from ultimate ruin down in Plassans. Or her end would have been different at any rate: it would have had its slice of sky and the smell of the trees by the river and the sugges-tion, at least, of human dignity.

It is difficult to pinpoint exactly where responsibility lies when righteous people surrender and allow their lives to disintegrate;

with Zola's deterministic assumptions the task is even harder. The reader is, on the one hand, shown all the factors that contribute to Gervaise's downfall, all the elements of contagious corruption to which she is exposed; on the other, the young woman's inherent weaknesses, her inability to deny herself to Lantier and to Coupeau alike, or to offer her children an example of rectitude, might seem to point to the fatality that resides within her. This is, of course, what the author wanted to portray, showing that there is no discrepancy between behavior and personality, and that the outer being moves inevitably in accordance with his or her inner dictates. If Zola has fully succeeded in his intent, however, the lasting impression for the reader is that of a Gervaise too tender and giving to resist the consuming forces of the city.

Central to the story stands the large tenement building in Rue de la Goutte d'Or; this building is not merely the physical but also the moral "theater" of the story. It stands by itself for all the sins of the city and for the city itself, for the visible ills of crowd and for dirt, with the rivulets of water and puddles in the courtyard, and the viscous stairways saturated with rancid odors. The hidden ills are only revealed when, after fermenting in the infectious atmosphere, they erupt in plagues, when proximity becomes promiscuity and unemployment drowns its sorrows in alcohol and indifference. The tenement building is, finally, the symbol of all those forces in city slums which conspire to assuage desire and kill the will.

It is important to notice that Gervaise's brief and relative affluence, and her contentment as mother and wife in the city of Paris, coincide with her residence in a quiet, small, and countrylike house in Rue Neuve de la Goutte d'Or.

> It was in a little two-storey [*sic*] house with a very steep flight of stairs leading up to only two flats, one to the right and the other to the left, the ground floor being the living quarters of a man who hired out carriages which were stabled all round a big yard opening on to the road. Gervaise was delighted, and thought she was back in the country; no neighbours, no gossiping to worry about, a peaceful corner that reminded her of a quiet lane in Plassans behind the ramparts and, as the final stroke of luck, she could keep an eye on her own window from her ironing-board, without even putting her iron down, by just stretching her neck. [P. 108]

It is here, away from the absorbing noises of crowded city quarters, that all the joys of a simple bourgeois existence unfold like flowers, the repeated marvel each morning of transforming the bedroom into a diningroom, the fluffy white curtains at the window and the religiously dusted furniture; here live the memories of Plassans, not those relating to a drunken father, but the days in the sun, by the river, and in the peace of country life. Work is nearby, and while ironing she can keep an eye on her house, with the uninterrupted sense of possession and naive pride that breed loyalty and continuity. It is in this small house that Gervaise meets the only friends she will ever have in Paris—the Goujets across the hall, the only other tenants on her floor and the only people that offer her the example of an orderly life in which sentiment and duty are not separable. Had Zola really wanted to emphasize the dynastic foibles in Gervaise, he might at least have exposed her to some destructive temptation while she lived still in the Rue Neuve; she is, instead, gracefully assimilated in the serenity of the atmosphere there, reinforcing with her presence the advantages of an intimacy that respects privacy, and of discretion that nurtures amity.

It is true that Coupeau's accident happens while they are still living in the small house next to the Goujets and that the young husband is already forgetting old aims and purposes; it is also true that residence in the big building is taken up with the inauspicious beginnings of debts and illness. Yet it cannot be seen as sheer coincidence that while in the Rue Neuve Gervaise's dream remains unchanged, even if now it appears as "an unclean thought" (p. 134), in defiance of the stark reality and as an indirect reproach to her husband's helplessness. She still wants a shop of her own, where she could exercise freedom of movement through a certain independence of means. Goujet advances her the money and she accepts, confident in her own reliability.

Where small size with a sense of space had dominated in the Rue Neuve apartment, the building where Gervaise now moves with her family offers the reverse image. Truer to the spirit of the city, its large size conveys a sense of restriction, and the multitude of people within increases the feeling of loneliness.

Gervaise let her eyes travel slowly down from the sixth floor to the ground and up again, overwhelmed by the enormity of the place and feeling as though she were in the middle of some living organism, in the very heart of a city, fascinated by the building as if she were confronted by some gigantic human being. [P. 60]

The building that arrogantly dominates the neighborhood contains no echo of Plassans, and the puddles of dye-water at the entrance suggest no vision of river banks. It is in itself all of a small city with a mechanism of its own dictating functions and directions for the people inside; it stands as a miniature and deformed vision of the city itself, contemplated through an imaginary and magnifying lens that broadens all ills while conferring the illusion of triumph to minute victories. Here, in this microcosmic Parisian world, Gervaise is condemned to perish.

It is then in Rue de la Goutte d'Or that appear the first signs of change in Gervaise, in the tenement building that symbolizes size, squalor, and all the other ills of the city. She is the proud owner of a laundry, well liked by all, and, at twenty-eight, still beautiful. But she is beginning to "put on a bit of flesh." Complacency replaces scrupulous behavior, and a kind of relaxed contentment abates the solicitude of older days.

> Her fine features were taking on a certain chubbiness and her movements the slowness of contentment. Nowadays she would sometimes dawdle on the edge of a chair while waiting for an iron to heat, with a vague smile on her round, jolly face, for she was getting fond of food, everyone agreed; but it wasn't a bad fault, quite the reverse. When you can earn enough to treat yourself to little luxuries you would be silly to live on potato-peelings, wouldn't you? [P. 144]

Her hypothetical musing here is presented in the form of general considerations, as if they really applied to most people and were universally held truths; yet these are merely her own rationalization and self-indulging thoughts meant to soothe an uneasy conscience and put guilt to rest. The future no longer exists when Gervaise begins to betray her past.

Gervaise's first signs of deterioration within the gray walls of the tenement building take the form of gluttony and a quiet indulgence for candies and cakes. As the placid owner lulls herself in a false sense of ease, the laundry shop, symbol until now of cleanliness and order, begins gradually to exhale a bad odor. ("In the heat all this dirty linen being raked over gave off a sickening stench" [p. 148]). Rather than a harsh rubbing of dirt from the clothes, so that these may regain their original whiteness, there is lazy chatter in the shop, with the girls giggling in the heat of long-drawn afternoons instead of applying themselves seriously to their tasks. There are salacious remarks and obscene gestures made, which are meekly condoned by Gervaise.

> She begged Clémence to get a move on, but the girl went on with her remarks, stuck her fingers into the holes, with allusions about the articles which she waved about like the flags of Filth Triumphant. And still the heaps went on piling up round Gervaise until, perched on the edge of her stool, she almost vanished from sight between the skirts and the petticoats. [P. 151]

Gervaise's "begging" of Clémence not only lacks the voice of authority but that of conviction, for she is herself submerged in the "Filth Triumphant" waved around her. Her laundry shop, which had been intended to be a heaven within the hellish city, no longer gives her asylum. Far from representing a private struggle against dirt and from upholding purity, the laundry is itself gradually drawn into the corrupting dynamism of the city, until it is so pervaded by it that it becomes indistinguishable from the most depraved elements around it. Like the building in which it is located and the streets that it seems to dominate with its height, it loses both identity and vigor, as it is absorbed in the "Filth Triumphant" of Parisian life. Its door is merely a transparent barrier that, far from keeping the city odors away, shuts in the rancid smells that have intruded within and permeated the air. Mesmerized by this filth, Gervaise begins slowly to sink, and, "feeling a bit giddy with the mountain of washing" (p. 152), she abandons herself to the smell of decay and the fascination, eventually, of her own failure. The symbolic value of her trade will then have followed faithfully the graph of her physical and spiritual health: stable and mounting at the outset, as Gervaise administers energetic slaps to remove dirt from clothes; wavering, when work is sloppy and the laundress undemanding; and degenerating at the end, as the shop is liquidated, with the decline of its owner's fortune and the disintegration of her life.

A very important aspect in this novel, and the one that lends it particular interest within the large frame of reference of Zola's work, is the inadvertent suspension—or so it seems—of hereditary factors in the shaping of Gervaise's destiny, and the encroachment instead of the city's diabolical forces. The poor woman's "immorality," or at least her lack of adherence to her own principles, is merely a surrender to something larger than she had been able to envisage; if it is true that she is partially aware of her betrayal of both frugality and probity, it is also true that her very gentleness and generosity have deprived her of the necessary strength to uphold old virtues in the face of the city's evils. The fatality would then seem to reside outside of her, and not within, even if she does acknowledge her share of responsibility. "Yes, it was their own fault if things went from bad to worse each season," she recognizes; "But you never admit things like that to yourself, especially when you are in the soup. They put it down to misfortune, God had something against them" (p. 318). Yet "misfortune" it is—the corroding elements of the tenement building in which the Coupeaus have come to live and the vindictive city that allows for no redemption and wields the worst punishment against those who are trusting and defenseless. Gervaise has come to know this by now, but she can only watch helplessly, unable to arrest the ravages against all that she had ever cherished.

Not everybody perishes in Zola's Paris; the Lorilleux, the Boches, all those who can compensate and accommodate, bend and sway with situations, do "make it." And there are also the Goujets, whose candor and single-mindedness preserve them from evil. Gervaise and Coupeau, on the other hand, lack the stamina to oppose their will to that of the city. For Coupeau, whose interest to the reader is limited to the impact he has on his wife's life, one cannot properly speak of tragedy; his is merely the failure to rise above the contaminating elements in which he was bred, of casually falling in Bibi-la-Grillade's footsteps. Coupeau, bred from infancy in seedy Parisian sections, betrays nothing and hardly anybody; had his wife been able to continue facing the city undaunted, in fact, had she not so meekly abandoned her original distrust of alcohol, he might even have been spared, perhaps, from passively following his friends to the corner bar. But Gervaise's defeat is a tragedy comparable, in its very modest way, to a new Theseus bravely entering a labyrinth but being slaughtered by an invisible

Minotaur—a Theseus without magic—human, weak, and perishable.

One might argue here that Gervaise, conscious at least to a degree of the forces she set out to fight at the beginning, should have measured her own strength accordingly instead of relaxing in false security. But this would be to ignore the malevolent will of the city, the monster Zola has created that preys upon innocence and generosity; for Paris is, in *L'Assommoir*, the sum total of collective ills, each in itself negligible perhaps—the poverty, the crowded quarters, the lack of roots, or the dominant dirt and prevailing disorder—but Cyclopean when viewed together and overwhelming for the defenseless individual. There is little resemblance between the Paris in Zola's *Love Story*, with its feline appearance and the seductiveness of a siren ensnaring the passerby, and the decaying forces at work in Gervaise's world, other perhaps than in both cases (as in *Nana* or *Savage Paris—Le Ventre de Paris* in its original title) the means of corruption are invidious and surreptitious. By showing itself for what it is from the beginning, lying in wait "between the hospital an the slaughter-house," Paris hides the strength of her weapons in the very act of revealing them; she thus dictates the false measures through which Gervaise will inevitably perish—for the poverty that, alone, had been feared is a mere manifestation of the city's pervasive ills.

One wonders if Gervaise could have held out, even though she did not. The reader absolves her sympathetically, echoing her thoughts and calling her fall a "misfortune," for what one likes in her is precisely the fact that she seemed to hold promises; "I must keep my head on things that matter," she says at the outset. "There is no future in fun and games" (p. 51). She is aware of the dangers that surround her and determined to combat them; together with her, the reader hopes that she will triumph, somehow, over the pitfalls strewn along her path, but only disappointments await at each turn. Gervaise's tragic fault is perhaps in the languor of her flesh, which mirrors the weakness of her resolve. Paris stands by like a beast of prey and, sensing her difficulty, pounces on her.

What Gervaise was incapable of discerning in the magnitude of evils around her is what one might call the image of the mirror within the mirror, limited in appearance but endless in effect. The many circles of hell that appear one after the other, each separate and yet encompassing all the others at the same time, present views that are both finite and limitless: the finite are of human size and hence give the impression of being governable; the limitless disappear in the illusion of distance, deeper and deeper within the mirror that reflects them. Unseen at the end, they become ignored, until they come back to haunt, each a fragment and a frightful unity. Once Gervaise, innocent and defenseless, steps within the first imaginary circle, with her arrival in Paris, she is in a way already caught; the possibility of escaping, or triumphing over the forces of betrayal, poverty and promiscuity are only illusory, both for her and for the reader. The reality is harsher and ungiving, composed of city blocks that lead in time to a figuratively dead-end road, Rue de la Goutte d'Or, and to a tenement building swarming with antlike people in endless motion toward ephemeral gains and dissipation. After the misguiding warmth of a shop of one's own, what follows is the nakedness of a room under the eaves. Paris pushes the defeated woman into a forgotten hole beneath the stairs at the end, and only there does the mirror of misery and fatality finally shatter. There death resides, beyond the last speck of the multiple reflections the city holds, in peace now, away from hunger and the dictates of the flesh.

In this carefully built novel where Gervaise is the principal character but Paris the dominant force, the movement is concentric and, to a considerable extent, symbolic. The story is introduced from an outer layer of Parisian life, with Gervaise in the Hotel Boncoeur at one of the peripheral boulevards, a stranger, unaccustomed to the vagaries and the impersonality of the city. She then moves first into a little un-Parisian house, in what turns out to be a temporizing measure, a protracted lull necessary before the eventual immersion into a more typical city tenement. The four years in the Rue Neuve appear on the one hand as the realization of a promise, the just reward for serious endeavor; but on the other, they represent the surreptitious movement deeper into the hellish circles of the city, a stealthy, satanic brew intended to dull the senses and to weaken resistance. The move to the Goutte d'Or is thus anticipated in passive acceptance through tantalizing promises of well-being and ownership; Gervaise is, at this point, already defeated without suspecting it. Pushed by the demon of "her shop," she borrows money that she will never be able to return, and she plunges in this manner, at an early stage of the story, into the mesmerizing city dealings she had sought to avoid. Unsuspectingly, she has surrendered to the threatening forces of disorder and decay that had appeared menacing at the very beginning—one endless night of wait at the Hotel Boncoeur.

It is not for the reader to allot responsibility and assign guilt; Zola leaves no room for judgment and hardly any for character interpretation. What prevails in his novel is a parade of "truths," visible, discernible to the naked eye, as scene after scene unfolds in tides of life in motion, irrepressible and uncontrollable. But life itself has a shape here, a dimension, a color, and depth, and, as the story progresses, what emerges beyond the crowd, the buildings, the streets, beyond Gervaise, Coupeau, and Lantier, is the mold that contains them all, the "body" of which people are merely a digestive apparatus, the city of Paris.

Notes to Chapter 2

1. Emile Zola, *Une Page d'Amour* (Paris: Garnier-Flammarion, 1973), pp. 367-68. The translation is mine.
2. Emile Zola, *L'Assommoir*, trans. Leonard Tancock (Baltimore, Md.: Penguin, 1974), p. 24. All subsequent quotations come from this edition.

3

D'Annunzio's *Child of Pleasure:* A City's Power of Seduction

To go from Zola to Gabriele D'Annunzio (1863-1938) might seem a larger shift in direction that it actually is, one that from a deep involvement with the barest of realities thrusts the reader into an unmistakably fictional world composed of vague yearnings and transient passions, in the shadows of a city larger than life. But Zola was a Romantic before he became fascinated with the principles of Naturalism, and even as he was well involved in the creation of his Rougon-Macquart dynasty, he did not abandon the sentimental longings that were so close to his nature. The forces of determinism often became, in fact, subordinate to lyrical musings in works such as *The Dream* or *A Love Story.* It is this latter work that no doubt inspired D'Annunzio's *Child of Pleasure.* Here, the French master's presentation of the seductive power of Paris is transformed into Rome's pervasive and corrupting charm.

D'Annunzio was born in the Adriatic town of Pescara, and he must have looked at the capital of his country with the eye of a provincial, both critical of and fascinated with the glitter of that large and cosmopolitan center. He is not well known to the American reader, for his gifts reside in the evocative and mostly untranslatable lyrical quality of his writing. He was above all a poet, but he also wrote dramas of merit (*Francesca da Rimini, Iorio's Daughter*) and was a much-acclaimed novelist. His better known novels, include, aside from *The Child of Pleasure, The Intruder, The Triumph of Death,* and *The Virgin of the Rocks.*

D'Annunzio's life was one of daring and romantic intrigue, making him, along with his renown in the field of letters, one of the most notorious Italians of his times. His march over Fiume to reconquer the lost city for his country in 1919, made of him an almost legendary figure, and his turbulent relationship with the celebrated actress Eleonora Duse conferred on him the halo of the irresistible seducer. Loyal to the Fascist movement and passionately patriotic at the same time, he retired in disillusionment over the Rapallo Treaty in 1921, and lived to the end in the town of Gardone on Lake Garda.

D'Annunzio's literary career is varied, both in genre and in stylistic approach, and it is difficult to define him within any specific movement. He is generally labeled a "decadent" both because of the richness of his language and for the fascination that the image of death appeared to hold in his work. His writing seems to aim primarily at rendering, in poetic language, the reality of situations, without much effort at penetrating psychological depths. Both his first and his last novels deal with the irresistible power of the city, Rome in *The Child of Pleasure* and Venice in *The Fire*. Both cities are presented as infused with vague harmonies of mystical and sensuous aspirations. The first of these two works has been selected for analysis because here one finds the additional element of country life away from Rome, through which the role of the city emerges with greater clarity.

The "eternity" of Rome is such an old subject, explored and exploited in so many directions, that it has become something akin to a cliché. What "eternity?" one wonders, aside from the considerable age of the city, which has, all the same, undergone so many changes and is still supposed to be the same! The sameness is of course arguable, even if it eludes definition. Yet the descriptions "eternal Rome" and "eternal city" remain, echoed perpetually by novelists, poets, or travelers. D'Annunzio, himself the product of a provincial upbringing, was fascinated by the capital of his country and, at the age of twenty-five, set about to write a novel in which Rome would be a central force, a kind of mesmerizing siren holding irresistible attraction. The theme is precisely that of the "eternity" of the famous city, weighed against the passing follies and ephemeral struggles of its inhabitants.

Writing from Francavilla-a-Mare on the Adriatic sea, only a few miles away from where he was born and brought up, D'Annunzio presents a vision of Rome that is not merely one of recollection in tranquillity and away, in this case, from the actual bustle of the city. It is a poetic rendition in which romantic inventiveness and traditional—even conventional—views are at play. Sitting by the very sea and pine groves he often celebrated in his poetic works, the author evokes a setting disturbing to the senses and quite different from the one so familiar to him. He recalls another blue, more mysterious and ethereal than that of the limpid waters in front of him, more intense and more remote—not a simple nature with a clear sky and warm sand, but the image of something both primordial and complex like the one he thought he had detected in Rome, where spirit and matter are never separate from one another. What he envisaged was a complexity of elements that would dictate passion and a hedonistic surrender to refined pleasures, a cerebral desire indistinguishable from the most pervasive sensuality. *Il Piacere*, as his work was called, connotes far greater sensuality in Italian than the English word *pleasure* suggests, a combination, perhaps, of *delight, enjoyment,* and *gratification*. Its setting could not be an uncomplicated town like Francavilla, nestled by the sea and in the shadow of a hill; it needed a place that would offer contrasts, alternatives, and admonitions against the vagaries of the senses.

The Rome of *The Child of Pleasure* is more than a spectator and less than a heroine. It is at once an energy that must be dealt with, and an unconcerned witness to the vicissitudes of the characters. Its power is undefinable and corrosive at once, in keeping, that is, with the decadent spirit of the society presented. Yet it would be too easy to absolve the hero of the story of his ultimate failure, of his betrayal of the ideals he had once cherished, and hold the city responsible instead. Rome is a catalyst here, more than it is a force of evil; it is the element of glittering distraction in the lives of those tempted by the monotony of vice. The people in the story are all too prone to look for asylum in the din and variety of city life, so that they can indulge the repetitive emptiness of acts that only have the illusion of variety; they feel secure within the city, protected from the temptation of self-analysis and harsh judgment.

In 1888, when Zola's theories of Naturalism were already reshaping literary views and the understanding of life's conditions, D'Annunzio was not quite certain yet about the direction his work would

eventually take. Still imbued with romantic concepts and the traditions of the earlier part of the century, he could not altogether renounce the appeals of poetry and lyric beauty; yet he could not stay
with the illusion that man is a world unto himself, when an important segment of that world was in fact proclaiming that the human
condition resided outside man. Unable perhaps to resolve the
dilemma between the dictates of Romanticism and those of
Naturalism, he combined the two. He thus made his main
character's personality dependent upon his environment—the
seductive quality of Rome or the peaceful restraint of the countryside—while endowing him at the same time with a dynamism of
sensuality that is only inspired and incited by the city, but not
altogether given by the city or culled from its presence.

The protagonist of the story is Andrea Spirelli, Count Fieschi
D'Ugenta, a poet and, potentially at least, a refined artist. He has,
however, a double personality and one that alternates with the
changes of the environment. He is, on the one hand, a gifted and
sensitive artist; on the other Andrea is a member of the rich Roman
aristocracy, one of the many bored and restless elegant people for
whom the city is merely the theater for savoring gossip, dances,
dinners, and receptions. There they collect "objects d'art" or love
intrigues without much appreciation for either. What distinguishes
Spirelli from his circle of acquaintances is precisely his artistic sensitivity and the possibility, therefore, of going beyond the emptiness of a mundane society and the attraction of a hedonistic existence. His gifted nature has offered him the chance of defying the
laws of heredity and of discerning the spirituality of Rome, rather
than surrendering to its sensuous appeal. The choices offered to
him are symbolized by the two women in his life: Helen and Mary,
representing in turn desire and purity, the voluptuousness of the
flesh and the lasting beauty of truth and sentiment. Yet the choice
is a missed opportunity, one that can only be contemplated in
retrospect when decisions are already irretrievable, for the story is a
reliving of events that have taken place at an earlier date and are
now beyond recall.

The story opens on a December afternoon in 1887, and it retraces
its steps to two years earlier, filling gradually the gap from 1885 until the present. It advances at this point only very slightly in time
from that early opening day, and it ends on a note of loss and emp-

tiness. It is not so much the tale of a love as one of the possibility of love and missed opportunity, a love, that is, which is squandered instead, along avenues of insatiable appetites in the shadow of a city that is both tacitly encouraging and strangely aloof.

> The year was dying gracefully. A late sun filled the sky over Rome with a soft, mild, golden light that made the air feel almost spring-like. The streets were full as on a Sunday in May. A stream of carriages passed and repassed rapidly through the Piazza Barberini and the Piazza di Spagna, and from thence a vague and continuous rumble mounted to the Trinitá de' Monti and the Via Sistina and even faintly reached the apartments of the Palazzo Zuccari.[1]

From the very first lines the reader is offered the vision of a city held within the languour of death ("the year was dying") and a renewed energy of life ("golden. . .almost spring-like"). The opening sentence presents the essence of the story through a city resplendent in wintry sun, soft and undulating with crowds and carriages mingling in continuous flow. The noise is only slightly audible, and yet it is a presence in Andrea's room; it blends with the smell of roses, delicate and pervasive. The themes of repetitiveness, perishability, tenderness, mobility, elusiveness, sensuality, and spirituality, which are the components of the entire work, are present in this initial paragraph. They are brought to the fore by the soft feeling in the air, the glorious steps of Trinitá de' Monti, the elegance of Via Sistina, the confused stirring of the crowd, and finally by the roses and the winter, the motifs of rebirth and death.

In his room carefully fitted to recapture the atmosphere of earlier days, Andrea waits for Elena. After two years of absence, this enchanting female who had held him captive to her sensuous beauty is coming to pay him a visit. The days of the past suddenly obliterate the two years' interval and fill the present with longing. The force of the imagination rekindles desire. The old passion, interrupted before it could run its course, stirs in Andrea, and he is filled with a kind of painful craving to hold, to possess, to relive. Everything is in place as in the past, the flames playing acrobatics in the fireplace, the tea table set with china, the big roses, open and inviting, filling the amphorae. Every detail is the same, evoked with care and culled from memory, with visions of nudity by the fire and petals of roses strewn on the rug.

Early in the story roses acquire the strength of a symbol volup-
tuously pervading the air with their perfume; they are both an
ethereal presence and a stirring one inflaming the senses.

> The room began slowly to fill with the scent exhaled from
> numberless vases of flowers. Full blown roses hung their heavy
> heads over crystal vases that opened like diamond lilies on a
> golden stem, similar to those standing behind the Virgin in the
> *tondo* of Botticelli in the Borghese Gallery. [P. 188]

Flowers here stand as a parallel to the city, both to its mystical
aspect ("similar to those standing behind the Virgin") and to the
pagan connotations, suggested by the velvety touch and the insidious aroma of the petals. Roses reflect also the perishability of
man's love and his ability to discover each time anew the joys of the
senses; they have, as love does, only one day of blossoming, soon
to fade before they live again. The endless sequence and perennial
rebirth of both love and flowers are mirrored in the ageless
presence of the city under its immutable sky. Implicit, too, is the
theme of death that the very blossoming of a rose suggests. And
death is already in the air, as the roses stand with their "heavy
heads" reflected in the delicate transparency of the crystal vase that
holds them. These roses recall as well other roses and other days,
when the rituals of love beheld the naked body of Elena and the
scattering of petals on the rug.

> She had a rather cruel habit of pulling all the flowers to pieces
> and scattering them over the carpet at the end of each of her
> visits and then stand ready to go, fastening a glove or a bracelet,
> and smile in the midst of the devastation she has wrought. [P.
> 190]

Each love stands alone, briefly poised in the center of an existence
as an undefined promise, a hope that soon becomes a fulfillment
and hence approaches inevitably its own end. This image of love
that repeats itself is echoed by the city; her life also runs in chapters
through history, in successive motion, with the Imperial Rome
followed by the Gothic, the Renaissance, the Baroque city, up to
the present day. Each "new" Rome is unique in itself and

simultaneously an echo of its past. The continuity and changeability of the city are reflected here in the motifs of flowers, women, and love, which are all equally perishable and renewable in time.

The present, so carefully built to evoke the past in Andrea Spirelli's room, is a stale imitation of it. When Elena arrives, she is strangely different from the woman he knew two years ago, resembling her only on the surface, but incapable of hiding now a kind of cold detachement; the illusion of warmth in their past intimacies no longer exists. "From Dreamland," reads an inscription on her purse, "a stranger here." Like the story of their love, Elena is both true and unreal, a creation reflected in the reality outside and trapped in the imagination. Her presence now, carefully anticipated as a vision of renewed seduction and expected surrender, acquires the magnetic quality of an unpredictable event and the fascination of mystery. "And in truth, she was even more desirable than in the former days, the plastic enigma of her beauty more obscure and more enthralling" (p. 199). Attitudes rehearsed ahead of time soon become authentic emotions, and the two acts, that of Andrea feigning love, and that of Elena feigning renunciation, are insinuated in the reality of the present and become the determining force in the life of Andrea. His desire, revived by a chance encounter and kept unsatisfied, will destroy, through its obsessive force, the precarious inner balance on which his salvation depends. In the room now pervaded by "an ineffable melancholy" the presence of Rome hangs as an inescapable fatality, deaf to the urgent call of desire and the appeal of the flesh.

> There was no sound but the dull deep inarticulate murmur of the city. Not a carriage passed across the piazza of the Trinitá de' Monti. As the wind came in strong gusts from time to time, she closed the window, catching a glimpse as she did so of the point of the obelisk, black against the starry sky. [P. 205]

The movement and the implied gaiety of two years ago give way to a forlorn image where the city appears suddenly as a desert, windswept and somber; yet there is a sense of vigilance in this Sphinx-like Rome, with its obelisk etched against the stars as a mute presence and a reminder of durability.

Andrea Spirelli is the last heir to a noble name, and he has cultivated the traditional refinement of his forefathers. Endowed

with a keen intellect and impeccable taste, he had led a life absorbed by studies, the worship of beauty, and a penchant for sensuous
pleasure, before meeting Helen. For a man ready for the experience
of passion, the encounter seemed almost predictable; desire erupts
and triumphs, while love is limited by a casual *"habere, non
haberi"* (p. 25) It is summertime, and Andrea waits. There is
suspense in the air, as Rome waits too.

> It was a St. Martin's summer, a "Springtime of the Dead,"
> calmly sad and sweet, in which Rome lay all golden, like a city of
> the Far East, under a milk-white sky, diaphanous as the firma-
> ment reflected in Southern seas. [P. 26]

The milky quality of the sky suggests a woman languidly dreaming
and sensuously displaying her graces. She can be held in voluptuous
surrender or cherished and contemplated as a "diaphanous"
presence. The vision recedes in the background as Elena sighs "mi
piaci, mi piaci," ("I like you, I like you"). It later echoes Andrea's
exultation, as he leaves the hothouse atmosphere of his mistress's
house.

> Thus began for them a bliss that was full, frenzied, for ever
> changing and for ever new; a passion that wrapped them round
> and rendered them oblivious of all that did not minister immedi-
> ately to their mutual delight. [P. 51]

The sensuous correspondence of the two lovers explores all avenues
of rapture: in the shade of Santa Maria in Cosmedin; at Villa
Albani, Villa Medici, or Villa Ludovisi; by the statues in the Museo
Borghese; or up the steps of Trinità de' Monti. Each stone or step
or road is an accomplice and a memory of their bliss, and the city
echoes Goethe's cry, *"Lass dich, Geliebte, nicht reu'n, dass du mir
so schnell dich ergeben!"* ("Have no regrets, my beloved, that thou
didst yield thee so soon" [p. 51]). This could have been a beautiful
parenthesis preceding a more complete and spiritual involvement.
It could have led to new heights and the aspiration of sentiment. It
was instead at the onset a culmination already, something that could
only deteriorate with time. Because the reader looks at the events in
retrospect and that day of summer wait is now but a memory in the
wintry sun, one can only lament the spent youth, the fading of a

dream, the decay, the emptiness ushered in by a brief period of orgy and pleasure.

Weeks and then months go by. Elena leaves, mysteriously, after a last meeting. Her carriage disappears by the Quattro Fontane, and the sentimental exaltation experienced only a few moments earlier "under the influence of a tumultuous sunset" fades with the noise of the wheels. Uneasily, the adventure is concluded, without explanation but without any sense of suspension either. It has—or it should have—run its course in the appeasement of the senses and the joys of the moment. Two or three months later a brief notice in the paper announces Elena's marriage to Lord Heathfield. Two years go by before the two lovers meet again, and only now, two years later, Andrea is for the first time shaken by a touch of jealousy. The name Healthfield assumes in his mind the shape of hands and lips that can hold and caress this woman who slips away from his arms. But jealousy or even sorrow, no less than boredom, are the province of the intellect with Andrea. Incapable of surrendering to spontaneity, mesmerized by the sensuous force of the city, he reduces all joys and pain alike to a manipulation of the imagination. Dictated through an assumed pose or a feigned interest, his emotions are in a way seized by the intellect and given a new life. Love thus becomes a contrivance like a mechanical toy, which must run its course once it has been put into motion; to stop it at any point before it reaches its natural end is to put into motion yet another device that clings to the imagination and directs its course. A new "toy" is born, a dangerous one at times, with wheels turning in rusty fashion and wearing out the very fabric that gives them life.

With the fading of the nineteenth century, the concept that love might be a fatality decreed somewhere in the stratosphere of the soul became less valid. D'Annunzio, with Gide, Proust, and others, became intrigued instead with the role that the imagination plays in the life of all sentiment. They seemed to agree in the assumption that a reality created by the mind is endowed with strength comparable to that of matter and all other verifiable truths. Love, with all its exuberance, its tenderness or passionate feelings, can thus be inspired by a place or a mood in the air. The object of love in such a case, be it a pensive delicate face or the alluring movement of a figure in the sunshine, becomes subordinate to the initial force that had inspired love. D'Annunzio thus made Andrea Spirelli's yearnings and Elena's appeal dependent upon the presence of Rome, so that the very composition of his lust and pleasure, of his obsessive desire, and, eventually, of his crushing emptiness is that of the city's sky, roads, and buildings, its streets and its mysterious voice.

The richness of the Roman sky and the intensity of colors in the city have hidden from Andrea's sight the presence of more ethereal beauties and the sense of the divine that often hovers in the air.

> Rome was his passion—not the Rome of the Caesars, but the Rome of the Popes—not the Rome of the triumphal Arches, the Forums, the Baths, but the Rome of the Villas, the Fountains, the Churches. He would have given all the Colosseums in the world for the Villa Medici, the Campo Vaccino for the Piazza di Spagna, the Arch of the Titus for the Fountain of the Tortoises. [Pp. 25-26]

Not in the glory of its past but in the dizzying richness of its present does Andrea cherish the nearness of Rome; not in the spatial symmetry of its arches and its forums but in the intricate composition of the Tortoises' fountain and the shaded villas does he find an echo of his desires. The sounds of bells from the many churches touch his senses before they can ever provoke flights of the spirit. They disguise sensuous pleasures within a mystical mantle.

> These fallacious ideas of purity and loftiness of sentiment were but the reaction after more carnal delights, when the soul experiences a vague yearning for the ideal. [P. 53]

The sacred and the profane, the temporal and the eternal, become indistinguishable one from the other, and raptures of the flesh are imbued with something resembling a mystical experience. Back in Rome after an absence of travels and studies, Andrea has surrendered to the warm breath of the city, and he allows his drunken senses to distort his vision and the ideal he had contemplated in solitude.

After Elena's initial departure there is a kind of lull. Other adventures—vague interests, horse races, and flirtations—fill the time for a few intervening months. Eventually, an incident resulting from a duel provoked by a jealous lover suddenly menaces to change the game of love into one of death. Having casually bartered his life for a passing fancy, Andrea is wounded, and he leaves Rome for a rest in the country. The setting is here one comparable to D'Annunzio's own provincial past. In Schifanoia, away from the enticing forces of the city, and in contemplation instead of the sea and trees swaying in the wind, he regains not only physical health but a new spiritual stability. His convalescence is transformed into a period of reappraisal that could lead—or could have led—to a rebirth and a closer relation with his old ideals of beauty and life. Andrea's nostalgic reaching out for the values he had once held sacred is as genuine as the fever that had pushed him earlier in the pursuit of Elena. Yet this dual nature in him does not exist simultaneously but only in keeping with the elements of place and atmosphere in which he finds himself. Where the Rome of monuments and obelisks attesting to the vagaries of man's passions had prevented a continuity of feelings in Andrea and the search for a spiritual balance to the joys of the flesh, Schifanoia operates in reverse manner. Here, the pristine nature, the vastness of the distant sea, and the gardens laid out with care seem to point to a greater and more harmonious order than the one created by man. Here, his old passionate urges seem distant, and Andrea begins to cherish more lasting values. A new strength pervades him—a new goodness and different hopes.

There are three stages in the development of the novel, each corresponding to Andrea's initial stay in Rome, departure to the country, and final return to the city. The first comprises the meeting with Elena, the blossoming of their passionate relation followed by disorder after her departure, and ending with the foolishness of the duel. The second, in Schifanoia, witnesses fresh poetical aspirations and the birth of a new love, one that is tender, generous, and spiritual. Maria appears in Andrea's life and their relation seems enhanced by their renunciation of physical surrender in favor of a purity more in keeping with an image of duration. But back in Rome, all hope of redemption is abandoned in favor of a sensuality that soon becomes dissolution. The ensnaring quality of the city will have triumphed once again and crushed all expectations of virtue and harmony.

During the time spent in Schifanoia, Rome is hardly a memory. Paradoxically, however, its presence is felt by the reader through the intentional denial of its presence and the contrast that inevitably arises out of an invidious comparison between the serenity of the present and the turmoil of the past. Instead of the inscrutable Roman sky, the blue of the sea stretches to heaven so "that the two elements seemed as one, impalpable and supernatural" (p. 95); not the stones of antiquity laden with man's passions, but "the wide amphitheatre of hills" (p. 96) gathers in the distance to meet the contemplative eye. "Where were now all his vanities and his cruelties, his schemes and his duplicities?" Andrea asks himself in the new peace that descends magically upon him. His very breathing becomes attuned to the rhythm of the sea and the wind, while memories of youth and purity lull him to ineffable tranquillity. This new pantheistic relation with existence points to the sacred force of nature as opposed to the ephemeral qualities of the city. Man's vision of the eternal is now given life and substance by the vastness of the sea, while before, crowds of people and buildings only obscured Andrea's vision and led him to disarray.

Just as the expectation of love in Rome had soon been rewarded with the meeting of Elena, Andrea, now transformed in a "vas spirituale," is inspired in Schifanoia by the gentle beauty of Maria. The two women, with their symbolic names representing, in turn, seduction and purity, are themselves to be seen as expressions of outside forces—the corrupting power of the city and the assuaging elements of nature. Maria is the tender mother of a little girl and the chaste spouse of a coarse man; she is suffused with melancholy and spirituality. Her personality—the feeling of love gradually blossoming in her soul, her struggle with the temptation of surrendering to the man who has whispered such gentle words in her ear, her supreme vow of renunciation—comes movingly alive through her journal. She leaves, finally, having triumphed over the fascination of love, finding solace in her child and in the oppression of virtue. Her triumph and her spirituality are also the triumph of a land where the sun and the wind still hold a promise of heaven.

This second adventure is also concluded uneasily. If this were the end of the idyllic love, one might see a comforting element in the incorruptibility of a gentle soul, and the triumph of virtue in the face of the greatest temptation. One should perhaps wish it to be so, and thus retain the illusion that every man, even one who had come so close to being contaminated by vice, could nurture sentiment and a poetic image of life. But the role of Maria is not over; it must yet show the vulnerability of the purest of beings when exposed to the forces of the city. In the languid air of Rome, Maria's strength will be diminished; she will surrender, vanquished, another victim of the triumphant city.

The brief summer months at Schifanoia are an interlude, a parenthesis during which dreams, desires, and aspirations coincide and contribute to a depth of understanding and a measure of maturity in the hero. But the real story takes place in Rome, and there Andrea soon becomes engrossed in more frivolous pursuits and the fever of sensuality. It is the month of October when he returns to his Palazzo Zuccari overlooking Trinitá de' Monti. There is in him an immediate stirring, "a lively reawakening of his old love for Rome" (p. 175), which recalls his old love for Elena and the desire to hold and to forget oneself within the joys of the senses. Deceptively, both Rome and Elena offer an image of languid surrender, of enticing promises and the gift of happiness. The room where Andrea retires as if in hesitation before abandoning himself to the charms of the city lulls him to a kind of torpor. Culled by the mixture of profane and sacred images around him—the bed, which is a high baldaquin, altarlike, the faded red and gold of the church drapes and the Latin inscriptions, the sacrificial pictures of grapes and wheat—both Elena and Maria appear in his dream, the features of one overlapping the other, blending and separating, confused at the end and indistinguishable from each other. As he awakens, the room becomes flooded by the golden luminosity of the Roman sun, suggesting the same diffused and enticing aura of the images in his dream.

Rome appeared, all pearly gray, spread out before him, its lines a little blurred like a faded picture, under a Claude Lorrain sky, sprinkled with ethereal clouds, their noble grouping lending to the clear spaces between an indescribable delicacy, as flowers lend a new grace to the verdure which surrounds them. On the distant heights the gray deepened gradually to amethyst. Long trailing vapours slid through the cypresses of the Monte Mario like waving locks through a comb of bronze. Close by, the pines of Monte Pincio spread their sun-gilded canopies. Below, on the Piazza, the obelisk of Pius VI looked like a pillar of agate. Under this rich autumnal light everything took on a sumptuous air. Divine Rome! [P. 178]

Framed by the window, Rome appears as a painting in which artistic rendition has created a reality more engrossing than truth. The city presents an image that is at once its own reflection and that of an imitation of the self, immediate and tangible yet out of reach and removed. The "clear spaces" alternate with "blurred" pictures, the "trailing vapors" from the rain contrast with the starkness of the cypresses, while the closer view of the pines is shrouded in "sun-gilded canopies" and the obelisk on the square directly below acquires the transparency of agate. But after Andrea's eyes have roamed the spaces of distant hills and the clusters of green, after they have taken in all the golden liquidity of the air and the sky, they finally rest on the pavement crossed by carriages and the movement of people. The regions of the spirit readily surrender to the appeal of the immediate, and Andrea's contemplative mood progressively shifts to the languid and the lascivious. Maria's purity is desecrated in his imagination, and he delights in falsifying the sentiment of love with the "refinements of sensuality." He catches one last glimpse of the sky before he surrenders completely to the spell of the street.

Life soon resumes its old mundane rhythm, full of masked balls alternating with dinners and concerts; but the intervening time between Andrea's first stay in the city and his return has created a psychological awareness that is itself only an imitation of the old one. The sense of wait and mystery that had conferred a certain youthful vigor to the earlier days is now missing. There are no longer any expectations or the illusion that a purifying presence might suddenly appear to arrest the decline of the spirit. There are hardly any hopes, in fact, outside the need for distraction and the urge for immersion into the social vortex. Gradually the opiate becomes a way of life, and only very rarely are vague memories of a distant past evoked by a starry night or the clear sight of pines against the sky. The story moves inexorably toward its unavoidable conclusion, as the link is made with the initial events at the beginning of the novel. The events introduced with the meeting with Elena in the room full of roses have retraced all the steps of the preceding two years and have come full circle back to that initial meeting. The presence of Elena is now disturbing to the senses yet devoid of the old passion so resembling love. What had been staged to imitate the old fervor in a traditional act of seduction, becomes, through

Elena's capricious refusal, a consuming fever. Elena's decision, itself a calculated imitation of purity and friendship, becomes an irritant and a stimulus to Andrea's senses. When he meets Maria again, he is in the grip of the frustration and desire that Elena's return had kindled.

The character of Andrea is the only one in the novel that assumes substance and credibility. All the others—the passing image of his cousin silently in love with him or the various people in the numerous salons, and even the two ladies who play a major role in his life—are but dimensions of his own vision, answers to a need or the complement to an aspiration of the moment. It is Andrea's world that comes alive through the pages of the novel, as it is the rise and fall of his hopes and his ambitions that the reader witnesses, in the constant presence of a city that is both an uncaring observer and a molding force. Andrea is a typical end-of-the-century hero, Baudelairian, Gidean, or Nietzschean in turn, in his vague longings and assumed postures. He is bent upon the conquest of his nature, reshaping and redirecting his life, removing from it all that is instinctual and spontaneous, and placing in its stead culture, refinement, and artistry. But when these efforts are applied to sentiment and love, the results are not always happy. Pleasure ("Il Piacere," of which the title speaks) becomes an intellectual contrivance, a cerebral stimulus that must take firm possession of the mind before it can reach the nether regions of sensuality. Emotions themselves are summoned by fantasy and its power of inventiveness; only images that have been entertained by the imagination are capable of arousing feelings. Love as such, or what one generally means by it—a strong attraction, a longing, or a natural communion—becomes totally subservient to the same cerebral stimuli that direct lust. Andrea's inability to distinguish between sentiment and desire, his search for an impossible appeasement are the dominating themes in the third and final part of the story. It is here too that the presence of the city is most keenly felt, that Rome becomes a cooercive element of vice not only for those who, like Andrea, offer little resistance, but also for Maria, who had until now found the strength to resist. Never an innocent bystander, the city now appears as a force and a mirage, and as a hot breath that turns man's attention away from the ethereal beauty of the sky in order to bend it toward the pavement. The possibility of redemption sug-

gested by the sound of bells echoing through the air and the purity
of lines of the columns and arches is but a mirage, the chimerical
blending of Elena's sensuality and Maria's chastity; the two faces,
superimposed one upon the other, become contaminated and inseparable.

The fact that Elena had disappeared from Andrea's horizons
before the adventure could pale of its own accord has left the note
of suspension or of incompleteness that exacts a price and demands
a conclusion. It is to be noted here that never has there been the
slightest suggestion to crown this relationship with the vows of
marriage when Elena was still a widow and thus perfectly eligible.
Marriage and the traditional bourgeois concept of family never
enter the picture here unless it be to show, indirectly at least, that
legally sanctioned unions have hardly any bearing upon love,
desire, or sentiment. Elena's sudden departure for England and the
eventual notice of marriage in the newspaper are never even
suspected to imply any sort of attraction for her new husband. She
was pressed with financial problems, and marriage was simply a
way of solving them. Andrea himself is the typical city dandy for
whom marriage, usually at a late date, is reluctantly accepted in
quest of wealth, purity, or both. One might speculate that Maria,
had she been free, might more readily have inspired a wish for continuity in Andrea than any amount of availability in Elena, while it
is this latter, or women in her image, who alone could persistently
have stimulated desire.

Elena's visit to Andrea after two years of unexplained silence can
only be seen as an act of provocation in keeping with the suggestive mellowness of the Roman air. One wonders otherwise why
she would have troubled to come, with her act of renunciation and
pretended piety, if not to play her role to the end according to the
unwritten laws of love games. She might have simply refused to accept Andrea's invitation when she accidentally ran into him, but
that might have aroused a kind of disdain, through which she
would soon be shrugged off. More prone to keep intact her image
of the irresistible siren, she chooses to affect languor and painful
renunciation, submission to a mysterious fatality, while retaining
the upper hand and a measure of domination in Andrea's life.
"Could you suffer to share me with another?" she cries
dramatically when her old lover comes near her. The answer should

be: yes, of course, why not? But there is a strict if unwritten code that does not allow for truth to triumph here; it must first be molded by fiction and be given life through the imagination. Only in solitude can Andrea recognize the abyss that separates lust from love; but in the duplicity of his own words and thoughts resides the strongest element of corruption:

> So it was true—she had never really loved him. She had not scrupled to break with him in order to contract a marriage of convenience. And now she put on the airs of a martyr before him, wrapped herself round with a mantle of conjugal inviolability! A bitter laugh rose to his lips, and then a rush of sullen blind rage against the woman came over him. The memory of his passion went for nothing—all the past was one long fraud, one stupendous, hideous lie; and this man, who throughout his whole life had made a practice of dissimulation and duplicity, was now incensed at the deception of another. [Pp. 210-11]

Once Andrea recognizes that there are no truths or pinciples that can act as bulwark against his desire, he knows as well that all ideals have been renounced. "Impurity crept through his blood like a corroding poison" (p. 208), and consciously, almost calculatedly, he surrenders to the appeal of lust, foregoing all possibility of redemption. After one last effort to cling to a remnant of goodness in him ("suddenly the beauty of the night filled him with a vague but desperate yearning towards some unkown good"), he obstinately turns away from the temptation of purity, "he bent his head and entered the house without turning again to look at the night" (p. 211). Symbolically, he leaves behind, with the balmy light of the stars, the image of Maria and all that she represents.

The sublimation of desire and her renuncation had been difficult for Maria, but not altogether devoid of beauty. It had been the price exacted by a temptation born in a languorous summer by the sea, but a compensation, too, for a sentiment that transcended greed. When she comes to Rome, the reader is prepared already for Maria's surrender. The city has brought about by now the capitulation of Andrea's aspirations; how could the innocent woman resist or even detect the falsity of the situation! Maria does not have the strength to take flight once again before the attraction of love, and yet she is not unaware; she knows that only pain awaits her, and her surrender is a sacrificial act, one of self-immolation. "I cannot describe to you," she tells Andrea, "the strange foreboding that has weighed upon me for a long time past" (p. 235). When she is ready to promise that they would meet again soon, there is a din and an outcry in the air, as if the city itself could not watch unmoved its own victory.

> She rose abruptly, trembling from head to foot, giddy, paler still than on the morning when they walked together beneath the flower-laden trees. The wind still shook the panes; there was a dull clamour in the distance as of a riotous crowd. The shrill cries borne on the wind from the Quirinal increased her agitation. [P. 235]

It is the city of Rome that clamors with the wind from its highest hill, for if it exacts evil, this Rome of D'Annunzio is not altogether evil. It is simply a city too complex and enigmatic to offer peace to those who are uncertain and perturbed, who lack strength and resiliency in the face of temptation.

The episodes that follow lead toward the unavoidable conclusion. Maria loves, but more in reminiscence of her idyll in Schifanoia than through the allurement of the present; yet it is the present that has undermined the strength she once had. Andrea takes her and whispers words of love in her ear, while he mentally superimposes the image of Elena on the madonnalike face he beholds. Maria must finally leave and join her husband in South America; in anguish and an oppressive sense of guilt, she prepares to leave the man she loves. Their last walk together is to the Protestant cemetery outside the walls where the poet Shelley is buried; "And forget me, for I can never be thine"—the verses come sadly to memory. Maria unwraps the black veil from her hat and ties with it the white roses she has brought for the poet.

> "How did you manage to get those roses?" he asked. She smiled, but her eyes were wet. "They are yours—those of that snowy night—they have bloomed again this evening. Do you not believe it?" The evening breeze was rising, and behind the hill the sky was overspread with gold, in the midst of which the purple cloud dissolved, as if consumed by fire. Against this field of light, the serried ranks of the cypresses looked more imposing and mysterious than before. [P. 302]

On "that snowy night," exasperated from a long and fruitless wait for Elena, Andrea had thrown a bunch of roses in front of Maria's door. She had spiritually retrieved them and nestled them in her heart, while the snowplow had mechanically buried them in any icy tomb. Could the roses of this last and mournful day be the same? In the allegorical meaning of the story, yes, they are the very same ones, nurtured by faith and love after being cast into the snow, and relinquished finally on a cold stone. They remain, on the tomb of the poet who had loved and died, the symbol of love and death, pervaded by the same golden light that had shined, at the beginning, upon rose petals strewn on the rug. More striking now, the theme of death is repeated in the dark cypresses, which are as ageless and imposing as the city in the distance and the chime of bells echoing from the Aventine.

The last scene is merely a reinforcement of what has already been suggested and developed. Maria abandons herself into Andrea's arms, mistaking the set expression upon his face for a pain similar to the one she suffers; but he is only consumed by jealousy and craving for Elena, and, in a last cruel irony, he murmurs her name.

> All at once, she struggled free of his embrace, her whole form convulsed with horror, her face ghastly and distraught as if she had at that moment torn herself from the arms of death. [P. 306]

The arms of death that, under the disguise of love, have wrecked her peace, now also claim her memories and the last shreds of ilusion. Nothing will be left if not squalor, the sense of having surrendered all into an immensurable void. After she will have left on the following day, her furniture is auctioned away, disposable as her feelings had been. Andrea walks in mechanically and buys a Buddha, the inscrutable God who seems to smile. The story closes as he finds himself following the porters up the stairs, an empty man behind meaningless objects, while "Rome, immense and dominated by a battle of clouds, seemed to illumine the sky" (p. 311).

This last image of the city that has borrowed the glow from the sky, shows a Rome that is triumphant and distant, perpetuating itself through the pages of history, watching generations of men, but remaining invulnerable, unheeding of their suffering and fleeting passions. D'Annunzio's Rome coincides, finally, with the image of the Buddha in the last pages—God-like, tangible, and remote at once, earthy and spiritual, seemingly fragile but immensely durable.

Notes to Chapter 3

1. Gabriele D'Annunzio, *The Child of Pleasure*, trans. Georgina Harding (Boston: Page and Company, 1906), p. 188. Miss Harding's translation follows the events chronologically as they were presented in the French translation, rather than as they appeared in the original Italian version. My study is based on the Italian presentation, while it uses the Harding and therefore the French translations. The initial paragraph quoted is in fact the opening one in the original 1889 novel in Italian. All subsequent quotations are from the same English translation. Also notice that the English title was regrettably taken from the French translation, *L'Enfant de la Volupté*, rather than from the Italian *Il Piacere*.

4

Rilke's *Notebooks:* Paris and the Phantoms of the Past

Where D'Annunzio's life was openly bent upon direct involvement with action, upon visions of heroic dimension and the contradictory forces that pushed him in turn amidst and away from society, Rainer Maria Rilke (1875-1926), equally self-centered but broodingly and tormentedly so, consciously sought his identity almost exclusively in the realm of poetry. The two poets do share an obsessive search for lyrical expression, and the effort for innovation and musicality in their verses. Rilke is—and few would quarrel with this—the greater of the two, the more melodious even, the more lastingly haunting in the images he evokes. His sources of inspiration came from his own inner world; his greatest loves were those he dreamed of in poetry; his affinity with action was primarily the urging of his restless nature toward intense peregrinations in search of an asylum.

Rilke led what was essentially an uneventful life. Yet his turbulent and sensitive nature often gave him the feeling that life was forlorn, beset by suffering and an inescapable sense of tragedy. Through writing, in his prose and, above all, in his poetry, Rilke endeavored to unburden his own anguish and to assuage his struggle against a pervasive and unremitting solitude. The separation of his parents when he was only nine years old marked him early in life with division and tension. He was almost thirty before he could accept that man's lot must by force be met in solitude and that wisdom lies within sorrow and pity. "At bottom no one in life can help anyone else in life; this one experiences over and over in every conflict and every perplexity: that one is alone," he was to write to

Friedrich Westhoff from Rome on April 19, 1904. "All compa-
nionship can consist only in the strengthening of two neighboring
solitudes" (Rainer Maria Rilke, *Letters. 1892-1910*, trans. Jane B.
Greene and M. D. Herter Norton [New York: W. W. Norton and
Co., 1945], pp 149-50).

Beset by poverty but having by now renounced all other means of
support outside of his own creative inspirations, Rilke went to
Paris in August 1902 in order to write a monograph on the French
sculptor Rodin. His stay in the French capital was often interrupted
by trips to Italy, Scandinavia, and Germany, but it is to Paris that
he came back time and again for inspiration and a tragic sense of
unity. The years 1902-10 were marked by intense literary activity.
The monograph on Rodin appeared in 1903, the year after he
published *Stories of God* and *The Tale of Love and Death of Cornet
Christopher Rilke*; in 1905 appeared the *Book of Hours*; in 1906-7
he translated Elizabeth Barrett Browning's *Sonnets from the Por-
tuguese* and wrote *New Poems*, followed a year later by *New
Poems II*. During these years Rilke worked also on *The Notebooks
of Malte Laurids Brigge*. The composition was painful and became
almost haunting for him. He soon came to consider his work as a
supreme effort to capture, within the pages of his book, the tragedy
of existence, his own and that of humanity at large. *The Notebooks*
was to remain for him, all through his life, his own poetic expression of man's need for communication and the artist's struggle for
expression. Through the meandering ways of *The Notebooks*, a
whole world of transient passions and squalor exemplified by the
magnifying presence of the city, was to assert its reality in artistic
language. "For Paris, which I admire so much and which I know I
must go through as one goes through a school,—is something con-
tinually new, and when it gives one the feeling of its greatness, its
almost limitlessness, that is when it becomes really ruthless and so
completely annihilates one that one must quite diffidently start in
all over again with an ardent attempt at living" (letter to Baroness
Von Nordeck zur Rabenau, June 20, 1907, in *Letters*, p. 284). Paris
became the lesson of life for Rilke, and his *Notebooks* is a lasting
image of and a defiance to the brevity of existence.

When Rilke left Paris for Munich in 1914 he did not know that
for years he would be prevented from returning by a catastrophic
and divisive war. Years of poetic maturity followed during which

the *Duino Elegies* and *Sonnets to Orpheus* were completed (1922). Rilke retired at the castle of Muzot in Switzerland, where he died of leukemia in 1926, soon after the publication in French of "Vergers suivis de quatrains valaisans."

The *Notebooks of Malte Laurids Brigge* was begun early in 1904 when Rilke, then close to thirty, first went to France. It was only completed six years later, in 1910. The composing proved painful for the young author, and it involved a struggle for the recapturing of a truth caught in the elusiveness of a haunting past. The result is a work that stands both as a kind of spiritual and emotional autobiography, and perhaps as the first fully significant step of the author into the realm of art. *The Notebooks* afford a glimpse of Rilke's ordeal in his confrontation with a reality replete with horrifying patterns of suffering. Painful as the slow composition of the work was, the writer was later to realize that he had the duty not to shy away from the horrible. His vocation was eventually to become the poet of inwardness; yet he first had to seize life, to embrace its outwardness, to accept its dismal aspects of poverty and misery and the omnipresence of death in the streets of Paris through which he wandered. Eight years after the completion of *The Notebooks*, in a letter to one of his female confidants, Rilke formulated the essence of that quest he had pursued in the French metropolis under the guise of Malte: "How is it possible to live, when the elements of this life of ours are altogether not graspable for us? When we always prove inadequate in love, insecure when we have to decide, powerless when facing death, how is it possible to go on being?"[1] The nightmarish patterns and compelling sense of reality of the *Notebooks* are the reflection of an imagination in turmoil; they also project the pathos of a frightful and unavoidable adventure in the realm of the unknown and the forbidden. The hero's search and that of the author coincide, both undertaken in despair and out of a need for clarity and order in a world of chaos. That neither Rilke nor Malte arrives at a coherent answer to the problems of existence does not detract from the validity of the search.[2] The bleak pessimism and pervasive feeling of loathing that dominate the first part of the *Notebooks* gradually usher in, if not a positive at least a more accepting attitude. The lingering note left at the end is one of energy and continuity that implicitly justify life.

The city of Paris is a drab and sad medley in this work, a place dominated by loneliness and malady, with faces of anguish along its roads and the recurring image of death. Malte, the protagonist of the story, is here both a spectator and a victim of the city, and his vision is intricately personal and, at the same time, objective and almost detached. Malte's eyes are like those of a camera, selecting details and magnifying them at times, moving along a spectrum of existence dictated by his own inner turmoil and fears. The protagonist's search is both personal and universal, a personal quest that extends beyond the self and reaches for the eternal. Malte's past rests in a twilight of memories of far-away Denmark and of a youth spent in oppressive loneliness. It is only in distorted fashion that he recaptures the morbid fantasies of the child he once was, in isolated and disjointed images that do not add up to the man he has become. When he comes to Paris he is twenty-eight years old, but he still carries within himself an unresolved childhood and the anguish of the incoherent fears that had weighed upon him during the early years of his life. That he must come to terms with that past before the present can hold any meaning for him is clear. But the confrontation with the past means a painful reliving of its torments in the light of an oppressive present, and a reshaping of his Parisian journey through the meandering paths of his Danish ancestry. Day after day will prove a new trial for Malte, seemingly hopeless at first but gradually revealing a glimmer of light in the miasma of city life. His pursuit slowly becomes a resolve, and the truth that he seeks will emerge out of his creative energy. Malte's search leads him to the only possible avenue out of his spectral world of revolving horrors. *The Notebooks* will oppose to the transient aspects of existence a lasting artistic creation.

The tension that is established with the opening words of the work is one that oscillates between recognition of new verities, with an implicit reappraisal of past assumptions, and the lingering doubts that rest upon years of longing and grieving. That tension also arises from contradictory wishes—from a morbid fascination with death and an unavowed but impelling desire to live. "So, then, people do come here in order to live; I would sooner have thought one died here."[3] The Paris that is contemplated through the word "here" is itself a recollection, a memory already, of the present that Malte is in the midst of living. The immediateness of the moment is in fact always pushed back and observed in the light of past experiences. The "here" of this initial sentence is indeed Paris. But Paris, while it stands as a whole, all around, in the streets, the buildings, the people, and even the noises, is cast filtered through an imagination that seeks access to its forbidden world. It is as if Malte were both within and on the outside of Paris, having just arrived and measuring the city with an appraising eye, and seeing it through the fog of years past, real and unreal, vital and decaying at once:

> I have been out. I saw: hospitals. I saw a man who swayed and sank to the ground. People gathered round him, so I was spared the rest. I saw a pregnant woman. She was pushing herself cumbrously along a high, warm wall, groping for it now and again as if to convince herself it was still there. And behind it? I looked on my map: Maison d'Accouchement. Good. They will deliver her—they know how. Further on, rue Saint-Jacques, a big building with a cupola. The map said: Val-de-Grâce, Hôpital militaire. I didn't really need this information, but it can't do any harm. The street began to smell from all sides. A smell, so far as one could distinguish, of iodoform, of the grease of pommes-frites, of fear. [P. 13]

Memory is emotionally selective, and Malte's notebook is thus a mirror of his state of mind. His walks along the Parisian avenues and the objects and people he sees are segments of a larger reality only vaguely sensed but still finding no correspondence within. What his eye singles out are recognizable shapes, the same that he carries within and bear heavy upon his soul. Malte has gone out presumably on his first walk in the foreign capital here, map in hand and eyes open to a world that is alien but holds no novelty for him. The images that come forward are framed in the recurring and alternating motifs of the act of living and that of dying. In slow succession, he sees first a kind of no-man's land, the "hospitals" in which people come both to die and to be born. The next image is one that denies life: a man who falls senseless to the ground. The crowd that gathers around him remains faceless and incongruous, hiding the vision of death without detracting from its horror. In relief to the oppressiveness of these images another picture is framed along the road. A "pregnant woman" comes forward carrying a message of life, "groping" but finding support in a "warm" wall. Another hospital, the smell of iodoform and then that of fried potatoes, repeat the fluctuating pattern established by the first images. Pervading all vision like an enveloping mist, there is the constant presence of "fear"—a fear that is Malte's life blood and seeks its correspondence on the outside.

Foreboding and anxiety, the senseless, the grotesque, often hold a fascination that defies the paralyzing effect of their presence. The images that rush to Malte's vision, frightful, frequently macabre, monstrous, and sickening, hold the attraction of a surrealistic world, both dismaying and bewitching, immediate, intimate, and immensely personal.

> I am learning to see, I don't know why it is, but everything penetrates more deeply into me and does not stop at the place where until now it always used to finish. [P. 14]

Malte's ability to discern within reality the hidden layers of the unconscious is new, directly related to the city to which he has come. Paris is the catalyst here that creates, with every event, a mirror of that event; it brings about a kind of emotional dissection that is both inside and outside the event that is contemplated. Malte observes the living portraits of fear, loneliness, and despair that he has always known; but for the first time he sees them, in spite of their familiarity, within a world that is not his own. If it is through his own isolation that he perceives, in the faces around, a reflection of his personal sense of loss and of his dread, he can now observe the random play of dread and loss upon features that are not his own, as phenomena outside of himself, unrelated to any direct experience.

> But the woman, the woman; she has completely collapsed into herself, forward into her hands. . . .The street was too empty; its emptiness was bored; it caught my step from under my feet and clattered about with it hither and yon, as with a wooden clog. The woman startled and pulled away too quickly out of herself, too violently, so that her face remained in her two hands. I could see it lying in them, its hollow form. It cost me indescribable effort to stay with those hands and not to look at what had torn itself out of them. I shuddered to see a face from the inside, but still I was much more afraid of the naked flayed head without a face.[4] [P. 16]

The emptiness of a Parisian street is a "bored" presence with which Malte must reckon. It—the street, or its very nudity—stretches in front of him like a reflecting mirror, throwing back the echoes of his thoughts. The "catching of the step" from under him gives here the foreboding and anticipation that Malte senses. He is a spectator and an actor reliving his frightful past and taking his first steps into a new world. The motion of going through an empty street is a painful discovery with a predictable end; but the steps now become a mission that will eventually lead to the double acceptance of life and death. The street is a guide that tyrannically leads Malte "hither and yon," to a confrontation with suffering and desolation. The woman, caught unaware, reveals a face not composed for Malte's scrutinizing eye; her everyday public mask "remained in her two hands," but inside out, showing the flayed skin and the vulnerability within. This poetic, surrealistic vision of the unknown woman who holds her face in her bare hands—and in so doing offers the portrait of Malte's own helplessness—is an appalling image of pain, but one that suggests an embryonic movement of reconciliation with life. If it is true, in fact, that Malte does not dare to look at "the naked head," and therefore at the total display of what is most hidden and most intimate in a human being, he nevertheless contemplates "those hands" and the segment of gruesome truth they represent.

It is of course difficult to establish to what degree Malte's struggle was that of the author himself. The reader does know that the poet was caught within the double vise of poverty and unresolved purpose during his stay in Paris, and one can only assume that this accounts for the images of desolation and the aimless wanderings in Malte's world. What is of concern here, however, is the role that the city plays both in projecting the evils with which life is replete and in suggesting the necessity for a measure of acceptance of those evils and a resolution of inner tensions. The city is not a casual background to the quandaries of Malte's existence; it is, rather, the force that brings all strife to the fore and dictates the painful dilemma of choices. Rilke had struggled for clarity there, and had, each day, come closer to heeding the imperious urge for artistic expression. When he yielded to the temptation of relief from the oppressiveness of Parisian atmosphere and went to Rome to seek peace, he was disappointed. The transparency of the Roman sun, he found, hid from view the depth of his search and prevented him

from accomplishing the task he had begun.[5] The work that had
been started in Paris could only be accomplished there. His hero
Malte is spared the added burden of flight from the gray city and
the vain hope that sunshine could reveal more acceptable truths.
Even Malte's trip to the theater in Orange, in the South of France,
can only be seen as part of his uninterrupted peregrinations and not
as an attempt at breaking away from them. He carries within the
tacit recognition that Paris is his own mirror, and that its enslaving
bond cannot be relaxed except through a full understanding of the
image it proffers.[6]

Caught within Malte's feverish vision, the large French
metropolis projects paranoid visions. Malte wanders through them,
in and out of objects and sounds, and catches in his frayed nerves
all the nuances of their presence. There is an anguished sense of
wait, and only an inner turmoil sporadically covers the din of the
city:

> Electric street-cars rage ringing through my room. Automobiles
> run their way over me. A door slams. Somewhere a window-pane
> falls clattering; I hear its big splinters laugh, its little ones
> snicker. ....These are the noises. But there is something here that
> is more terrible: the stillness. I believe that in great conflagra-
> tions there sometimes occurs such a moment of extreme tension:
> the jets of water fall back, the firemen no longer climb their
> ladders, no one stirs. Noiselessly a black cornice thrusts itself
> forward overhead, and a high wall, behind which the fire shoots
> up, leans forward, noiselessly. [P. 14]

Within the noises, even the mechanical and strident ones, there is
hidden the presence of a humanity in disarray, but one that is at
least alive with its screams and its calls. In the silence that at night
descends suddenly upon a motionless universe, however, Malte
watches the terrifying phantoms of his imagination. His prostrate
figure yearning for sleep becomes the prey of the city's now spectral
force and hidden violence. The very use of the present here, "there
are the noises. But there *is* something..." suggests the recurring
pattern, the daily trials that the young man has fixed from memory
in his notebook.

Memories, for Rilke as for Proust, are not culled through a
cerebral process of a mental storing up of thoughts, but through an
eruption of images within the vagaries of the imagination, an

associative power of colors, shapes, sounds, and smells that is sudden and often unconscious. But in Proust there is a collective image that gradually emerges, one composed of many layers that rest upon each other with an ever widening and deepening perspective. In Malte's rambling journal, however, there is no focal point, no symbolic cup of tea or kaleidoscopic sun ray upon a pavement to give a point of reference to his "remembrance of things past." The images are disconnected, with no sequential order, each contained in its own frame, frozen in time and immutable in an endless present. Yet little by little a new sense of reality emerges out of Malte's nightmarish contemplations, one that does not consist in an avoidance of but in a willful consenting to the horrors of life.

The image that Malte constantly sees, wherever he looks, the "face in the mirror," is of course his own. His walks along the streets of Paris are hence a kind of pilgrimage, a retracing of each step of the past in the light of the present. The person he addresses at each turn is his other self. That part of his self is still out of reach, on the other side of the psychic cleavage he carries within. But he seeks at each turn a coincidence and a blending with it. "Have I said it before?" (p. 15), he repeats as he tries to bring his intellectual and emotional beings closer to each other. "I sit here and am nothing. Nevertheless this nothing begins to think and thinks, five flights up, on a gray Parisian afternoon..." (p. 28). In those thoughts what had been only a dream begins to be a vocation, as Malte sets upon the road that will transmute his anguish into poetry and a work of art. The "gray Parisian" air will not allow him flights of fantasy; he must measure his call with the reality around him, and the reality he had smothered in the early recollections of his youth. "Twelve years old, or at most thirteen, I must have been at the time" (p. 30). Slowly, the tacit suffering of that child of long ago comes to the surface. It is contemplated in dismal solitude by the young man who desperately needs to distance those years in order to face the future.

There remains whole in my heart, so it seems to me, only that large hall in which we used to gather for dinner....This lofty and, as I suspect, vaulted chamber was stronger than everything else. With its darkening height, with its never quite clarified corners, it sucked all images out of one without giving one any definite substitute for them. One sat there as if dissolved; entirely without will, without consciousness, without desire, without defence. One was like a vacant spot. [P. 31]

The images that emerge from the distant past, dark, oppressive, bringing along all the repressed pain of the voiceless child that Malte once was, become alive in the equally oppressive Parisian atmosphere. The role of Paris is thus gradually delineated as that of an analyst drawing out of Malte, as with a patient, the reality he must slowly confront. The city's voice is inaudible but imperious, and Malte will heed it. He will look at all the images he carries buried in his consciousness and reappraise them with new maturity and new strength.

Malte says, "I kept on the move incessantly" (p. 46). With self-scrutinizing clarity he knows that the constant act of moving has been his unspoken manner of rejecting a reality too painful to accept. He also knows that all of his perceptive powers are directed by his inner anguish and that he will continue to detect on the outside a replica of the phantoms he carries within. He runs both away and toward those phantoms, realizing that they can no longer be avoided and yet recoiling from their presence. "Somewhere or other I saw a man pushing a vegetable cart before him. He was shouting 'Chou-fleur, chou-fleur,' pronouncing the 'fleur' with a strangely muffled 'eu'" (p. 46). Would Malte have noticed the muffled sound if it had not silenced the word "flower," standing for beauty and renewal? That question does not really come up in the text, but a similar one crops up in Malte's consciousness: "Isn't the main thing what the whole business was for me?" he asks, implicitly acknowledging that all reality, of objects, sounds, and sensations, is but the echo and the reflection of one's own voice and inner visions. "The sweet, lingering smell of neglected infants was there, and the fearsmell of children who go to school, and the sultriness out of the beds of nubile youths" (p. 48). The "neglected" new borns, the smell of "fear" exuding from school children, and the sweltering cloyness associated with youths who have no knowledge of love are the images that come forward in Malte's Parisian journey. They repeat the pattern of his own life and the bewildering loneliness of his growing years.

I said, did I not, that all the walls had been demolished except the last—? It is of this wall I have been speaking all along. One would think I had stood a long time before it; but I'm willing to swear that I began to run as soon as I had recognized that wall. For that is the terrible thing, that I did recognize it. I recognize everything here, and that is why it goes right into me: it is at home in me. [P. 48]

The "walls" that have "been demolished" are the barriers he himself had erected around a vacuum. There he had crawled and lived in isolation, seeking protection from the evils outside. The images that are here evoked are nighmarishly vivid. Each segment of Malte's life stands encapsuled in walls that have tumbled down and have finally left him exposed and frightened. One barrier remains, a last impediment between him and a final reconciliation with all the horrors of life. "I began to run as soon as I had recognized that wall," Malte says. At each running he relives the torment, in anticipation and the effort to avoid it, of that obstacle in his way. But that wall fills the streets of Paris with the same bleak houses of his youth, the same sterile lives, and the omnipresent image of death.

The line of demarcation between life and death in Malte's world is one tied to the element of fear and, to a lesser degree, to that of longing. Death is that which is fearful, the distortion of images, the corruption of thought—the face of the woman that bewilderingly clings to her two hands, the neighbor's wrestling with the mathematics of time, the shadow weighing in the darkness on the weeping child's bed. Death is not the figure of Christine Brahe leaving her grave to walk erect and unconcerned through the dining room, or the flighty image of Frederic IV's morganatic wife casually appearing in grandfather's talks. Death is the feeling of oppression that emerges from a wall standing sneeringly in the way or the loss of warmth from those one loved. All the figures that had been dear to young Malte have receded into the engulfing shadow of the grave; but as they moved away, Malte has caught their last receding step within his memory and feverish imagination. It is that step, that last motion before eternity, that is within the composition of the wall erected on his path and nourishes the passionate vagaries of his mind: Chamberlain Christof Detlev's ultimate struggle with a force stronger than his, or Maman's last outing to the Schulinses' house. It is of no concern either to the reader or to Malte himself if those images—of grandfather's powerful railings against the impending death or the Schulinses' spectral house in the eerie setting of his youth—are framed within any semblance of empirical reality. They are Malte's tyrannical truth with which he still must come to terms. They are the last erected wall along his way and the last psychic obstacle against creation.

Alone in the foreign capital peopled with shadows, Malte recognizes the nature of death: it resides in loneliness, disarray, and the irrationality of motion constantly at odds with the folly of existence. But the monstrously large Paris itself, when contemplated in the light of the mystery of life, becomes a speck in the realm of eternity. Malte's own losses can thus be assimilated within a larger concept of death, one that is visible upon all the anonymous faces in the streets of Paris. The death of each individual slowly emerges as only a step along the road of unrecorded history, a repetition in time of all the facets of existence. Christof Detlev, Count Brahe, Ingeborg, beautiful Abelone, and even the haunting image of Maman are contemplated, one by one, by Malte, until they blend within a larger frame of reference. Only there are they invested with a measure of their own tenuous continuity and the rightful perspective provided by time and memory. The figures of King Charles VI of France, that of Ivan Grosny and the false Czar that suddenly emerge from the pages of history books upon Malte's consciousness, do not diminish either his personal sense of loss or the importance of the lives of those he had loved. But they can now be viewed in a different light, which embraces a spectrum of existence larger than that of the individual. The Paris with a thousand deaths and a thousand lives at every corner gradually reveals to Malte a new dimension of death and a measure of life. The milling crowd that seems to have only a semblance of life upon a mask of death imparts a lesson that he has been loath to accept, that of the inseparability of life and death within all visions of eternity.

An entirely different conception of all things has developed in me under these influences; certain differences have appeared that separate me from other men, more than anything heretofore. A world transformed. A new life filled with new meanings. For the moment I find it a little hard because everything is too new. I am a beginner in my own circumstances. [P. 67]

Assertively, the vast city in which Malte has sought refuge has pushed him on. It has led him to weigh the cumulative force of his own past against all that is the past, and to recognize that within a seemingly aimless existence the individual has his own legitimate role. The small universe of his youth in far-away Denmark imparted greatness to familiar figures. That greatness is not diminished with the knowledge of their relative insignificance within the magnitude of life. But the ghosts that once composed Malte's reality are gradually reshaped, "transformed," and given a new perspective through which his fears and hopes assume equitable dimensions. He now notices "certain differences" that separate him from the others, and with this his life assumes a degree of importance it has not known until now. What counts even more is that implicitly the other faces around him assume individual contours too, within the grayness of city life. The city thus becomes a repository of human memory in which Malte has found the very shape of his own past. Paris embodies a condensed reality of life projected through its images of desolation, sickness, and death. "I am a beginner in my own circumstances," recognizes Malte as he considers his private world from the perspective of a larger model of life. He can now identify, within the antlike existence of the city, a coincidence with the strong individualism of the past.

Malte's *Notebooks* is, in the final analysis, his lasting answer to the horrors projected through the magnifying lenses of city existence. Malte does not come to terms with those horrors, and in that respect his efforts are a failure. But in his very act of struggling, his anguish crystallizes into words, and the nightmare of his long Parisian night finds a voice that will be heard long after he himself disappears. If the ominous presence of death is not diminished, the limitations of one man's life at least will have been challenged:

> The existence of the horrible in every particle of air! You breathe it in with what is transparent; but inside you it precipitates, hardens, takes on pointed, geometrical forms between your organs; for whatever of torment and horror has happened on places of execution, in torture chambers, madhouses, operating-theatres, under the vaults of bridges in late autumn: all this has a tough imperishability, all this subsists in its own right and, jealous of all that is, clings to its own frightful reality. [P. 68]

Malte recognizes here the "imperishability" of the evils of life. They cannot be pushed aside, disguised, or forgotten; surely they cannot be conquered. But in giving them a voice, Malte finds a way of cloaking his own terrors within the sphere of art:

> But do not imagine I am suffering disappointments here—quite the contrary. I marvel sometimes how readily I give up everything I expected for the reality, even when the reality is bad. My God, if any of it could be shared! But would it BE then, would it BE? No, it IS only at the price of solitude. [P. 68]

His uniqueness as a human being has been both challenged and reaffirmed through the proximity of people and immense suffering. That uniqueness, which has rested on a romantic image of the world and of his place within it, now finds a measure of strength in a willful affirmation of the self, in solitude and a chosen path. Malte's world had been an island, a self-contained image that, with the fears and the pain, had held some comfort and a sense of belonging. No matter how puzzling that world might have appeared to the child he once was, his own life and that of those around him had been held in a common bond. Within those bonds he had found what was an unchallengeable identification, comprising a family, a town, and a country. At this point all of that has to be reappraised, measured against the nameless deaths on the faces of the anonymous crowd and reaffirmed in the light of all the wretchedness of Parisian existence. "At the price of solitude" a poem is born that will contain the essence of his minute life within the larger spectrum of existence, and his own spark of eternity. Borrowing Baudelaire's prose poem, Malte writes here:

> Mécontent de tous et mécontent de moi, je voudrais bien me racheter et m'enorgueillir un peu dans le silence et la solitude de la nuit. Ames de ceux que j'ai aimés, âmes de ceux que j'ai chantés, fortifiez-moi, soutenez-moi, éloignez de moi le mensonge et les vapeurs corruptrices du monde; et vous, Seigneur mon Dieu! accordez-moi la grâce de produire quelques beaux vers. [P. 53][7]

Paris has brought to fore the meaninglessness of existence but, at the same time, the necessity of a full realization of one's being within the vacuum that entraps him. In the foreign words of the foreign capital, Malte borrows the very language of the city that has revealed to him the unavoidability of horror: the same poetic language that has insinuated as well, within those horrors, its own imperishable light.[8]

In the same period, or only a short time later, in which Rilke was striving for a lasting expression of man's brief existence and for an artistic mold into which to pour his vision of life, there existed unknown to him, in the same city of Paris, another man waging the same battle. Marcel Proust, from his cork-lined refuge in a fashionable Parisian district, was also measuring the insignificance of a lifespan against eternity, and endeavoring to defy those limitations in the same manner as the young Rilke from his squalid tenement room. Both Rilke and Proust concluded that the essence of art rests upon the crystallization of one's understanding of life and the translation of that understanding into a language that is at once very personal and timeless. Both proceeded with the Platonic assumption that all knowledge is a remembrance, and that the only valid perspective for the present is given by a reliving of all of the yesterdays. The artist's impelling necessity to seize a fleeting reality and fix it into lasting language finds impetus in the discernment of past experiences seen in the light of the present. For Proust, his search for a valid expression led him to a projection of images with an ever-enlarging and varying focus, as if new and bigger frames were constantly added to the initial one. The result was a multifaceted landscape that expands tangentially in ever-growing dimensions. For Rilke the acquiring of a cohesive mental view of existence was equally gradual; but for him the final impact came not in physical isolation from the world but in confrontation with it. His inner quest could only find expression after a spiritual collision with the city and a contest that could not avoid failure except within the enduring realm of art. Only with a lasting artistic creation could he fitfully oppose the baleful forces of death and despair in the city of Paris.

Although the question never occurs, one could wonder why Malte came to Paris. But with the question, an answer is immediately formulated; it is one that does not give reasons, however, but simply accepts the fact that Malte *had* to come to Paris. Only in this large, gray, foreign, and discordant metropolis could he establish the necessary link between past and present, from which would emerge his artistic creation. He retraces slowly his steps and relives one by one all those images from his past which have left furrows in his soul: the death of his mother, that of his father, of a house, of a dog. He trembles in evoking the face of the child he once was, and the fear, the pain, and anguish upon that face. Tenderly he watches over that child who stands aghast in a world he does not understand, struggling with the phantoms of a seemingly endless night. He remembers when the young Malte was kneeling on a chair and tracing on a paper, by candlelight, heroic knights and primeval horses; when the wonderfully red crayon fell and rolled toward the dark wall across the room, he clambered down and groped, lost in the immensity of the thick rug. Suddenly, from the wall, another hand, thin and disincarnate, "came groping in similar fashion from the other side."

> The two outspread hands moved blindly toward one another. My curiosity was not yet used up but suddenly it came to an end, and there was only terror. I felt that one of the hands belonged to me, and that it was committing itself to something irreparable. With all the authority I had over it, I checked it and drew it back flat and slowly, without taking my eyes off the other, which went on groping. [P. 84]

These phantoms from the far-away past cannot be simply dismissed, at will, and called puerile fancies. That wall of long ago is the same that Malte recognizes in Paris, the unchanging nightmarish barrier that prevents the full apprehension of life. Only a spectral hand reaches out from it, a kind of aimless tentacle from which Malte recoils. As he contemplates in retrospect the bewilderment he had then felt, he recognizes that the child had already felt despair at not finding the words that would relate his experience. That same anguish grips him now, measured, however, in the poetic language that gives reality to his suffering. "To live through once again the reality down there, differently, conjugated, from the beginning" (p. 85): that is the horrible task that Malte has undertaken through the urging of Paris, to reconstruct in words the frightful experience of his past and bring it to life. The alien city has projected for him, it now appears, spectral hands and faces of death so that he could catch in them a glimpse of eternity and perceive, in the passing of time, the renewal of life.

The longings and dreads of childhood, the suffering of later years, assume their rightful proportions when contemplated in the shadow of history and past kings. Malte has learned that life has the face of anguish, that it dwells not behind but within the fearful wall. He has also learned that he must not run away from that wall, but stare at it and, with love and compassion, accept the spectral hand proffered to him. "This, then, is to your liking," he addresses God, "in this you take pleasure. That we should learn to endure before all and not to judge" (p. 179). The final lesson taught by the city is the most difficult to accept: the humility that, upon discernment of the need for love on the withered faces of passers-by, accepts that love be denied. "This city is full of people who are slowly gliding down to their level" (p. 180), people, that is, who have been worn out and bent down by life, without warmth or promise. "They walk along past the houses, people keep coming who screen them from view, they vanish away behind them like nothing" (p. 181). They disappear leaving no trace, but they reappear around a bend, with different faces and yet always the same. The city has denied man his uniqueness but has conferred upon the human face a touch of eternity. The destitute people along the streets, with their nakedness and vulnerability, the grimaces of pain and the image of squalor, are the perennial shadows of a life that denies love. But love, together with hate, suffering, and hope, finds expression within a mask that is the synthesis of a larger truth: the "shadows ordered in the semblance of a face" are the artistic mold that contains the essence of existence, purified and enhanced.

> This was the strong, all-covering antique mask, behind which the world condensed into a face. Here, in this great incurved amphitheatre of seats, there reigned a life of expectancy, void, absorbent; all happening was yonder: gods and destiny; and thence (when one looked, up high) came lightly, over the wall's rim: the eternal entry of the heavens. [P. 195]

In the large open theater of Orange, Malte has come to seek the forum for a poetic synthesis of life and to observe the gigantic play of existence take shape in surrealistic truth. Here the individual makes room for larger concepts that go beyond him without, however, denying his own entity. The plurality of existence, composed of movement and the stillness of death, emerges from the stage of the large amphitheater. There the world is envisaged, the heavens and eternity. Above the recurring image of the wall, a glimmer of light is now visible, as is the entry into the heavens. That light, that glimmer of eternity, "the eternal entry of the heavens," is the poem that surges from Malte's conscience and takes the shape of words. The implicit challenge to God ("We who have undertaken God, can never finish" [p. 99]) is to strive for a measure of His timelessness and fix it upon the written page. That challenge bows to a life barren of love and warmth, and it accepts that the demands of art reside outside love and unity.

The final pages in Malte's notebooks are dedicated to the image of the Prodigal Son who wandered away refusing the gift of love. The oppressive solitude that had paralyzed Malte's youth gradually appears to him no longer as a calamity but as the condition for his being. Alone, without friends in the cruel city where he has come, without the warmth of those he has loved, he knows that his task consists of reshaping life and of giving it the form of art. Like the legendary Prodigal Son, "he recognized more clearly from day to day that the love of which they were so vain and to which they secretly encourage one another, had nothing to do with him" (p. 216). As Malte concludes his journal of anguished search, his task begins. Art, like life, has no conclusion, as it is each time renewed and re-created, at each beholding. Malte too has learned the lesson that Rilke had detected in Rodin's creation and its answer to the problem of opposition between life and art.[9] Paris has shown him that life does not lie within the perishable comfort of love but in the calculated repetitiveness of all the horrors that go into its composition and their projection into eternity: the grinding of lives and deaths, the suffering, the neglect, the perennial sense of loss and fear, the whole past united with the present.

Notes to Chapter 4

1. Letter to a lady, L. H., November 8, 1915, in Rainer Maria Rilke, *Briefe* (Leipzig: Insel-Verlag, 1938), 4:86.
2. In a letter to his wife Clara, dated October 19, 1907, three years before the completion of The *Notebooks*, Rilke expressed the double anguish—his own and that of his character, Malte—at the difficulty of coming to terms with the horrors of life. "And all at once (and for the first time) I understand the fate of Malte. Is it not this: that this test was too much for him, that he did not

pass it in reality, although in his mind he was convinced of his necessity, so much so that he sought it out so long instinctively that it finally clung to him and never left him?'' (R. M. Rilke, *Briefe aus den Jahren 1904—1907* [Leipzig, Insel-Verlag, 1930], p. 432).

3. Rainer Maria Rilke, *The Notebooks of Malte Laurids Brigge*, trans. M. D. Herter Norton (New York: W. W. Norton and Company, 1949), p. 13. All quotes are from this edition unless otherwise indicated.

4. Malte's experience here is possibly related to a similar one witnessed by the author. See in this connection part of a letter (July 18, 1903) he wrote to Lou Andreas Salomé: ''One evening late in autumn a little woman stood next to me in the light of a shop window....I suddenly looked at her strangely clasped hands. There out of these hands, slowly, quite slowly, rose an old, long, thin pencil; it grew and grew taking a long time before it was completely visible, visible in its entire wretchedness....It seemed to me that a whole destiny unrolled before me...'' Rilke, *Letters. 1892-1910,* trans. Jane B. Green and M. D. Herter Norton [New York: W. W. Norton and Co., 1942], p. 110).

5. To Salomé, Rilke writes on May 12, 1904, from Rome: ''However that may be—in any case more modern and more serious countries have since educated my senses to be subdued and simple, so that they now feel what is glaring and strong, schematic and uninflected in Italian things as a relapse into picture-book instruction'' *(Letters. 1892-1910,* p. 157).

6. The haunting image of Paris often appears in Rilke's correspondence during this time, and also later. One adjective that recurs time and again is *''schwer''* (heavy, burdensome). In his earliest letters from Paris in 1902 he declares, ''Paris ist eine schwere, schwere, bange Stadt....'' To Lou Andreas-Salomé, much later, after he had freed himself of some of his Parisian anguish, on October 21, 1913, he was to write to the same haunting feeling about the French city: *''schwer''* was the word for Paris. On December 21, 1913, to Princess von Thurn und Taxis, declaring himself ''surfeited'' with Paris, he pronounced the city ''a place of damnation'' (*''ein Ort der Verdamnis''*). I might also mention a famous line in the first *Duino Elegy*, composed in 1911, only one year after Rilke had concluded *The Notebooks*, which identifies the beautiful as ''the beginning of the terrible, which we can hardly tolerate'' (*''des Schrecklichen Anfang, den wir noch grade ertragen''*).

7. The English translation of Baudelaire's poem reads, ''Unhappy with all and unhappy with myself, I would very much want to redeem myself and to grow a little proud in the silence and solitude of the night. Souls of those I have loved, souls of those I have sung, give me strength, sustain me, keep away from me all lies and the world's corrupting exhalations; and you, Lord my God! grant me the favor to produce some beautiful verse.'' (The translation is my own.) To Salomé Rilke was to write on July 18, 1903: ''A prayer of Baudelaire's; a real, simple prayer, made with his hands, awkward beautiful as the prayer of a Russian—He had a long way to go to get there, Baudelaire, and he went on his knees and crawling'' *Letters, 1892-1910,* p. 108).

8. Many studies exist on Rilke's very rich and very personal language. Among others, Hans Egon Holthusen calls the intensely personal and lyrical expression "idiopathic" *Rainer Marie Rilke: A Study in His Later Poetry,* trans. J. P. Stern [New Haven, Conn.: Yale University Press, 1952], p. 9).
9. See Rilke's *Auguste Rodin* (Leipzig: Insel-Verlag, 1930), p. 7: "Rodin was lonely before his fame. And fame, when it came, has perhaps made him lonelier still."

5

Proust's *Remembrance of Things Past:* Venice and the Reality within the Dream

Many are the ways that lead to artistic realization. For Rilke it was an early dream, an "idée fixe" that impelled him, from a young age, toward poetic expression. Marcel Proust (1871-1922) came to it slowly, hesitantly at first, uncertain of its meaning. Gradually the will to write gained ascendancy in his life; it acquired the shape of a mission until, during his last years, it became obsessive and exclusive.

In a study of the city in modern fiction it would be difficult to ignore the degree of influence exercised by the very presence of the city in the artistic lives of the authors. With Proust, who was a dandy deeply involved in all the intrigues of social existence well before writing became for him a dominant passion, the city had a decided role in the shaping of his art. It inspired the fluctuating visions and urbane movement that are so intrinsic to his work, and it also allowed him leaps of fantasy into places sharply contrasting with its din, its size, and patterns. Perhaps, then, Proust's artistic vocation should be traced, mystically, to a time considerably earlier than his birth, when his own father broke away from family traditions and left the hometown of Illiers for Paris. Had he stayed in his native village, Marcel would have been later deprived of one of the great sources of inspiration for his *Remembrance of Things Past*. Illiers, transfigured into Combray, became the focus of his evocative power and artistic inspiration, linked to memories of youth and to vacations away from Paris in the grandmother's old house.

Proust was born in 1871 in Auteuil, near Paris, but grew up in

Paris. As a young man he was a faithful frequenter of fashionable salons and artistic circles. He was at once the typical "snob" so convincingly illustrated in his works, and the dispassionate observer endowed with the ability to discover all that was false and pretentious in those circles. His interest in the visual arts was more conventional and wordly, perhaps, than it appears in his discussions and lengthy expressions of admiration for certain painters. This chapter does not deal, however, with the visual arts as such or with any of Proust's works as a whole. Rather, I am concerned with his presentation of Venice as it appears scattered through the pages of *Remembrance of Things Past.*

Proust was not a traveler by nature, preferring to cherish the thought and anticipation of beauty rather than contemplating it directly. He was almost thirty years old when, in 1900, he went to Venice for the first time, accompanied by his mother. It is there that Marie Nordlinger, Reynaldo Hahn's cousin, who was also there, helped him revise his translation of Ruskin's *Stones of Venice.* What he wrote later in his *Contre Sainte-Beuve* (Paris: Gallimard, 1954; the translation is mine) reveals the tension that exists between previously imagined realities and their actual meeting.

> Before arriving in Venice ... mother was reading to me Ruskin's dazzling description which compares her in turn to the coral reefs of the Indian Sea and to an opal. Naturally, when our gondola stopped in front of her, she could not have in our eyes the beauty that for a moment she had had in our imagination, for we could not perceive things at once through the spirit and the senses. [4:122]

His portrait of Venice eventually became the blend of a vision long fermenting in his imagination and its actual discovery in a brief and poetic encounter. Proust's image of Venice is thus an artistic rendition of his own lived experience and, above all, of what his imagination saw within a constantly changing reality. It is there precisely that his originality rests, in the proffering of a reality that includes within its definition the presence of his very personal dream.

When Zola, Dos Passos, or D'Annunzio write about Paris, New York or Rome as corrupting, dying, or mesmerizing cities, when the situations they set forth resemble more unavoidable fatalities than individual choices, the reader knows that their assertions are dictated by a personal understanding of societies, of traditions, and of the role that the city plays in the lives of human beings. That knowledge does not, however, prevent one from accepting the realities such as they are presented or from entering into the created worlds of the authors; their premises and conclusions become the reader's for a time, and one sees in them verities of prophetic value inspired by creative intuition. Such is the reality of art as man has come to understand it, one that takes shape in a suspension of disbelief and in the intellectual and emotional relation one establishes with the world that lives within the literary work.

When at the turn of the century, with the disaffection from Naturalism, a new concept of art and reality was thrust upon the public, it was at first either rejected outright or received with uneasiness. The new form that emerged, both in the visual and in the literary arts, required a certain amount of sensuous response that the viewer and the reader were not accustomed to granting. They were, in fact, asked to acquiesce to a different "suspension of disbelief," one that did not merely involve the discarding of preconceived knowledge and factual understanding, but a certain forsaking of all notions and measures. D'Annunzio belonged more or less to that generation, and he cultivated the art of sensuous responses in literature; but he was too steeped in nineteenth-century traditions to be able to break away completely from them. Dos Passos was too involved in the problems of social values and directions of society, and, while in his novels he abandoned linearity and introduced cinematic flashes and seemingly disconnected episodes, he remained strongly indebted to Zola's ideas and traditions. When *Swann's Way* appeared in 1913, Thomas Mann was still the author of a nineteenth-century masterpiece in traditional form, *Buddenbrooks*, and James Joyce was still groping for full original development. The first author to free himself from all nineteenth-century traditions, and not only in manner and language but in the very notion of and relation to reality, is Marcel Proust. One is almost tempted to say that without him contemporary literature and artistic concepts would not be the same. What is of concern in this study is not, however, his undisputed originality and the place he holds as a precursor of new attitudes and artistic perspectives. The interest here is in his presentation of the city—Venice in this instance—which, along with the flowers, the cathedrals, or the people he describes, is to be seen in a different perspective from those accepted until then.

Proust discarded all notions of reality that consisted in a presumption of objective truths outside of man himself; the greatest enemies in his artistic universe could be considered, in fact, to be Zola and his school of Naturalism, with their assumption that not only buildings and streets, but families, relations, and atmosphere exist independently from the individual and his sensibilities. The "reality" of Proust's Venice is thus not to be seen as a force, real or imaginary, or as an immutable stage for lives and events. The mystical quality, even, with which his vision is imbued, has no religious fervor outside his own very individual relation to it, and it contains no truths or axioms that the reader must accept as a prerequisite. His presentation is so personal, in fact, that it may even be considered hermetic, a private domain precluded to the outsider. The reader cannot, as he might with Dos Passos, Zola, or Balzac, enter his world and make it his own, nor can he partake of the author's experiences and make of them an extension of his own understanding of life. If beauty is in the eye of the beholder, the beholder of beauty in Proust's work is none other than Proust himself, and one cannot borrow his sight. The reality he contemplates is suffused with too many shades of personal visions and intimate understandings for it ever to be the reader's, and his sense of truth is enveloped in the intricate pattern of his dreams, fears, and expectations. One cannot enter the domain of Proust's life and make it his own, nor can one divest himself of his own consciousness in order to accept the author's. But if the reader cannot invade the Proustian world, he can let it come to him, he can acquiesce to its presence and allow Marcel's dreams to unfold before him. And that is, parenthetically, the sense of beauty that Proust wanted to convey—an evolving of images, from the outside, which is superimposed by the reader's own experience and understanding of life, a coincidence of the viewed and the contemplated, the reality of the imagination and the evocative force of external reality.

In the *Gazette des Beaux Arts* of April 1, 1900, in an article on the English aesthetician Ruskin, Proust wrote that "The appearance of things alone reveals their profound nature" and that "a painting is beautiful to the degree that the ideas it translates into images are independent of the language of images."[1] If one changes the word "painting" for "Venice"—for his presentation of Venice is indeed a kind of painting, a personal travelogue and a pilgrimage in search of beauty—one may see that Proust meant to offer his own vision and only incidentally to suggest a mirror to the reader's dreams and an echo to the reader's feelings, and not in any way to substitute that vision for his reader's.

Proust's views were largely borrowed from Ruskin, who had conceived of beauty as something intrinsically existing in its own right, whose discovery rests upon a personal training of powers of perception. It is in the contemplation by the observer and in the meeting of two mystical forces—one coming from the observer and one originating in the work of art—that beauty finally lives. The subjective property hence implied in beauty through a personal discovery gave rise in Proust to a new concept in which reality is a microcosmic vision permeated with sensations and a passionate, more than rational relation with truth.

The process of arriving at a synthesis in *Remembrance of Things Past* follows a threefold movement very systematically. The first is the "imaginative process" where images evolve out of reflective dreams that are evoked through the power of sensations—dictated by shapes, that is, colors, sounds, smells. A world is here created that is by its very nature in a state of perpetual flux, for there is no external correspondence to what the imagination alone has envisioned. The second part of the movement—and usually at a much later date, after the "invented" reality has had ample time to take root and establish its presence irrevocably in the consciousness of the protagonist—is the meeting with external reality. This is invariably a shock that thrusts Marcel into a phase of disarray in the effort of finding a coincidence between the inner and the outer images. The third movement—which is ultimate and the one that will last in time—emerges however not out of a coincidence or superimposition of one truth upon the other, but out of a meeting of the two. A tension is established between them—between, that is, the gestative years shaping the vague contours of a personal dream and the shocking, tangible voilence of the present. Within this tension, gradually, a new shape emerges, a new truth, both personal and lasting, which is the work of art.

To trace Proust's presentation of Venice amounts, then, to retracing the path of his dream, one arising out of imaginative renderings of the city in paintings or books and the images and associations they conjure in his mind. That his first contact with the placid and multifaceted laguna, or with Saint Mark's glittering dome, or with the implacable white of the Doges's palace standing sentinel by the waters comes to him second hand emphasizes both the fallacy and the truth of an experience by proxy. The image contemplated in a dream that has no experience of it outside the dream itself cannot coincide with the shock of real discovery or in any way resemble a direct contact with external reality.

> The idea which I have formed of Venice, from a drawing by Titian which is supposed to have the lagoon in the background, was certainly far less accurate than what I have since derived from ordinary photographs.[2]

Titian, the Venetian painter straddling the fifteenth and sixteenth centuries, contemporary of Giorgione and leader of a school known for its emphasis on lights, deep shadows, and sensuousness of shapes and colors, is the first to introduce Venice to the young Marcel. It is hard to imagine what sights were conjured up through the reproduction of a painting that is itself an artistic and personal rendition of the city, but it must have been something resembling the wonder experienced by a child upon hearing a love story. One basks in a vague warmth composed more of images and unclear shapes than of feelings and sensations; and if there were any feelings, these surely were linked to the picture on the wall and not to the lagoon by the Adriatic Sea, to the shapes on the canvas and not to those against the Venetian sky. Yet out of these initial imaginative explorations into a city that still remains an abstraction for Marcel, visions are born that will one day confront the external reality and help reshape it. That confrontation will represent the segment of truth contained in all vicarious experiences.

The dimensions of a city are of course larger than any painting or words could suggest. Yet a painting or a single word even—the name of a city, Venice—encompasses within its limitations a uniqueness of associative power that the actual city cannot rival. By its very uniqueness, a name contains a universe; it holds an identity distinguished from all others and assumes shapes recognizable among thousands. Where an actual city may possibly suggest another through the narrowness of certain roads or the style of a church or buildings, a name has the singular force of conveying echoes that belong only to itself.

> How much more individual still was the character that they assumed from being designated by names, names that were only for themselves, proper names such as people have. [1:296]

"Venice" for Marcel soon assumes the ineffable contours of spring, with lights and flowers sweeping across paths of variegated waters amid Moorish columns and glittering facades; and by association, each time he feels a slight softness in the air, the vision of that Venice he does not yet know surges up miraculously from the confines of his unconsciousness and assumes the shape of his longing—simplified perhaps, but comforting in its reliability and the repetitiveness of its images "committed to the safe custody of names" (p. 297). Such is the role of the imagination, which colors all reality—to create worlds that hold the magic power of resonance through time, so that a spark may ignite and become one with the elements of life.

There is in Proust neither love nor beauty that can exist without having first been awakened within the imagination. Wordsworth's stress upon recollection in tranquillity assumes here a mystical aura; it becomes the kindling of a memory pertaining to an unlived experience—or rather, the memory of an experience that has been lived only in the imagination. A name or a figure on a canvas—or, in the case of Venice, the name of an image on a canvas—creates its own echoes and memories, and within these there reside expectations of truths that go beyond both name and image. This is presupposing an inherent truth within beauty, which will eventually communicate itself to the receptive mind and feelings. Proust was, of course, much influenced in these assumptions by Ruskin, the English moralist and aesthetician whom he discovered through Robert de la Sizeranne's book in 1897, *Ruskin and the Religion of Beauty*.[3] Proust's natural subjectivism in his relation to the world around him found an encouraging voice in Ruskin's precepts, a voice that widened his frame of reference and extended it from the mere self to the universe of art and beauty outside him. It is through Ruskin that he began to look at paintings and cities as objects mysteriously linked with his sensibility but endowed with a personality independent of his own, a flavor and a compelling fascination resembling those held by a cherished lover. Venice becomes for him at once the focus of his yearnings, the promise of joy and the repository of a mystical truth, which would surge up and envelop him in a sudden revelation upon his first contact with the magic of its beauty. In the following passage Marcel anticipates seeing a famous actress's rendition of *Phèdre*.

> But what I demanded from this performance—just as from the visit to Balbec, the visit to Venice for which I had so intensely longed—was something quite different from pleasure; a series of verities pertaining to a world more real than that in which I lived, which, once acquired, could never be taken from me again by any of the trivial incidents—even though it were the cause of bodily suffering—of my otiose existence. [1:339-40]

The performance of the Berma in Racine's *Phèdre*, and Balbec with its romantically stormy waters on the Normandy coast, and Venice—all become enmeshed here in the same wistful pursuit in which the anticipations of pleasure and fulfillment are inseparable from the suggestive power of art. Sunrays springing from canvases in a picture show (p. 415) would rekindle his memory of the yet unsavored beauties of Venice and the longing for the eternal mellowness he associated with it; or Venice would suddenly surge up through the words of the painter Elstir, evoking the amphibious liquidity of boats and people, the sensuously captivating brocades, the glittering colors of fabrics in one of Carpaccio's paintings (1:673-74). These images proffered by Elstir out of his own understanding of the old Italian master's view of Venice—and hence through the blend of two artistic visions, that of Elstir and the other of Carpaccio himself—are added to Marcel's own growing image of that city and its visualized if yet elusive reality.

Little by little the Venice standing as in wait by the Adriatic Sea while Marcel chisels out in his mind the images of the city becomes merged with a dream so personal that it will never detach itself from it. That dream will one day supersede the reality, which will in turn blend with it. A new vision will thus emerge, composed of both dream and reality, fluid and interchangeable.

> One of my dreams was the synthesis of what my imagination had often sought to depict, in my waking hours, of a certain seagirt place and its mediaeval past. In my sleep I saw a Gothic fortress rising from a sea whose waves were stilled as in a painted window. An arm of the sea cut the town in two; the green water stretched up to my feet, it bathed on the opposite shore the foundations of an oriental church, and beyond it houses which existed already in the fourteenth century, so that to go across to them would have been to ascend the stream of time. This dream in which nature had learned from art, in which the sea had turned Gothic, this dream in which I longed to attain, in which I believed that I was attaining to the impossible, it seemed to me that I had often dreamed it before. But as it is the property of what we imagine in our sleep to multiply itself in the past, and to appear, even when novel, familiar, I supposed that I was mistaken. I notice, however, that I did frequently have this dream. [1:819]

The synthesis of all images, the crystallization of a city, can only come within the dream, wakeful or in sleep, as in the passage above, for dream is often the composite of an inner and an outer reality, the order that takes shape out of confusion, and the blending of the past with the present. The hand of man (the "Gothic fortress") and that of nature ("the green water") stretch in unison toward an ideal unity that combines the two worlds. These will henceforth live together in cohesive beauty, assimilated one to the other through the power of a creative imagination, nature having "learned from art," transmuted and embellished through "the eye of the beholder," a new truth reflecting what is real and what is contemplated. Doubts will occasionally arise ("I supposed that I was mistaken"), but the doubt itself will be an element of the new truth, and the dream will reappear, obstinate and vivid. The dream is, of course, the creative inspiration and vision of the artist. But where literature had sought, within the Romantic movement, either to imbue all objects so completely with the artist's passionate contemplation, or, with the Realists, to divest it of all emotive connotations, Proust made of objects and towns—of Venice—the amalgamation of these two disparate movements. He showed that a city is simultaneously an external reality and the reflection of a contemplated vision, and that the imagination helps form reality and give it a meaning more lasting than mere shapes. "The supreme effort of the writer as of the artist," he had written in 1907 in "Journées de Lecture," "can only lead to lifting partially for us the screen of ugliness and meaninglessness which leaves us without curiosity in the presence of the universe."[4] Within the vision of the city offered to the reader, one can thus discern an element of beauty, a Venice that, born of art, will retain a dimension of the author's contemplative imagination.

What has been until now a vaguely conceived desire for Marcel, images mirroring his childhood and accompanying his adolescence, soon changes aspect. The Venice that appeared as a smile at the horizon of his simple fantasies, often kindled by the mere reproduction of a Titian on the wall or the evoked presence of a Carpaccio painting, now becomes laden with the passionate longing, jealousy, and frustration of his new love for Albertine. With the presence of the young woman in his house and the tension contained in that anguished love affair with its craving for a possession beyond flesh or spirit, Venice now appears as "the other," the cherished promise of deliverance from his torment, of comfort and beauty in an unimaginable future, the purified essence of a love faithfully in wait. His desire for Albertine soon becomes a destructive sublimation of the self within the other, and hence the desecration of the other's most intimate essence—of her mysterious present and her undisclosed past. It is a love that strives to act as a vise and hold Albertine prisoner of Marcel's consciousness, so that she can be disposed of, be cast away and replaced by the other love—that Venice that remains wrapped in the blue light and the glaucous liquidity he had envisioned in his early dreams:

> How many persons, cities, roads does not jealousy make us eager thus to know?. . .Perhaps the habit that I had formed of nursing in my bosom several simultaneous desires. . .apple trees in blossom, storms at sea, a desire for Venice, a desire to settle down to work, a desire to live like other people—perhaps the habit of storing up, without assuaging any of them, all these desires, contenting myself with the promise, made to myself, that I would not forget to satisfy them one day, perhaps this habit. . .had become so prevalent in me that it assumed control of my jealous suspicions also. [2:437]

His thought of Venice, then, and the promise that the name of that city holds out, come into his consciousness no longer as a mere desire that he would "satisfy one day," but already as a partial realization of that desire, the positive element that erects a system of balance against the weight of his suspicion and his jealousy of Albertine.

Equivocation and a craving for freedom now accompany his images of Venice: "I should have liked. . .to set off for Venice, but how was I to manage it, if I married Albertine. . .?" (2:397); irresolution and implied regret: "I really believe that I came near that day to making up my mind to break with her and to start for Venice" (2:454); hostility and a suggestion of rancor: "If my life with Albertine was to prevent me from going to Venice. . ." (2:497); unrequited yearning: ". . .that Venice for which the Spring weather too filled me with longing. . ." (2:498). The dream is now accompanied with restlessness and discontent. It assumes the reverse aspect of his bondage with Albertine, often taking the shape of a wonderful and intimate freedom, "I might at that moment be dining in Venice in one of those little restaurants, barrel-vaulted like the hold of a ship. . ." (2:501-2). Venice becomes the only alternative to his obsessive love for Albertine, the image that, if translated into actuality, could alone replace the force of his present passion: ". . .the appeal of some reality that addressed itself to my imagination, as might have been this evening, a picture of that Venice of which I had thought so much during the afternoon" (2:577). Venice and Albertine thus become inadvertently united in his mind, through the very opposition that they present to each other, in the irreconcilable simultaneity of the presence of the girl and the city in the life of Marcel, and the tension that results from the negation of one through the other. The distant city that had first been an image of restful beauty now appears blended with the passionate desire inspired by Albertine, but acquiescing to his love, devoid of the stark and painful reality of the present. The city has slowly become a substitute for Albertine, and it holds the temptation of an alluring courtesan, seductive in Fortuny's fashionable dresses that evoke it, with their sheen and the softness of brocades and velvets.

While the very presence of Albertine in Marcel's Parisian apartment molds and increases on the conscious level the desire for the envisioned "mistress" on the Adriatic, what has in effect happened is that that far-away Venice becomes, indeed, so intrinsically blended with the yearning for Albertine that the city ceases to exist for a time in its own right—or it stops, at least, being a desirable object in his imagination when not superimposed, as a magic transparency, over the image of the girl. Like a prisoner's envisaging the joy of walking freely along the roads outside, but anxiously looking for asylum and a roof over his head the moment he is given freedom, Marcel draws away from the thought of Venice and clings to the image of Albertine after she is gone.

> That Venice where I had thought that her company would be a nuisance (doubtless because I had felt in a confused way that it would be necessary to me), now that Albertine was no more, I preferred not to go there. Albertine had seemed to me to be an obstacle interposed between me and everything else, because she was for me what contained everything, and it was from her as from an urn that I might receive things. Now that this urn was shattered, I no longer felt that I had the courage to grasp things. [2:;721]

Already in *The Pleasures and the Days* Proust had asserted the superiority of dream over reality; but dream is born out of an imagination that needs to be nourished before it can, in turn, feed the dream. The imagined reality of Venice, long preceding the appearance of Albertine in the life of Marcel, seems suddenly secondary and dependent on the disappeared girl's ability to give it consistency. It is she who is now "the urn" that contained the Venetian dream, and not the power of his imagination; yet it is precisely his own imagination that, having first made of Venice the comforting antagonist to his unhappy relation with Albertine, now endows the latter with that same role. Venice is thus as real or as unreal as the girl and his love for her—she, a memory now of an unlived happiness; the city, a memory as well of an equally unsatisfied desire. But then, all of Proustian reality falls in this same category, one that shrinks from contact with the immediate in order to hold a more lasting truth that embraces at once the past while projecting itself toward the future. It now becomes evident that there is no such thing as "physical" reality alone, and that the most tangible of objects—or persons—exists more and with greater intensity in the realm of the imagination than in its "chemical" balance. Just as Albertine's attraction becomes enhanced when she is absent, Venice's lure is diminished when the city is suddenly thrust in the sphere of the possible and the immediate. Before it can regain its old ascendancy it must return to its original place, where the resonance of its mere name created an echo enveloped in a dream. Venice must disassociate itself from Albertine in order to live again in its individuality, and it will have to resume the wavering consistency of a wish if it must be endowed with life.

After a kind of protracted convalescence following the obsessive need to contemplate the disappeared girl's phantom through a discovery of her past and her very ephemeral essence, Marcel, free at last, goes to Venice. How much more real the discernment of the senses is than that of the imagination; but how much richer the shock of the first meeting is when the poetry of the imagination, filtered through years of wait—years of maturing in sorrow and in the discovery of love, in accumulated anguish and the treasuring of a smile—has anticipated that meeting and endowed it with ineffable beauty!

> When at ten o'clock in the morning my shutters were thrown open, I saw ablaze in the sunlight, instead of the black marble into which the slates of Saint-Hilaire used to turn, the Golden Angel on the Campanile of San Marco. In its dazzling glitter, which made it almost impossible to fix it in space, it promised me with its outstretched arms, for the moment, half an hour later, when I was to appear on the Piazzetta, a joy more certain than any that it could ever in the past have been bidden to announce to men of good will. [2:821]

This reality so long contemplated in the dream has assumed the dimension of fantasy, ethereal, suggestive, and immensely vast in the reverberations that, emanating from it, embrace the whole past that nurtured it. The Golden Angel reaching for eternity in its gesture that seems to hold the sky, retains firmly in its arms Marcel's evanescent past, the belfry of Saint Hilaire and the years of Combray, the vagueness of his young dreams and their passionate intensity. "Impossible to fix in space," it seizes the whole of space and infinity; transcending its immediacy, it stretches through a measure of time and space conceivable only in the imagination. Where one might have read into the experience a religious significance,[5] none exists—unless it be the religion of art itself, encompassing at once Venice, the Golden Angel, and the author's depiction of their glittering loveliness. No mysticism could equal a contemplation of a beauty that, born of a word, a gesture, or an image caught within reality, coincides with an inner vision before it becomes an actual contingency again—only to come full circle again and reenter the creative realm of the imagination.[6]

The magic of the first encounter with Venice reaches for a past in which Marcel is on familiar ground; instinctively he turns to memories that have already fused the real and the unreal and created, through a very personal relation with objects and events, an intimate truth that transcends both objects and events. This first encounter is too new to suggest by itself its own echoes and to go beyond the immediacy of the moment. It can but lean on other images and associations in order to be held in all of its glory. Only on the following day, after San Marco's Campanile has been able to detach itself from too close a present and dictate its own truth within the inner eye of the imagination, does it begin to assume its own contours and unambiguous identity.

> But on the second morning, what I saw, when I awoke, what made me get out of bed (because they had taken the place in my consciousness and in my desire of my memories of Combray), were the impressions of my first morning stroll in Venice, Venice whose daily life was no less real than that of Combray, where as at Combray on Sunday mornings one had the delight of emerging upon a festive street, but where that street was paved with water of a sapphire blue, refreshed by little ripples of cooler air, and of so solid a colour that my tired eyes might, in quest of relaxation and without fear of its giving way, rest their gaze upon it. [2:821]

A whole night has gone by since his arrival, and now Marcel can surrender to a new sense of wonder, the realization that Venice, this dream come true, the promise that for so long had been permeated by other wishes, mingled with different realities, is something so different from and yet so very much resembling the world he already knew. Like Combray, it has its aura of Sunday festivity, but its gaiety is peculiarly its own, reflected as it is by roads that are waterways of tranquillity and comforting densities filled with blue.

Perhaps he would have discovered the depth of the "sapphire" and its solidity without Ruskin's *Stones of Venice* and without the anticipation of beauty that had for so long nurtured his musings; but, deprived of the element of "recognition," the discovery would have taken longer and it might not have been altogether the same. For the Venice of Marcel is not a surprise or a sudden discovery; it is, rather, a creation, the work that, after years of gestation and waiting, finally sees the light and breathes, in its newly acquired shape.

The shape of Venice is here linked to poetry and love, to spontaneous reminiscences, to nostalgia and the personal emotional ties associated with it and coinciding with its discovery.

> From a long way and when I had barely passed San Giorgio Maggiore, I caught sight of this arched window which had already seen me, and the spring of its broken curves added to its smile of welcome the distinction of a loftier, scarcely comprehensible gaze. And since, behind those pillars of differently coloured marble, Mamma was sitting reading while she waited for me to return. . .that window has assumed in my memory the precious quality of things that have had, simultaneously, side by side with ourselves, their part in a certain hour that struck, the same for us and for them; and however full of admirable tracery its mullions may be, that illustrious window retains in my sight the intimate aspect of a man of genius with whom we have spent a month in some holiday resort, where he has acquired a friendly regard for us. [2:822-23]

The arched window is no longer merely a Gothic heritage of beauty or the memory of Venice's Byzantine past; it is a frame contemplated from a distance both spatial and temporal, and it encompasses a beloved face. The "broken curves" are a girth surrounding a life that is its very own and a segment of history too, a blend of the two existing harmoniously together within a perception that embraces them both. That window so inextricably joined to the memory of "Mamma" is, however, not only the segment of a past evoked in a constant present. That window is also Venice itself opening onto the perennial splendor of its view—a view that is now rendered so intimate and comforting by the presence of a loved face. Along with arched windows and the emotional relation they inspire, what Marcel discovers is a world that coincides miraculously with the one he had entertained in his mind and partially invented during the long years of wait preceding the actual meeting with the city. What had appeared to him in that distant dream as "an arm of the sea cut the town in two; the green water stretched up to my feet, it bathed beyond it houses which existed already in the fourteenth century. . ." (1:819, already quoted earlier), now holds similar images:

> My gondola followed the course of the small canals; like the mysterious hand of a Genie leading me through the maze of this oriental city, they seemed, as I advanced, to be carving a road for me through the heart of a crowded quarter which they clove asunder, barely dividing with a slender fissure, arbitrarily carved, the tall houses with their tiny Moorish windows. [2:823]

To what extent the oriental flavor of Venice—or the "carving" of roads through fascinating mazes and the beckoning of lights at their end as in fairy-tale tunnels—is dictated by the past visions in his youthful dreams is difficult to say. One does know that they run parallel, even when the passing of time and the cumulative layers of personal experiences have withheld from those visions a total conformity with the present. This is not to say, however, that there is not a new Venice born of the actual meeting with the city. Its newness comes not only from the transformation of a familiar dream in the hands of time, but also from the impossibility of having invented, in the past, images with no correspondence in his world. This new Venice that is no longer merely an echo of days in Combray, is composed, to be sure, of San Marco, San Giorgio, the Doges's palace, but also of little *"calli"* meandering by narrow slices of deep sea, of simple people and children inhabiting an "ancient, plebeian quarter" with the natural right of those who are at home, and the sudden apparition among them of "Corinthian columns" and an "allegorical statue" (2:824). "In order to form an idea of an unknown situation," he had written after the shock of Albertine's disappearance, "our imagination borrows elements that are already familiar and for that reason does not form any idea of it" (2: 679). Had he been completely honest with himself, he might have recognized that, though the imagination cannot fully represent an unknown situation, it can nevertheless anticipate it to a great extent. The Venice that had assumed in his mind the pain and the intensity of his love for Albertine will not disassociate itself even now from that image.

> Sometimes at dusk as I returned to the hotel I felt that the Albertine of long ago invisible to my eyes was nevertheless enclosed within me as in the dungeons of an internal Venice. [2:831]

Combray, the "budding grove" by the sea at Balbec, Albertine, Fortuny's dresses, Titian, Carpaccio, are all imbedded in the colorful mosaic of the Venice Marcel finally meets, new, transfigured, and recognizable at the same time. It is a Venice that will create echoes from its own inner voice and reappear magically, at the bent of a road, like the Martinville belfry tower, or in half-wakefulness upon a night, like a forgotten element of his past. It will indeed come to life again suddenly on the pavement of Paris, years later, surging from the enchanted confines of his unconscious memories.

> A deep azure blue intoxicated my sight, impressions of coolness and dazzling light hovered near me. . .it was Venice, about which my efforts at description and the supposed "snapshots" taken by my memory had never yielded me anything, but which was brought back to me by the sensation I had once felt as I stood on two uneven flagstones in the baptistry of Saint Mark's. [2:922]

It is here, within memories and the images contained in them, that the "real" Venice resides, in the impressions and the sensations that emanate from those memories—the ones that coincide with truly experienced events and those dictated by the accumulation of time and the working of the imagination.[7]

It is, of course, impossible to decide exactly where imagination helps create reality and at which point reality itself is the stimulus, the catalyst that puts into motion the workings of the imagination. With Zola, with Dos Passos, or with any of the authors who defined reality in terms of factual happenings or objective "truths" determinable in shapes and sizes, the question hardly occurs. The reader in those instances accepts the author's premises, and follows the paths of "reality" traced for him. Proust does not allow this to happen, both by affinity with a world that shuns definitions and by an artistic concept of reality that rests upon a fluidity—and hence a suggestiveness—of presentation. One cannot establish, then, if it is truly Venice—whether in its name and resonance, in its images in paintings or books, or in its very appearance—that dictates Marcel's reactions and understanding of the city, or if the reality of the city is totally dependent upon his ability to discover it and reinvent it in his own fashion. And one comes closer here to an understanding of Proust's reality, for, through the reader's very inability to pinpoint the line of demarcation between Proust's associative power and the verifiable truths of his world, the imagination begins to assert itself. Within the working of the reader's own imagination then, one will find the mirror of the reality proffered by Proust, and the reader will look upon a Venice that is inconsistent, beguiling, evanescent, in a perennial state of flux, but a Venice, too, that is immensely true, faithful to one's individual comprehension and the dimensions of the world.

Notes to Chapter 5

1. The original text reads "L'aspect des choses seul révèle leur nature profonde" and "Une peinture est belle dans la mesure où les idées qu'elle traduit en images sont indépendantes de la langue des images." (The English translation is mine.) These observations are made in an article on the English aesthetician Ruskin, "Pélerinages ruskiniens en France."
2. All quotations from *Remembrance of Things Past* are taken from the C. K. Scott Moncrieff translation in two volumes (New York: Random House, 1934). This first quotation appears in the first volume on p. 31.
3. See in this connection Maurice Bardèche's *Marcel Proust Romancier* (Paris: Les Sept Couleurs, 1971), 1: 127-64. Also, Jean Autret, *L'Influence de Ruskin sur la vie et l'Oeuvre de Marcel Proust* (Geneva: Librairie Droz, 1955); and idem, *Ruskin and the French* (Geneva: Librairie Droz, 1965).
4. Marcel Proust, *Pastiches et Mélanges* (Paris: Edition de la Nouvelle Revue Francaise, 1921), p. 250: "Le suprême effort de l'écrivain comme de l'artiste n'aboutit qu'à soulever partiellement pour nous le voile de laideur et d'insignifiance qui nous laisse incurieux devant l'univers." First published in *Le Figaro*, March 20, 1907. The English transation is mine.
5. See in this connection Elliot Coleman, *The Golden Angel* (New York: Coley Taylor Inc., 1954). Mr. Coleman's thesis sees a desire for purification in Proust, through art, beauty, the soaring Angel that mirrors a religiosity beyond the author's conscious beliefs.

6.   Mr. Bardèche calls the recurring images in *La Recherche*—whether they be the Martinville towers, the river Vivonne, or the Vinteuil sonata—a "leit-motiv," a kind of fixed mental mosaic of which the protagonist is a prisoner. The guiding reality in that case is not a spontaneous and sensuous relation with life, but a cerebral force that dictates images and superimposes them upon outside reality (Bardèche, *Marcel Proust Romancier*, 2:46-49).

7.   A detailed study of the myth of Venice in *Remembrance of Things Past* would deserve a whole volume. The city is indeed nothing less than a myth recurring throughout the Proustian novel, and my study is in no way exhaustive. I have only chosen it as an example of the role of the city in literature in order to emphasize both its tenuous and obsessive reality. The many allusions to the Adriatic city, first dreamed of by Marcel, talked about by Swann, artistically described by Elstir, at last visited in *The Fugitive*, are listed in the index to the Pléiade edition.

6
Bely's *Saint Petersburg:* A City Conjured by a Visionary Symbolist

Bely, which means "white," was the pseudonym chosen by Boris Bugaev, born in 1880 (d. 1934), the son of a famous mathematician who was authoritarian and hostile to all that was poetical, fanciful, and decadent. Boris's father, whose image will appear hauntingly in his fiction, was married to a much younger woman, beautiful, capricious, neurotic, and just as domineering as her husband. Her main fear was that Boris might be swayed by his father into becoming a methematician. She sensed that his temperament was rather that of a mystic and of an artist. But Boris's education was altogether neglected, and he was, contrary to all expectations of his gifted parents, a backward child, as was, according to Sartre, Flaubert himself, "the idiot of the family." In a curious novel, *Kotik Letaev* (1922), Bely attempted to probe into the secrets of a child under five and to relive the sensations and impressions of a two- and three-year-old. The volume was hailed a marvel of paleontological psychology and as an acute imaginative reconstruction of the processes through which a child acquires language, interprets metaphors, and builds his own world.

Young Andrei's mystical and poetical bent met with the outraged scorn of his father who, like many Russian liberals in those days, branded it as a betrayal of the scientific and materialistic philosophy that alone could, through a positive and objective analysis of the faults in Russian culture, improve it. The young man, to avoid causing his father to be ashamed for his betrayal to poetry, adopted a pseudonym. He became a habitué of a circle of promising young men immersed into irrationalism and dreaming of a Second Coming. Vladimir Soloviev was their inspirer. All espoused one form or another of decadent cultism or of ethereal and often raving symbolism. Bryusov and Balmont, poets promised to a brilliant future, Sologub, Merezhkovsky and his wife Zinaida Hippius, gravitated around Soloviev or his strange doctrines. The title of one of Soloviev's poems, "Ex Oriente Lux," is indicative of those young men's revolt against Western rationalism. Bely entertained obstinate dreams of a feminine beauty, as chaste as that which haunted the thoughts of English Pre-Raphaelites, identified with Sophia or divine Wisdom. He also found that mystical ideal embodied in the wife of his friend and co-Symbolist poet, Aleksandr Blok. His intricate carnal and spiritual adventures recall those of Shelley, and even more those of the German romantics Novalis, Brentano, and the Schlegel brothers.

The early works of Bely were poems and "Symphonies," as he entitles them, in prose, and he always remained an experimenter in poetic prose, musical and extremely artistic; it has been pointed out that English translations do not altogether do justice to its beauty. Meanwhile, and through the vicissitudes of his disturbed and sentimental life, the poet-turned-novelist fell under the sway of the mystical anthroposophist Rudolf Steiner, at whose "School" in Germany and Switzerland he went to reside. He underwent what he considered as mystical experiences himself, and, like not a few of his compatriots, he obstinately pondered over the destiny of Russia. When the Revolution of 1917 overthrew the Czarist regime, he, as well as several other Russian poets, hailed it for a time as a spiritual revolution. He soon had to realize that the Marxist emphasis on economic materialism and the "Americanization" of the country, advocated by Lenin himself, pointed to an orientation very different from his lofty dreams. Blok died in 1921. Other poets who had also set their hopes on the spiritual renewal of Russia (Yesenin in 1925, Mayakovsky in 1930) put an end to their own lives. Bely's last years were torn with anguish and hesitations between his desire to believe in Russia as the land that would redeem and save mankind and the brutal lie given to his illusions by the rulers of Russia who succeeded Lenin. He died in 1934.

Saint Petersburg served as a background or as a setting for several novels of the nineteenth century. There Dostoevski roamed as a student, was arrested and nearly shot for conspiring; there he was buried, along with other celebrated writers and artists, in the churchyard next to the convent built in honor of Alexander Nevsky of the thirteenth century. The most impressive avenue in the city, the Nevsky prospect, the bridges over the Neva, the Moika canal, the quays palely lit by the winter sun or resplendent during the long summer evenings, often figured in Dostoevski's short and long novels—*The Humbled and the Offended, White Nights, the Eternal Husband, Crime and Punishment.* It was reserved to Bely, a later novelist even more torn by painful contradictions, to make the city central to a richly orchestrated novel, *Saint Petersburg* (1911). While many Russian critics honor the work as one of the masterpieces of their prose and the best piece of fiction by a writer of their Symbolist era, the author and his strange novel were frowned upon or relegated to oblivion by the rulers of Russian intellectual life during the Stalinist era. The book does not seem to have deeply influenced any of the novelists who, since Ivan Bunin, have been singled out for conspicuous honor by the Swedish Academy; not even a fellow poet, Boris Pasternak, acknowledges to it much credit for his own rendering of Russian life. But exiled Russians, Dimitry Mirsky and Vladimir Nabokov, have lavished unstinted praise upon it. Translations into English were slow in appearing; the reputation of Bely as a master of musical prose doubtless frightened off translators and publishers, fearing that the same misunderstanding that long kept Pushkin's prose and poetry and Tuchev's discreet, moving verse from being adequately conveyed through other languages, would impede the enjoyment of Bely's deft creations. The author's early works in prose had indeed been entitled "Symphonies," and the musical pattern along which they were presented was not too felicitous. Half a century after the full promotion of other "musical" and intricately textured masterpieces to the rank of classics (*Ulysses, The Magic Mountain*), *Saint Petersburg* deserves to be granted its eminent place ungrudgingly. It stands among the novels of this century in which a city is the true moving force and the arbiter of fate.

Saint Petersburg was for 200 years the capital of Russia. Like Alexandria of Egypt, it was the deliberate and, in several respects, the artifical creation of a sovereign whose vision and willpower defied tradition as well as natural forces. It took little time for both cities to stimulate the imagination of writers and to become rallying points for scholars and scientists and a repository of art works and of books. Only Chicago and perhaps Buenos Aires have acquired, with the same promptness, within hardly more than a century, the same individuality fostered to a large degree by poets and novelists celebrating or indicting the mysteries, the confusion, the refinements, and the underworld of a metropolis. Berlin, also an artificial creation along the banks of an unglamorous river, and Washington, D.C., planned, like Saint Petersburg, geometrically and designed to become a characterless administrative center, took much longer than the Russian capital to stimulate the imagination of writers and painters. It is to Pushkin, Tolstoi, Dostoevski, Bely, and others that the city of Peter the Great owes its letters of nobility. The mystique created around Leningrad, in an imponderable yet considerable way, played a role in the fierce resistance that the besieged capital put up against the Germans, one of the longest and most cruel sieges in history, through the 900 days of August 1941 to January 1944.

When compared to Kiev and to its rival, Moscow, Saint Petersburg appeared to many Russians as a vulgar and ambitious upstart. There were no hallowed medieval memories linked with it, no Byzantine domes, no autochthonous buildings appearing to have been erected in harmony with the landscape. Like Washington, regularly praised by European visitors but decried by Americans from New England and from the mid-Western plains, Saint Petersburg often incurred the contemptuous comments of the tranditionalists among the Russians. The patriotic but reactionary historian, Nicholas Karamzin, early in the nineteenth century, had called the city "the immortal mistake of the great reforming Czar." From the very earliest time of its foundation, Saint Petersburg was opposed, and usually sacrificed, in people's imagination, to Moscow. The latter was the genuinely Russian city, embodying the Asiatic and southern origins and aspirations of the Russian people. Everything in the capital established north of the Baltic Sea, in contrast, appeared to lack Slavic authenticity. The harbor and its islands recalled Amsterdam, the many canals were in emulation of Venice, the straight boulevards, the palaces, the statues had been designed or made by Italians, Frenchmen, or Germans. The geometric regularity seemed to fulfill a foreign, Cartesian dream, and to have forcibly expelled any traces of Russian mysticism and any yearning for the Asiatic chaos.

What paltry rivulets are the Spree, the Tiber, even the Thames and the Seine, beside the broad, majestic, rolling Neva! Hardly another river in Europe carries such a volume of water. Its long wintry spell used to provide the city with ice; carriages drove safely on it. Its triple stream (Big, Middle, and Little Neva), always ready to rise in whirlpools and floods, was a constant threat to the houses. The wide network of canals could not always be relied upon to drain the marshes and to tame the chafing stream in its days of wrath. The peril of drowning was incessant. The autumnal fogs that shrouded the city were dreaded as unhealthy and turned the classical, spacious avenues into phantasmal scenes. Its two fortresses, Kronstadt and "the Castle of the Key" (*"Schlüsselburg"*), which once protected the city from the then warlike Swedes, gave it a fierce appearance. Opposite, on an ancient island, the Peter and Paul fortress looked even more forbidding. The gilded spire of the Admiralty rose like a challenge to the traditional round cupola. Even the cathedrals (Peter and Paul, and the one consecrated to the Dalmatian Saint, Isaac), lavishly adorned with marble, porphyry, and bronze, were more imposing in their ponderous neoclassicism than they were inspiring. No mountains or hills were in sight—only flat suburbs and overcrowded islands where dwelled the administrative clerks and the industrial laborers. No wonder that sultry, disgruntled men of letters became haunted by the thought of the vengeance that an artificial city might wreak some day upon its rulers, in the guise of a gigantic flood or a revolution.

Andrei Bely's *Saint Petersburg*[1] is, as the title indicates, a novel about the controversial and contradictory city of Peter the Great. It is also a symbolic prophecy of the impending doom of Russia, harassed by a recent defeat (in the Russo-Japanese War) and by an abortive revolution. A conflict of two generations is exemplified by the estrangement between father and son, at times recalling the painful struggle and pathos in Turgenev's *Fathers and Sons*. The futility of the plottings, of the endless and aimless talks by nihilists and utopians, offers a picture of the would-be revolutionaries even more ludicrous in their earnestness, and as inefficient in their powerlessness to act, as that of Dostoevski's *Demons*. The characters, fewer in number than in almost any other great work of Russian fiction, are powerfully delineated in their pathetic contradictions. The fogs in the city atmosphere, the cold, geometric beauty of the avenues and of the canals, the weight of the past and the memory of the ruthless founder, control the behavior and the dreams of the puppetlike inhabitants. Nowhere is there to be found in the large volume a carefully organized and detailed description of the scenery, of the streets and houses of the city, or even of the Neva of which one senses the constant presence. The outward appearance of the characters is also missing, and they all shift and blend in the grayness of the air leaving no marks on the memory, such as the effect associated with the creations of Balzac or Tolstoi. But it is through the minds of these pale, ghostlike actors who fret about the city, vainly endeavoring to elude their ironic destiny, that Saint Petersburg is filtered, misty, elusive, and at times overpowering.

The initial two pages of the novel might be somewhat disconcerting for the unprepared reader, setting the tone of the narrative with insolent sarcasm that is purposely broken up by acid aphorisms. Rabelais or Swift come to mind here, rather than the more classical presentations and neatly told stories with logical sequences of events fixed in time and place. Bely refutes all the factual, descriptive sentences that, in guidebooks or geographical manuals, claim to sketch the appearance and life of a city. All logic and established patterns of the past are derided here, and Petersburg appears as a reality born of the imagination. Assertive in its pervasive reality, the city echoes the world of Gogol and Pushkin; the latter's presence is subtly evoked through the repeated allusions to the "Bronze Horseman," which delicately merge with the wavering structure and leitmotiv of the novel. The symmetry, the rectilinear avenues, the uniformity of the houses, the obedience of the servant population and of the office clerks—all conspire to make of Saint Petersburg the city of mechanized bureaucrats. The aging senator and high government official who will stand at the center of the rambling novel has himself taken on the gait and mental habits of a computer. The placidity of his unvaried existence has, however, been rudely shaken of late.

The senator has a composite name, Apollon son of Apollon, which points ironically to the identity of a Christian man who is neither serenely godlike nor visited by the Muses. Ableukhov is his family name, an abbreviation of an Asiatic appellation; the contrast it presents to the surname emphasizes the clash between the Eastern and Western traditions. The city itself mirrors the same tensions, standing as the most westernized in the Czarist empire but torn by conflicts and chaotic turmoils. In the very first paragraph, in sharp, seemingly unconnected sentences, the sedate high official is derided through the remarks of his servants; he is pictured as a self-controlled, deliberate man, ever conscious of his rank and of his duties. He sedulously sharpens his pencil "to a refined pointed end" (p. 4), jots down his few thoughts, and makes ready for the carriage that the lackeys have punctually prepared for him. Yet, in that picture of a pompous state official of sixty-eight, absorbed by the feuds between bureaucrats and safely ensconced in his director's armchair, the sarcastic novelist has slyly hinted at the destructive forces at work. A letter with a Spanish stamp has arrived that very morning, and the servants gossip about the wife who, a few years ago, eloped to the other end of Europe with some unmentionable lover. The senator sends her some money every month. Their son has been educated without a mother, and his father never knew how to express his affectionate concern for him. Ritually, every morning, he asks the servants the same question, "Is Nikolai Apollonovich still in bed?" and, ritually, the answer is "yes."

Outside, even graver signs of disturbance are shaking off the senator's quietude: revolutionary ferments are seething and menacing banners have been paraded along the streets, daring to caricature Apollon's ridiculous green ears. Later, he will encounter the threatening eyes of petitioners, be insulted while riding in his carriage by insolent pedestrians, and suffer at the thought of his own son wandering among those "déclassés" and malcontents. The pomp of grenadiers and hussars parading in all the brightness of their helmets and breastplates stands in contrast to the rumbling discontent of the working class, which every morning pours out from the islands across the Neva where it is quartered, away from the stately palaces of the dignitaries. This military pomp contrasts no less with the petty calculations of the leftist youth, at a loss to discover how to break the authority of the Czar and of his administration. They do not have contact with the working classes, nor are they familiar with the political literature of those who have hailed the riots of 1905 as an exercise for the day when they will take over the weakened regime. Ladies prattle about those revolutionary plots, at the center of which is Apollonovich, the senator's son. The conspirators, egged on by "agents provocateurs," have secured from that indolent and hesitant young man the promise that he would blow up his home, and his father presumably with it, by means of a mechanism hidden in a sardine can that would eventually explode. During the forty-eight hours into which the novel is concentrated, suspense will be built up, until it will be too late for the Hamlet-like, would-be parricide to stop the diminutive infernal machine he has hidden in his room. Clumsy in his attempts at communicating with his son, too shy to manifest his tenderness toward him, too weak and weary even to make him mend his ways, the father vaguely senses that the company of dubious characters kept by his son will lead him astray. But both seem to be paralyzed into inaction through some spell cast by the city.

Nowhere is the scenery of Saint Petersburg elaborately described. Still, through vignettes, a few touches of color, repeated allusions to the greenish water of the canals, to the air saturated with moisture, to the splendor, but also to the unhealthiness of the Russian metropolis, are hauntingly recalled. The streets of the city, the author remarks early in the book, are endowed with the eerie power of transforming the passers-by into shadows. One might almost believe oneself in Dickens's London on a foggy day. The canals, through which the founder of the city had hoped to emulate his favorite harbor of Western Europe, Amsterdam, are a symbol of stagnation and of corruption. The time of the year is October, and violent gusts of autumnal wind moan along the broad, exposed perspectives. Soot rising in whirlpools from the chimney stacks lends a funereal air to the houses. In section 14 of the second chapter of the book, Bely unveils the symbolic meaning of his novel, which is nothing less than an anticipation of the city's impending doom, itself a forewarning of the collapse of Russia, condemned to die so that it may be born again.

The central motive is Falconet's famous statue of Peter the Great. The lawgiver and the indomitable architect of the harbor and of the navy was, rather than the conqueror and warrior, the figure that Falconet chiseled, at the request of Catherine the Great. A disciple of his, Marie Anne Collot, had sculpted the head. The

horse is one of the noblest ever modeled since Leonardo da Vinci
and Verrocchio. A snake, presumably the symbol of the envious
resistance by the Russian Boyards to the inflexible Czar bent upon
westernizing them, coils around the pedestal and lends balance to
the enormous mass. The mere transporting of the block from the
Finnish countryside, where a peasant had first detected it, proved a
Herculean task. Human lives were ruthlessly sacrificed by the
modern Pharaoh who brooked no opposition to the fulfillment of
his dream.

Bely does not resort to subtle enigmas in order to let the reader
guess the trend of his ominous reflections on the gloomy future of
the statue and of the city caught in its shadow and its destiny. He
addresses the statue, and Russia, in an eloquently poetical page in
which he assumes the mantle of a prophet envisioning a tragic
future:

> Beyond the bridge, in St. Isaac's Square, a cliff rose out of the
> mist; fronting it, the enigmatic Bronze Horseman loomed, hold-
> ing out his green bronze arm; above the shaggy buzby of an
> Imperial grenadier, a rearing horse shot out of its front hoofs. . .
> A shadow concealed the Horseman's huge face; but the palm
> of his outstretched hand was bathed in moonlight.
> Since that pregnant time when the Bronze Horseman had
> galloped here and had rooted his horse in Finnish granite, Russia
> had become divided, as had the destiny of the Fatherland; weep-
> ing in anguish until the ultimate hour, Russia had been severed
> in half.
> Russia, that bronze steed is your symbol. Your fore hoofs are
> plunging in darkness, in emptiness; but your hind hoofs have
> taken deep root in the granite soil.
> Will you break loose from the riveting granite, just as some of
> your witless sons have broken loose from the soil? Or, perhaps,
> breaking through the fog, you will leap through the air and then,
> with your sons, vanish in the clouds?. . .Or, frightened perhaps
> of leaping, you will again set down your hoofs and, snorting,
> bear the great Horseman away from these illusory lands into the
> perspective of spacious plateaus?
> But this will not be.
> Having reared and measured the air with his eyes, the Bronze
> Horseman will never set down his hoofs. He will leap over his-
> tory; and great will be the tumult when he does so. He will cleave
> the earth: the very hills will crumble from the fear assailing them,
> and this fear will make the native plains arch themselves into
> hills. . . .And Petersburg shall sink. [Pp. 71-72]

The defeat sustained by Russia at the hands of the Mongols in the thirteenth century and the destruction of the Russian fleet at Tsushima in 1905 are conjured up, as are the famous and frequent murders of rulers in Slavic history, as a forewarning of the cataclysm that will engulf, along with Saint Petersburg, the whole of Western civilization.

> The ultimate Sun shall rise and dazzle my native earth. But if you should fail to rise, O sun, then the shores of Europe will fall under the heavy Mongolian heel, and the foaming, raging sea will once more descend to the bottom of the ocean—into the primordial, long-forgotten chaos.
> So rise, O Sun. [P. 72]

Bely's poetic prose is an invocation with the forceful tone of a prophecy. The prodigy occurs: the clouds open up, a patch of turquoise drifts across the heavens. A weirdly brilliant moon shines and spreads its radiance over the Neva, on the domes and spires of the city. Towers are transmuted into stony cliffs, facing the world of man from a distance across the water. Clouds again engulf that visionary scene. Caught in his own fantasies and fears that project the oscillating waves of assertive durability and the perishability of Saint Petersburg, Nikolai's dreaming friend helplessly holds the bomb that has been entrusted to him. The fantastic visions that magically unfold to his feverish sight reveal, in the transfiguration of elements, the future invasion of the hallowed land of Russia by hordes of Manchurians and Mongols. The proud city is chastised for its rationalist arrogance. Chinese and Moslems will revolt. The Second Coming is at hand, and it will work apocalyptic havoc. Some of the fears inspired by the Chinese fellow-Communists of this last quarter of the twentieth century and by the presence of twenty-five million Moslems, only half-assimilated, in the southern regions of the Soviet Republics, which probably haunt the modern rulers of Russia, might have been prophesied here by Bely.

The night had been a disturbed one for father and son. The former, while donning his bemedaled uniform for some parade, gloomily brooding over his solitude and over the threats against stability and hierarchy in Russia, vainly endeavors to reach out to his son. The son had been fretting all night, obsessed with nightmarish visions. He wants to convince his intellectual self that he hates his father, as the symbol of all that he detests in the rigid order that stifles all attempts at reforming Russia. Yet, physically and otherwise, he knows he is very much like his progenitor. And he resents living like a parasite, lacking determination, vaguely studying Western philosophy as an alibi for his playboylike aimlessness. Father and son meet over a meal, embarrassed, shy, pathetically unable to communicate with one another. Outside the gloomy mansion, brief pictures of the ever changing colors of the waters and clouds of Saint Petersburg are sketched by the novelist: deep green-blue canals, phosphorescent patches of red piercing through the mist, glimpses of the islands from which the revolutionary uprising may emerge. The supreme art of the novel is thus to associate the strange and swift changes in the sky and in the watery reflections of Saint Petersburg with the turbid emotions of the characters.

The fourth chapter of the novel evokes a visit by perturbed Nikolai to the Summer Garden, planned and planted by Peter the Great himself. Once a rare and delicate spot with fountains and exotic trees imported from Western European lands, it appears now, to the anguished walker, as a desolate spot. "Frenzied birds circle and swoop above Peter the Great's small house" (p. 112). The leaves swept by the wind whirl around gloomily. As Nikolai walks away in dejection toward the Neva, an unreal, enormous red sun hovers over the wide river. Red is a recurring symbol throughout the volume: the windows reflect the ruby glow; the spires, the palaces appear steeped in a flaming conflagration to the Hamlet-like, irresolute, and self-torturing young man; "Sparkling torches burst everywhere into flame" (p. 115). An ominous twilight of gods and men alike is heralded by those portents in the air. The geometrically planned city of orderly state officials and meticulous clerks and ushers seems ready to be engulfed into chaos. Red, Bely hints, is the emblem of that destruction.

Old Apollon, who had gathered that the red domino who played pranks at parties and insolently broke up the quietude of his friends was none other than his own son, is seized with the premonitory symptoms of a heart attack. As he rides through the streets of the metropolis, he is accosted by strange, ghostlike characters, who utter for him enigmatic warnings of what is to come. His son, on his own side, writhes in doubts and dread, as his fellow conspirators blackmail him into keeping his word and starting the explosion destined to wreck his father and the stately house. A friend of his, Lieutenant Likhutin, tries to hang himself, and makes a mockery of his halfhearted suicide attempt, like one of the tragic buffoons of Dostoevski. At one time, it occurs to the lonely and distressed senator that he had missed something through proudly ignoring the common people whom he feared. He becomes an almost touching old man when gently helping a poor girl, pursued by some persistent follower, to her home. His son comes across his father, "a thin little human figure hurrying along the sidewalk" (p. 123), and flees from him so as not to appear too compassionate. Neither of them has the courage to break away from the coils of fate and from the paralyzing habits that enmesh them. Meanwhile, once again, as Nikolai roams around the spectral city pondering his promise to turn into a parricide, an apocalyptic vision flashes upon his wearied mind. The clouds over the Newsky prospect open up. A red gleam transfigures the houses and the canals, and illuminates the statue of the Bronze Horseman. The symbolic gesture of Peter the Great's raised arm has lost its imperious significance. The arm seems to shake, the horse's hoof crashes down on the huge granite. The statue now speaks and utters a cry that seems both threatening and irrevocable: "to destroy—irretrievably" (p. 167). Nikolai understands that it is his own fate to destroy, to wield and suffer utter ruin, and to be "irretrievably lost." The deed must then be performed. Pushkin's poem again provides the epigraph for the sixth chapter, "Pursued where'er he went / By the Bronze Horseman / Wildly Galloping" (p. 188).

The suspense is further prolonged through confused, hectic meetings of ineffectual revolutionaries never weary of discussing and prophesying. Nightmares haunt them, in which, recurrently, the landmarks of the doomed city, the bright arrow of the Admiralty building, and the dome of Saint Isaac's loom in the eerie mist, and the Horseman flees from his rock amid a resounding clatter. All the rulers of Russia, the Alexanders and the Nicholases, had been pursued by the galloping bronze giant. All of them, like the Wandering Jew, or like the hallucinatory Evgenij in Pushkin's poem, had been mere playthings tossed about the vengeful tragedy arising from Peter the Great's "hubris."[2]

The suspense becomes more anguishing as the visionary novel enters its seventh and eighth chapters, the final ones. Nikolai, remorseful and torn, imagines the stone buildings of his native city carried away in a wild dance of death. Memories of his childhood invade his anguishing mind, snatches from Goethe's "Erlkönig" learned from a German governess (*"Es ist der Vater mit seinem Kind"*; "It is the father with his son") echo in his ears as the wind howls outside. He yearns for the imaginary purity of his younger years, while cranes are obstinately flying and uttering their shrill cries above the roofs of the houses. Dante, likewise, in the Paolo and Francesca canto of his *Inferno*, had, in one of his most grandiose comparisons, as he watched wailing shades pass him by amid the winds of hell, been reminded of "cranes chanting their lays, making a long line in the air with their numbers" (*Inferno,* canto 5, 46-48).

Nikolai, more than ever rent asunder between his remnants of filial tenderness and what he takes to be his duty and loyalty to his fellow revolutionaries, keeps on hesitating. He might still get hold of the sardine can and throw it into the Neva. Almost complacently, yet shivering with a voluptuous dread, he imagines the bomb exploding, the plaster falling and the rugs burning, then his father's funeral and himself following the coffin in mournful, hypocritical dignity. Like Bely himself, Nikolai had long nurtured a grudge against the name, the flesh, and the blood that he had inherited from a father who had never understood him. Still, what right had he to set himself up as a supreme arbiter and to execute a final punishment, all in the name of an idea?

Meanwhile events are rushing on. The older Ableukhov has lost his grip on the details at the office and has forsaken his once exemplary punctuality. He seems to hear obsessively the thudding of horses' hooves, as if, after the defeat at the hands of the Japanese, the horsemen of Genghis Khan were threatening to take over Saint Petersburg and mete out to the city the fate of Sodom or Gomorrah. His repentant wife is now back from Spain. He brings her to the house in a mood of meek reconciliation. He even associates their son with the would-be happy family reunion. Entering his son's room, he notices a strange object clumsily wrapped up, with a clicking mechanism inside it. He takes it to his own study to examine it further at his own leisure. Nikolai, in a supreme fit of repentance, looks in vain for his sardine can in order to stop its time mechanism. During the night, while he lies awake in anguish and terror, the terrific crash occurs. Nikolai catches sight of the pathetic and frail body of his father running in the corridor. He offers to assist him, but is rejected. Soon after, the father dies of a heart attack. The secret of the explosion is not found out.

Nikolai, for whom his dying father had generously provided, leaves Russia, as if in search for valid answers to all the unspoken questions, to far-away and foreign lands. He travels to Tunisia, then to Egypt, to confront the Sphinx and to ponder over the *Book of the Dead* and other ancient texts. He will only return to his mother country to look for comfort in loneliness and meditation, at the country place he has inherited from his father. The city of Peter the Great no longer means anything to him. No longer would he look to the future for signs of a more liberal Russia, free from the nightmare of the Bronze Horseman and from the Czar who had built an artifical and Europeanized country.

> He lived alone, never called on anyone, no one ever visited him; he was often seen in church and, lately, he had been reading the philosophical works of Skovorod. His parents had died. [P. 310]

The structure of Bely's novel contrasts, in its apparent simplicity, with the broader expanse and symphonic construction of most of the classics of Russian fiction, from *Dead Souls* to *Doctor Zhivago*. Its casual, at times ironical tone might rather remind one of the longer stories of Chekhov. Nowhere does the narrator seem to take himself too seriously or to dissert upon the mystical significance of the catastrophe toward which is directed the attention of the reader. No claim to philosophy of history or to moralizing about the nihilists is put forward by the discreet and ironical author. The scope of the novel is, from the start, a narrow one. The working classes, the shopkeepers, the professionals of revolutionary movements are kept out of Saint Petersburg exactly as they are kept out of Proustian fiction; the only exception is that of the servants. Other novels revolving around cities, from Balzac, Hugo, and Dickens to Zola, have not resisted the lure of moralistic declamation against the monstrous destructiveness of that modern dehumanizing congeries of people. The favorite images or comparisons were those of volcanoes, blazing furnaces (or, at best, crucibles), and sewers. The symbolic masters of the cities were greedy speculators, unscrupulous politicians, Don Juans avid for sexual domination, or triumphant prostitutes like Nana.

Bely is less encyclopedic and in no way drawn to gruesome pictures of violence and vice. He is neither a social reformer nor a Savonarola vituperating against luxury. His metropolis is nowhere called a Babylon or a Nineveh, to be destroyed because of its disregard of all moral laws, or a Babel arising against some divine decree. He prefers a tone of irony to that of a solemn denouncer of monsters. His pity extends to the very characters whom he ridicules most insistently: the feeble and awkward Nikolai who plays at being an apprentice of revolutionary destruction and is embarrassed with the ludicrous sardine can that has been palmed off upon him, and the even more pathetic father, unable to shake off his official self and to uncover what is human within him. The sections of the novel are disconnected, so as to reflect the confusion of the minds unable to grasp the significance of events. The apparent disintegration of the novel—or at least of the novel's classical structure—thus runs parallel to the mystifying quest and faltering resolve of the characters. The motif that runs all through the work, persistent, emphasized again and again through the allusions to Pushkin's famous verse tale, is always the same: the father, the son, their servants, and their friends all grope their way clumsily in the fog and under the incessantly changing skies of the Russian capital. They are but shadows in a visionary merry-go-round. A curse pursues them: the curse of their Tartar blood in the case of Apollon and his son, but also the curse of the Bronze Horseman. Peter the Great, the admirer of Dutch efficiency, exemplified in the arsenals and shipyards of Holland, the "Flying Dutchman," had tried in vain to erect a city of harmonious and geometrical boulevards and concentric canals, reneging not only Asia but the mystical forces by which Russians are nurtured. This novel in which the city commands the puny destinies of the feeble individuals is also a highly personal novel. Bely, all his life pursuing some mystical "Advent" that might endow his own fate with an ulterior significance, attributes to Nikolai his own ambivalent feelings of hate and affection toward his father, the implacable mathematician. He also identifies with the forlorn Evgenij in Pushkin's poem, desperate when his beloved's house and his own dwelling were carried away by the flood, fleeing like a madman the pursuit of the galloping Bronze

Horseman, and finally meeting with death on one of the islands beyond the Neva.

Notes to Chapter 6

1. All quotation from *Saint Petersburg* are from the translation of Bely's novel by John Curnos (New York: Grove Press, 1959). A recent translation of Bely's novel by Robert A. Maguire and John E. Maimstad (Bloomington, Ind.: Indiana University Press, 1978) was not available when this study was in progress.
2. Bely himself would eventually succumb to a kind of doom, a pervasive sense of fatality not unlike the one that haunts his novel. After the completion of his apocalyptic novel, he was to live through Nicholas II's overthrow, then his gruesome assassination, and, in 1929, he was to write a perceptive technical study of the Pushkin poem that he had used symbolically in his *Saint Petersburg*.

7

Romains's *Death of a Nobody:* A City's Collective Soul

The exasperated mysticism of Bely, his reaching out into the domain of the supernatural and the leaps of his fervent imagination that oscillate in turn between the sublime and the grotesque, find little parallel in modern literature. Yet, on a much smaller scale and one that is no doubt less inspired, a young writer in France, early in this century, endeavored to attribute to life mystical forces encompassed in the realm of the prosaic. His name is Jules Romains—a pen name for Jules-Louis Farigoule, author of many volumes that were collected under the general title *The Men of Goodwill.*

Born in 1885 in Saint-Julien-Chapteuil, Romains was only twenty-one when he began to think of the novel as a means to project collective rather than individual forces. He formed a small group with Duhamel, Vildrac, and Arcos and formulated his doctrine, illustrated already in his early stories and plays, in *Death of a Nobody* in 1911, and in *Lucienne* in 1922 (the latter is the first volume of a trilogy entitled *Psyche*). The long series *The Men of Goodwill* was started in 1932 and continued to the end of his life in 1973.

Romains's assumed principle of cosmic unity does not lean upon any religious dogma, but at the same time it does not reject it either. Rather, the author envisioned a kind of mystical unity that is at once within and beyond religious experiences. Implicitly there is the acceptance of the proposition that there are forces greater than those apprehended by man alone. ''Romains' merit is not to have composed a religion 'ex nihilo,''' writes the critic Cuisenier, ''but to have rejuvenated existing religions or to have given life at

last to what until now were only abstract concepts.''[1] I am not sure
that the mystical unity of all elements, such as Romains presents it,
is entirely convincing, or that the translation of a vague spirituality
finds an echo in man's actions and injects a soul into all matter. All
the same, his venture had some originality, and the modest influence that it exerted upon the world of letters is well worth con-
sideration.

Romains could hardly have been aware of Jung's principle of the
''collective unconscious'' or his assumption that there is a constant
interrelation between objects and human beings. But he was acquainted with Durkheim's philosophy based upon a postulate that
all moral and social facts are kindred in spirit, even when removed
from individuals' consciousness. These are indeed the axioms that
Romains set out to illustrate in his work, and he began to write of
events, the minutest and least remarkable of them at times, as if
they were chain reactions originating with the individual but exten-
ding gradually to neighborhoods and even to entire cities. Events,
he assumed, were souls in action endowed with a kind of cosmic
energy that constantly renewed, expanded itself, and thrust
echoes into the distance.

Where Balzac and Zola had presented a complex image of France
during their times in their numerous novels, with the assumption
that only out of their entirety—that is, the collective total of these
novels—could there emerge a cohesive image, Jules Romains proceeded on a different hypothesis. He too aimed at offering a
socioeconomic history of his country, but history, he assumed, is
discernible in each of its smallest components: the minutest of
segments contains an intimation of their totality, for each fragment
is indispensable to the integrity of the whole. That such lofty ideas
were not perhaps adequately illustrated in Romains's work, that
they remain less convincing than he envisaged them, should not
detract from their value and the new social scope they injected into
literature.

The city has come to evoke, quite naturally, images of crowds
pushing along the streets and crossroads, noise, confusion, and tall
buildings' dwarfing the individual and reducing his aspirations to
repressed sighs. Words such as *anonymity* and *alienation* easily

come to mind, as easily as *congestion* and *loneliness*. The absence
of nature, of open spaces, the narrow slices of sky above and the
cluttered pavements below—all help to convey a picture of the impersonality, distance, uncaring, and unaware existences of people
who, side by side physically, are in effect remote from one another.
But contrary to this accepted view and the often assumed image of
multitudes composed of disjointed and inimical islands,
Unanimism sees a unifying current, an invisible thread tying the
single parts into a mythical whole, a collective "being" with a
unified awareness. What is needed for this "collectiveness" to
spring to life is but a spark, an event, born within the amorphous
mass, which separates itself from the whole. In so doing, it
becomes the catalyst for a gradual and united awakening.

The American writer Waldo Frank, who came himself to be
strongly influenced by the movement of Unanimism, wrote in the
introduction to his own translation of Romains's *Lucienne*:

> Unanimism is roughly an aesthetic expression for the sense all
> these writers seriously share, of the actual organic unity of life
> beyond the conventional units of individual things and persons.
> In philosophy and religion, this sense is as old as the Ionians, as
> the Hindus, as the fundamental Jewish wisdom that stretches
> from Pentateuch to Spinoza. France is creative above all in
> aesthetic forms. What Romains has done is to give organic ex-
> perience, and substance in modern terms, to a conviction which
> heretofore has remained mostly in the limbo of speculation.[2]

The aesthetic expression of which Frank talks can be summed up in
a positive view of humanity, a current that runs through all beings
and through all inanimate things to compose a cosmic oneness.

Romains' attempt to create a world that breathes in unison
would have required, to be successful, a life-giving, imaginative
fertility that few novelists have possessed since Tolstoy, Balzac, and
Zola. After the lapse of almost half a century since the first
volumes of *The Men of Good Will* appeared, the reader is tempted
to be severe to that tedious and often repetitive series of novels.
Their creator does not always appear as a man of vision, and one is
at times inclined to see him almost like an ox yoked to a plough or,
as brother novelist Francois Mauriac preferred to put it, like a
galley slave to his oars. The preface and the comments on his

painstaking saga-novel by the author are annoying with their professorial tone and their frequently preposterous claims. The novelist is lavish with geographic, historical, and sociological remarks on how and why Paris grew as she did; he appears to know all about the configuration and psychological characteristics of the districts of Paris (Montmartre, the Latin Quarter) with which he is most familiar. He can explain the mechanisms of financial deals on the Bourse, of publicity in the Department Stores, of the contrivances of politicians. Still the visionary force that alone would magnify the thousand scattered details and endow them with dynamism and with some significance is missing. The novelist had courageously endeavored to expand the art of fiction beyond the tight, constricting limits that tradition had imposed upon it. He refused, as he stated it, to make the whole life of a city like Paris revolve around a single individual. He rose against the convenient assumptions of the picaresque novel in which the same character perfected his own education through traveling across several lands, observing and often duping people from varied social strata, multiplying his amorous feats. He turned just as resolutely against the personal novel, especially dear to the French since Constant and Stendhal had practiced it. He repudiated limiting the usual plot to the love affairs of a couple (even with occasional third partners intruding), to the self-centeredness of a family cell, or to the narcissistic contemplation of an artist or writer watching himself grow and decline. For Romains the lives of all are enmeshed into a network of relations with one or more groups and unfold within the context of a city. No portrayal that is confined to a family, even if it is achieved with the mastery of Thomas Mann in *The Buddenbrooks*, not even the complacent evocation of a loose group of teenagers such as Gide assembled in his *The Counterfeiters*, could ever comprehend the variegated existence of a vast city. Romains unabashedly assumed the lofty position of the omniscient novelist, from which his successors of 1970-75 (Butor, Robbe-Grillet, etc.) are desperately, perhaps vainly, struggling to free themselves. Yet if he mastered all the ecological and social problems that the modern metropolis appeared to him to contain, he failed to render the collective life of "Paris at five in the afternoon," as he had proposed to do, for instance, in the eighteenth chapter of his first volume, *The Sixth of October*. Unanimism implies a single-minded collective soul emanating from or embracing the multiplicity of persons from all classes forging links among themselves. But the soul is not always present in the string of episodes and unexciting incidents of *The Men of Good Will*. The scores of characters leading their parallel lives remain as gloomily isolated from each other as the stiff, upright ladies, gentlemen, children, and pets in Seurat's painting *La Grande Jatte*. Yet there is a positive force in Romains's novels, one that opposes the disintegrating movement of modern life, and more particularly of city life. What is affirmed here is that inner repository of hope and continuity which resides, consciously or unconsciously, in every human being, the will to survive and to channel all efforts toward a kind of mystical unity, beyond the mere confines of a lifetime.

With the Greeks fate lived in the tension that existed between man's freedom and the necessity of his action, in the oscillating movement that went from the divine plan to the human will. Jules Romains's Unanimism is an answer to that same necessity which the Greeks called fate; but the world he envisaged is demythicized, removed from the anthropomorphic values of ancient times; it is a world that is essentially optimistic instead and leans upon spiritual virtues in order to combat the forces of disarray and loneliness. Romains's philosophy asserts that beyond humanity and its doings, beyond its struggles and its passivity, there is a kind of undefinable and nameless energy that directs all contacts—of people, animals, and even objects—toward undiscernible aims, not in keeping with any pattern of logic, and yet not unreasonably. A spark suffices to ignite a chain reaction linking man to man, one hand or voice touching the next and then the next. That spark is the catalyst through which life's great factor—its soul, or mystifying element, its integrated movement or essence—for one brief moment at least, takes shape. That moment becomes the essential truth, the goal toward which all steps are directed, and it ultimately justifies all the aimlessness and the struggles waged in solitude and anguish.

In *Death of a Nobody* the catalyst is death, the apparently insignificant end of an insignificant man, Jacques Godard. That this individual should have been entirely unremarkable is surely by design; it would have been too easy to relate the persistent memory of someone dead to the importance he held when alive, to his past vitality or inspirational force. But Jacques Godard was truly a "nobody," one of the many thousands of unknown workers retired and living in a large city, too insignificant to have ever stepped out of the banal mold life had assigned him, or to leave a trace behind him. His death at the very beginning of the book holds no surprise or pathos; he is but briefly introduced before he is discovered lifeless one day in his room. In the immediate silence that follows, it is difficult to imagine that the simple death of this lonely man could ever bestir the city outside, that it could even be noticed, that it would be an element of importance in the life of the building where he had spent years almost unnoticed and unheard. But buildings, as all objects at large, become impregnated with the life that is breathed on them, and they retain a memory and an unconscious meaning well beyond the presence that inspired them. The listless crowd of Paris amid which Godard has passed silent and undemanding, will now halt its movement for an instant and offer him quiet homage. The crowd is a city crowd, composed of disconnected currents each intent upon its own path, the traditionally indifferent and hurried crowd along the pavements of a large city. It is now held back briefly, as it stops to form a link of interaction and feelings evoked by Jacques Godard, the "nobody" to which the title of the novel refers. He has stepped out of line in order to join eternity.

The first few pages of the novel dealing with Godard before his death are an introduction to the essential theme. This theme deals with a scattered group of people that acquires a new consciousness and dimension in the presence of a small void in its midst. When Godard was still alive he was part of a mere statistical order:

> Jacques Godard's life, as far as his own consciousness was concerned, was a meager affair; in the consciousness of others it scarcely existed at all.[3]

Only death brings to the fore in this instance the uniqueness of a man's life and of his end. The porter who discovers Godard's inanimate body is the first to come to grips with the essential meaning of an existence.

> I don't believe in heaven or hell, but all the same one doesn't slip out of life as easy as all that. [P. 14]

The simple statement of the porter, without any transcendental quality, is an almost instinctive refusal to allow the death of man to pass unnoticed, to acquiesce to the dictates of anonymity of a large apartment building in the city of Paris. He muses about the customary rituals of flowers and tears, of farewells that sadly contrast with the indifference of life, and his thoughts become a precious possession, the gift of a pensive moment in contemplation of death. For one moment at least he is the sole possessor of the secret, shared only with the silent room, the drapes, the bed, the still air around. "I am the only person who is in the secret," he tells himself, savoring the privilege in which others will soon partake too. There is at once a sense of regret at having to part with the exclusivity of his "possession," and the quiet awareness that the gift would have little value were it to stay with him alone. The crowd of the vast city is as yet unaware of the event that will form a link in its midst; it remains unseen outside the building where the death of a nobody is, quietly, already beckoning for recognition. Romains does not mean here to give undue importance either to one inconspicuous death or to an anonymous multitude along the streets of a large city. What he shows, rather, is the meaning concealed within each aspect of that multitude, of which Jacques Godard remains himself a part; yet no meaning can emerge without the conscious effort of bringing together the disparate elements, so that they may stand, for one moment in time, as a unity and in common awareness. The nature and secret beauty of cities lie in their complexity, which is revealed through individual elements that must in turn be joined to the whole before they can be fully perceivable—for the details themselves do not become apparent until they are shown within the larger scope in which they are contained. It is the mass that gives life to its components, which, implicitly, are insignificant outside of their unifying context. In this resides the importance of the city, in its projection of vast crowds and houses, streets alive with movement, through which man is revealed in his collective needs and aspirations. If the individual as such does not acquire importance in Romains's unanimistic portrayal, he gains a certain dimension within the larger scope in which he is cast.

The assumption that truth is more discernible when magnified rather than in its minute details is not a new one, of course. Diderot in *Le Rêve de D'Alembert*, has shown, by reverse procedure, that individual cells each have a distinct life within the body that contains them, but that they cease to possess an autonomous existence when detached from the body. Almost the whole of Balzac's literary production points to essential verities that become evident only in exaggeration and even in distortion. Through the magnified frame of reference that he creates, one sees in old Goriot the image of paternal love, projected in enlarged dimensions and hence the "monster" of paternity, or in Cousin Bette the distorted portrayal of envy and perversion. Rather than broaden individual characteristics, Romains reduces the size of men and women by not assigning them roles of either heroic dimension or central importance; but he places them within an expanded context that confers on them, if not excessive significance, at least a measure of humanity that renders them identifiable. The expanded context within which life assumes meaning and purpose in *Death of a Nobody* is the "teratological" presence of Paris.

During the brief acquaintance the reader makes with Godard before he dies, one learns that "the appearance of Paris disconcerted him" (p. 1). Yet the reader knows that he had never beheld the city as a whole, with its sprawling masses of roofs in varying sizes and colors, above the large or small streets, linear or curved, and that the dynamic tangents of the Parisian world in which he lived remained for him unperceived to a great degree. Still he sensed that his own life did not begin and end with himself alone and that a speck of his existence at least was to be found in the vast city around.

But from up here what astonished him even more than the size of the town was its complexity. What extraordinary differences between blocks of houses! What a tangle of lives underneath that covering! The rumpled panorama of roofs and walls lay like a heaving, tumbled blanket over living forms still more furiously agitated. His eyes searched the distance for his own quarter and his home. After long hesitation he marked down a little white reef rising out of the mist. . . .Then he felt oddly moved. An uncomfortable kind of regret took possession of him, like the sinking feeling of a man who has missed a treat. [Pp. 2-3]

From the top of the Panthéon where, after long years of residence in Paris, he has impulsively climbed for the first time, he understands suddenly that not to have seen it all is almost the equivalent of having missed it all. The flighty image he now discerns of a Paris buzzing with vitality, stretching in all directions and well beyond the reach of his own eyes, is a little compensation, an unexpected gift after a whole existence spent in monotonous and insignificant privacy. Only through this brief but encompassing perception at the closing of his life can he feel integrated with the world in which he had lived as a stranger. The search for his own house among the thousands around reinforces here both the importance of that "white reef," symbol of his identity, and the insignificance of a single residence, a family even, or a person, that are transformed into diminutive segments, in meaningless "reefs," when separated from the whole. The little white wall that Jacques Godard finally distinguishes from the others in the distance, assumes its significance in relation to the larger mass to which it belongs. It also represents at once its own and Godard's limitation, and their reciprocal continuity.

Mystifyingly, one must assume here that Godard's brief contemplation of Paris's rooftops and his unvoiced sense of unity with the huge city for an instant, thrust their own echoes. The one instant will live on in an expanded consciousness that has brought together the small man on top of the Panthéon and the large metropolis beneath. Through this mysterious unity, that continues after Godard dies, neighbors will come together. It is indeed the death of the practically unknown lodger next door that will now give them a realizatin of their own individual worth within the group they suddenly form. The neighbors are a complex group of individuals who had lived in close proximity to each other without, however, ever reflecting about the tenuous threads that linked their lives.

> Nobody knows their neighbors in tenements in Paris. But when trouble comes— — [P. 30]

"Trouble" means death here, the element that has forced the neighbors to come together and evoke the departed one, in secret unity with him for the first time, and also with themselves. In the bustle of everyday Parisian existence, individuals stand alone and without recognition of each other; they blend and oscillate, invisible and unaware of the crowd that they compose. But now in the presence of death the beehive movement of the apartment building comes suddenly to a halt, miraculously uncovering a view never entertained before. Just as Paris unfolded the magic complexity of its roofs and buildings to the wondering eye of Godard suspended one day, as his life approached its appointed end, between heaven and earth, the stillness now uncovers the intricacy of the city's most intimate architecture, that of its human components.

As the news of Godard's death spreads, people come forward, in small groups, with each person becoming aware of those around him and of his own place among them. In humble offering to this novel sense of unity and to the conjured presence of the dead man, a wreath is bought by the lodgers of the apartment house and inscribed, plainly, "Offered by the tenants." With these simple words, the theme of reciprocity is subtly introduced, for the word *tenants* is more complex than it seems at first. "People will think he was the landlord," someone objects (p. 30). But the word is allowed to stand, with its ambiguity and the suggestiveness of its meaning. Jacques Godard hence becomes the cotenant and the landlord at once, symbolically sharing and providing a home for himself and for his new-found friends. The simple inscription on the wreath can thus be seen as the expression of a larger concept that embraces both the donors and the recipient at once, making each in turn donor and receiver. The correspondence that is established between objects and individuals, and even between simple words and people within listening range, is an echo, born somewhere in the heart of the city, that is thrust into space in a succession of movements that go from one to the other in ever widening tangents. What started on the top of the Panthéon, that embracing glance thrust upon the city and, implicitly, upon the people within, by an unknown Jacques Godard, has borne the fruits of acknowledgment and cast lights that reverberate in the hearts of men.

The anonymous world of the city is, on the one hand, a machinelike apparatus that swallows up lives so that no trace is left of them; but, on the other hand, the city is like a reservoir of energy, forever sending waves across the spaces and linking minute worlds to its own large sphere. "No, it's maddening, but I shall never be able to see him clearly; it's all a blur" (p. 45), laments Godard's father, from the far-away village where news of the death

has reached. Paris has absorbed all life from those who have come
there to seek asylum, and taken in its stride man's purpose and his
dreams. No memory is left, even with the closest kin, of features
once loved and soon disappeared in the meanders of city life.
Stronger than memory, however, the city sends out waves of
energy, which give new impetus to forgotten elements. Symbolic of
her mysterious force, the telegraph poles stretch across the
distance, tall and visible from afar: they are the tangible illustration
of that unity which is established between the city's complex realm
and the small crowds of distant hamlets. Jacques Godard's old
father, himself scarcely alive in the consciousness of others, suddenly assumes a face, a name, an individual importance through
the news transmitted by the enigmatic wires leading from the city to
the recondite corner of his existence. At the telegraph office, the
girl asks,

> "Do you know who this is—'Godard'?" "Godard. . .Godard
> . . .Yes." "Not in the town, is it?" "No. Why?" "A telegram
> for Godard, without the extra payment. Can't be delivered."
> "The Godards are not far off. . .not much over a mile." "So
> they had a son?" "Perhaps. Why?" "'Your son died to-day at
> his lodgings.'" "Godard's boy is dead?" exclaimes the old
> woman. [P. 33]

The existence of the old man, having no resonance in the memory
of the girl at the office and only a vague echo in the old lady's
reminiscence, assumes some significance with the news of the son's
death. The son himself, whose possible existence was classified with
a hesitant "perhaps" until now, suddenly becomes "Godard's
boy," a real entity, somebody's relation, whose presence unexpectedly raises from the ashes of a forgotten past to appear amid
the streets of his native village. It is as if father and son came
together again after these many years of separation, as if, with the
laconic words that have crossed the distance from Paris to the
village along the mysterious telegraph lines, Jacques Godard's
spiritual presence had been swept in to cling, for one enduring moment, to the old man's consciousness. This same Jacques Godard
who died in Paris, and whose reality had been at best of a statistical
order when alive now invades with the mystical force emanating
from the city the lost hamlet of his childhood. The girl, the old
woman, the little boy who carries the telegram, and all the others

who come in contact with the news of his death, all behold his ephemeral appearance in their midst and recognize him.

The theme of reciprocity, central in *Death of a Nobody*, establishes an oscillatory movement that embraces objects and people and confers to each through the other a certain vigor and a measure of importance. As the story advances, it gains momentum, and its added dimension extends to larger areas and to greater numbers of people. The previous cause-and-effect, progressive movement becomes one of simultaneity. Images no longer project tangents in successive order, but they begin to form spatial arches oscillating from one point to another. These images present visual flashes in cinematic fashion, establishing links between dissimilar actions and people in the two worlds of Paris and Godard's native village. The tenants in the city and the boy by the small town's bridge, the old man by the diligence and the little girls collecting offerings for the wreath, are juxtaposed, their movements repeated, their acts retold in the new light that pairs and synchronizes them on a shared screen. The two worlds many miles apart from one another are thus united (a) mystically, through parallel actions and reactions in the two separate places; and (b) physically, through the long road that goes from one to the other and joins them at the two ends. The small coach first, and then the train carrying the old father to the son's funeral, will retrace the length of that road; each turn of the wheels will reduce the distance from the village to the city, until finally the two worlds will symbolically coincide, with the arrival at the tenement building and the old man's facing his dead son's residence.

The building is itself a living organism and a presence, a town within a city, as it were, full of cubicles and squared-off areas with people living in each of them their separate and anonymous existences. They stand as in hiding beyond barriers of floor levels, halls, walls, and only rarely do they meet and greet each other in their impenetrable privacy.

Over there, in Paris, the house was suffering the night to stab deeper and deeper into its heart, and slowly was giving over its inmates to sleep. In a room on the fifth floor was an old lady who had gone to bed immediately after supper; . . .A few minutes later a little girl on the second floor fell asleep. . . .Souls were peeling off one by one their wrappings of the day. [P. 82]

One by one, the antlike population of the apartment building falls to its assigned place, each room now holding an image of sleep, some restless and others peaceful, all quiet, under the mantle of slumber that Paris seems to hold protectingly over them. Old Godard also falls asleep in a corner of the railway carriage, itself full of cubicles and people enveloped in darkness, an "apartment building" in motion that advances toward the city that is its goal. Rest is the unifying factor in the mysterious correspondence that is established between the people in the large Parisian house and those in the moving mechanism. The new dawn will bring them closer and synchronize their actions.

When the old father arrives in Paris and the link is finally completed between the city and the village, he stands captive of the force that has drawn him here. He discovers the house across the way and hesitates before surrendering to its secret life.

> The old man lifted his head and looked at the house on the other side of the street, which he had just been told was the house he wanted. [P. 94]

He has reached his destination, and with his presence in Paris a new cycle begins, one in which the event of the son's death sends fresh waves across the city, through its intricate streets and into remote quarters.

There are two striking aspects to Romains's presentation of Paris. The first, more traditional, projects the city as a large magnet that draws life into its orbit from all directions; no individuals are visible there, no identifiable groups within the anonymous movement of people and their separate goals. The other Paris that comes out of the pages of *Death of a Nobody* is one in which all the disparate elements that go into the composition of the city carry, each in itself, the hidden power to synchronize, at any given point, their movement toward a common purpose. It is this latter aspect that becomes increasingly emphasized as the story advances:

> It was not only the house that the death had drawn together. In distant quarters men had put on their Sunday clothes, and by unfamiliar routes, by tram and omnibus, by streets they were not accustomed to tread, with many false casts and fetching wide circles, they gathered about the coffin. [P. 105]

Drawn by Jacques Godard's death, people go, as if in agreed resolve, beyond the imaginary confines where their lives have until now evolved in isolation. A sudden harmony is created out of the chaotic distance that life in the city imposes upon its inhabitants. Buses and streets become symbols of a single destination, and the clothes with their Sunday sheen are the visible link in the shared purpose of the people. The rays of communication that had so far traveled in direct line—from the event of the death to the discovery of the body by the porter, the imparting of the news to the individual residents in the building, the sending of the telegram, the oscillating movement from city to village—now extends in all directions and spans a network of connecting lines that seems gradually to encompass the whole of Paris. It is so that Jacques Godard, from being a mere particle among the myriads, becomes by virtue of some mysterious current an element thrusting a cycle of revolving actions. These, through a series of leaps and bounds, send as it were their own rays across the distance. Thus it is that out of the very principle of the individual's isolation a new concept of strength evolves, inconspicuous at first in its single manifestation but becoming increasingly relevant in its extended and pluralistic form. Human beings are here microcosms within the macrocosm of the city, and their importance resides in their collective role.

Godard, the retired railroad widower who had lived alone and inconspicuously in a fourth-floor flat of a Parisian apartment house, had no lasting ties in life, no children of his own to whom to transmit a single inherited trait; but from his departure springs a new type of bond, a voice that echoes in the streets and across the quarters of the city. The paternity that had eluded him during life suddenly takes shape, and from his sterile existence a new vitality emerges.

The procession passed on, its dead man seemed to them a thing of dread; they loved and venerated him, as the worshipper loves the god of his choice; they were one with him. [P. 117]

In the humble respect and identification that the group bestows upon the dead man, a part of him lives, a germ of recollection and an identity. This amorphous child of Jacques Godard, the little Parisian group born of his ashes, will thrust more echoes along its way, offsprings of a secret power that reaffirms each time life within the streets of the city.:

A hand-cart with an assortment of sweets and cakes spread under a little awning of painted cloth jolted by, close to the pavement, and the sight of it increased the cheer of the walkers and whipped their souls into eddies. They became voluble, and told long stories that required gesticulation. Memories came crowding into every head at once; the image of Godard seized the opportunity to mingle with them, and, as if taken by the hand, was swept away in a circling dance that forced it to seem happy. The patch of sky was bright blue and if the houses on the boulevard were barriers, it was merely as its banks are barriers to a river. [P. 109]

The image of Godard is a supernatural presence here, transmuted, from the dead man, into a vision of light and joy. It is a radiance that embraces the whole city and confers to it a peculiar splendor and a mystical unity under the canopy of the sky. A friendly and almost adventuresome mood dominates ("told long stories"), as the little procession winds its course along crowded streets, forming gay and light arabesques ("a circling dance"). Houses that have stood as barriers against the city's invading throngs of people are now simple embankments ("banks") for the containment of energy. In this moment of communion walls acquire the transparency of the air, revealing their inner life and the secret of their being. Paris will have found a voice at last to whisper its mysterious ways and its links with eternity.

The suggestiveness of the group that is as one large offspring of the dead man's soul is, however, short-lived. Much as a child's indebtedness to his father is sporadic and of little duration, so does the group soon stop recognizing the source of its passing unity, the feeling of oneness it had lived upon a day, in its slow walk behind a simple hearse. Yet that day remains a prism fixed in time with its reflecting and multifaceted colors. People resume their interrupted everyday existence, their solitude and anonymity. They go about their routine tasks and rituals, scattered along the many avenues, faceless and incongruous within the vast city. But what was born on that day long ago with the discovery of Godard's lifeless body is a creation, a poem of which humanity is the subject and city life the hidden song. That creation will sparkle anew for an evanescent moment, miraculously, and reappear as a vision within the heart of people; an engine driver lost in reveries will evoke the day, or a man walking the rain-soaked Parisian boulevards:

But what he felt was no longer merely the fun of focusing a
memory or rummaging for a name. . . . "Well, he was a man
who died. That is all." He kept hold of this idea and he perceived
it was filling his heart. It persisted so vigorously and with such
amplitude that he said to himself: "This is the first time I have
ever really thought about death. [Pp. 148-49]

The memory of a once-lived experience will one day suddenly erupt
and bring to the fore forgotten features—an incident, a face, a
name. Continuity is not limited to matter here, or to progeny; it is
rather a spiritual force that is communicated in the presence of life
itself, from man to man, to object, to sounds or passing visions.
Seen as such, the city becomes its natural habitat, with large crowds
of dissimilar characters emanating currents of vitality among all. A
long time after his disappearance, Godard's spirit, or soul, or
perhaps his essence, lingers on; it invades the mind and heart of a
young man and, through the reality of death, dictates a new sense
of life. "Life, life, life" (p. 150), said the young man in exultation,
conscious finally of the gift he holds in his veins. And he reaches
out at large toward the space and the movement that surrounds him,
eager to live his own portion of existence in full consciousness.
When he reaches the end of his trail one day and joins the dust of
timelessness, there will perhaps be an echo that will be heard by
others, born on this day of joyful communion with his world.
Maybe the very stones of the city will hold his voice in abeyance
and project it anew one day to a receptive heart.

Jules Romains's aim was to show the complex relationship of
man and matter, and the unifying force that integrates them. He
has contributed something new to the vision of life, that of cities
being repositories of continuity and unity, rather than of disrup-
tive, confusing, and alienating elements, such as they are traditionally portrayed. The image of man and city that he offers is thus
an essentially positive one, even if the importance of the individual
may appear diminished. Larger than the anthropomorphic interpretation man tends to give to the world around him, there is a soul
that emerges from the city, he appears to say. That soul may be in-
comprehensible, but it still transcends the existence of single persons in order to create something larger and unperishable, which is
the coincidence of man with his universe.

Notes to Chapter 7

1. André Cuisenier, *Jules Romains et l'Unanimisme* (Paris: E. Flammarion, 1935), p. 35. The translation is my own.
2. Waldo Frank, in his Introduction to Jules Romains, *Lucienne*, trans. W. Frank (New York: Boni and Liveright, 1925), p. 6.
3. Jules Romains, *Death of a Nobody*, trans. Desmond MacCarthy and Sidney Waterlow (New York: Alfred Knopf, 1944), p. 7. All subsequent quotations are from this edition.

8
Dos Passos's *Manhattan Transfer:*
The Death of a Metropolis

If Romains's clearly optimistic view of the city's collective power is to be considered exceptional, the bleak outlook of John Dos Passos (1896—1970), from the opposite side of the spectrum, is perhaps no less so. Neither Balzac nor Zola had perceived many redeeming qualities in the life of a big metropolis, nor had D'Annunzio, Rilke, or Bely. Yet they had all left an interstice in the desolate wall erected by the city against man's hopes, and a glimmer of light could filter through occasionally and point to a path of redemption. With them, the city's evil was matched by human frailty, its coercive strength by apathy and sloth. Implicitly then, one could envisage that if ever it could be measured against individuals of integrity and relative stamina, the city might not unavoidably be the victor. Feeble as such a hope might appear to be, it still could not be ruled out as altogether preposterous. Man could lay claim to some individual worth with those authors, and retain the right to assert his will when confronted by adverse forces. Dos Passos, however, leaves no such redeeming possibility in his presentation of the city.

Dos Passos is an author of contradictory leanings and passionate commitments. When he came home after the events of World War I, he looked at the forces of progress in his country with new eyes. The ordeal of war had marked him deeply. Powerless as he had felt against its destructive thrust, the war still loomed in his imagination as a giant machinery in motion, diabolically grinding away thousands of lives for the benefit of a few. Thus, from discerning

141

massive elements of corruption in the promotion of industrialism, to an outright condemnation of capitalism as its inspiring and demonic force, the step was a relatively short one. Nurtured by revolt and inspired by a messianic spirit in the defense of the poor, Dos Passos hence set out to show that a large city, symbol of industrial progress, was but a furnace emitting poisonous gusts upon the lives of the individuals.

Manhattan Transfer was published in 1925. It portrays the largest city of the United States as a repository of mutually destructive forces, directed both against man and against itself. New York is here a city in the grips of decadence, the prey to a decaying impetus borne out of the evil perpetrated onto others, but also mirrored in its own energy. Its last gasps of life are caught for an instant, before its inevitable plunge into the abyss of total annihilation. The pages of the book *Manhattan Transfer* thus stand as witness of the impending doom, a recorded history of the final stage of a city in disarray. Lulled into complacency, pushed by greed, and deafened by the cacophony of machines, this metropolis of the New World stands for the sins of civilization and subjugation of man.

Dos Passos felt an overwhelming sense of outrage at the injustices that were committed indifferently, and even sanctimoniously, at the expense of defenseless individuals. His insistence on detecting masses mesmerized by a system of craftiness and exploitation soon identified him, however, with anarchist and communist groups. In fact, while a strong socialist sympathizer at the time, and a member of the executive board of the leftist *New Masses*, he never became a full-fledged communist. The years 1932—34 were actually to be the zenith of his socialistic sympathies. From then on there was a constant shift toward more conservative political attitudes. While the first two volumes of his *U.S.A.* triology, *The 42nd Parallel* and *1919*, published respectively in 1930 and 1932, are clearly still identifiable with the old ideals, the third volume, *The Big Money*, appearing in 1936, shows signs of skepticism. If it constitutes an implicit condemnation of the capitalists, the revolutionaries do not fare any better. The excesses of the Spanish Civil War, the trials of the Old Bolsheviks, rivals or dissenters of Stalin, increased his disillusionment. The events of the Second World War brought about a total reversal of position and a repudiation of Communism.

Dos Passo's gradual disaffection with the causes he had considered vital in his younger days coincides with a decline in the mastery of his art. His later books, *Adventures of a Young Man* (1939), *Number One* (1943), *The Grand Design* (1951), *The Head and Heart of Thomas Jefferson* (1954), *Mid-Century* (1961), and *The Best Times* (1967), do not measure up to his earlier achievements and may account in part for the critical neglect he has suffered. There has also been too close an identification between the ideas he espoused and his artistic production. While he was himself responsible for this to a large extent, one can now, through the perspective afforded by time, recognize his merits. One can also separate Dos Passos the man from Dos Passos the artist, and not hold *Manhattan Transfer* or *The 42nd Parallel* either as models of their author's deep concern for the helplessness of the masses or as ironic heralds of his eventual repudiation of liberalism. *Manhattan Transfer* stands on its own artistic rights as a lasting and obsessive portrait of fatality at work.

Nightmarishly modern and caught within an endless cycle of renewal and decay, New York has offered through the years the vision both of man's greatest hopes and of his ultimate aberration. It is the city proverbially known as "the melting pot" and, at the same time, one that has been regarded as an unparalleled source of evil and that has often spelled disaster, threatening to upset the very fabric of society. Yet New York continues to survive, baffling its supporters' promises of rebirth and its detractors' prophecies of doom. Change and renewal have not altered its image, and it stands now, 200 years after its inception, virtually the same as Dos Passos saw it 50 years ago, modern and decrepit, glittering and tarnished, gloomy and unpredictable, a city whose reality resides in tension and the denial of tranquillity.[1]

Dos Passos's view of America's largest city is a pessimistic one. Fearful of the chaos and the destructive quality he thought he saw in man's pursuits of material goods, he considered New York the symbol of his country's thirst for ephemeral wealth and the source of abandonment of old ideals and lofty purposes. His portrait of the city in *Manhattan Transfer* does not merely forecast doom for an eventual future; it announces it as a force well at work, a presence that has already filtered through all walks of life. The daily dramas of existence that he portrays are not only struggles for survival; they are, most of the time, empty gestures accompanied by death rattles and the agony of man's impossible contest with powers far greater than his. Such a view offers no room for optimism, unless one sees in it an admonition, the lesson against the decay that resides within passive renunciation of those ideals originally poured into the very foundation of New York; in the act of depicting the city's inevitable end, Dos Passos reaffirms the importance of spiritual values and the necessity of preserving them.

> *There were Babylon and Nineveh; they were built of brick. Athens was gold marble columns. Rome was held up on broad arches of rubble. In Constantinople the minarets flame like great candles round the Golden Horn....Steel, glass, tile, concrete will be the materials of the skyscrapers. Crammed on the narrow island the millionwindowed buildings will jut glittering, pyramid on pyramid like the white cloudhead above a thunderstorm.* [2]

It has often been said that death is the force that transforms life into destiny; only then do deeds, frozen in time, hold the awesome quality of immutability. What remains of the great cities' life of long ago is now recorded history, in which man's glory and his toils have joined destiny. But Rome's lot, or that of Athens or Constantinople's, is New York's lot too, and to wonder if this great city whose vitality is seemingly stronger than the cement of its composition could possibly be spared the fate of Nineveh, can be only a rhetorical question. Corroded by hidden ills, even if still unconcerned by the impending "thunderstorm," the proud city of glittering steel and glass will soon sink into rubble—for Dos Passos's presentation of New York is, more than a challenge, a recording of history in the making along the paths of destiny.

Barring the work of earthquakes or of other cataclysmic forces, cities do not die overnight. The nature of their heartbeat cannot be measured either by its acceleration or diminishing pace, and none of their components can be examined singly in search for a clue to their health. The bloodline or nerve centers of a metropolis are totally polymorphous, interdependent entities of foreign bodies held together by that nebulous thread called atmosphere. It is when this atmosphere becomes tainted that the disintegration appears unremitting, much like the gradual wearing of strongly woven cloth. *Manhattan Transfer* is an account of that process of wear and tear, of the thinning out of the fabric in which resides the life of New York. From the first to the last page, stone by stone gives way as the characters, one by one, surrender to the destructive elements of the city in decay. The increasing distance that emerges between them and all dreams of purity traces the way toward the final end. That end, already visible at the beginning, projects a future held in the grips of a fading present. Dos Passos's presentation is thus, in a way, the portrait of a city's death in the making, and an admonition, possibly, against those elements which bring about the disintegration of a city under the guise of unavoidable fatality.

The story opens with the arrival of a ferry in New York's harbor.

Three gulls wheel above the broken boxes, orangerinds, spoiled cabbage heads that heave between the splintered plank walls, the green waves spume under the round bow as the ferry, skidding on the tide, crushes, gulps the broken water, slides, settles slowly into the slip. Handwinches whirl with jingle of chains. Gates fold upwards, feet step out across the crack, men and women press through the manuresmelling wooden tunnel of the ferry-house, crushed and jostling like apples fed down a chute into a press. [P. 3]

The view is presented suggestively from a vantage point, the eye following the gulls' plunge into the turgid waters along the bloated ferry coming from faraway lands. Neither the sky above nor the ocean behind is in view as the focus centers upon the narrow frame of the harbor; an image of desolation amid the mechanical churning of the slowly advancing ferry already dominates; loneliness, dirt, greed, and anonymity are all too visible. New York lies in wait while faceless beings are disgorged in its jaws.

At the beginning of each chapter there are brief "captions" such as the one quoted above, which are seemingly unrelated to the events and the intrigues of the story. They project, in reportage fashion, self-contained images that establish a pattern of both isolation and repetitiveness mirrored within the stories. These stories, although enriched by the human element, remain to a great degree nebulous; the men and women caught in the strangling grip of the city are not meant to move the reader either individually or as a whole, for they are only cogs in a revolving wheel, a statistical

order devoid of tragic dimension. People come alive in quick succession, appearing, disappearing, recognizable and yet altered,
aged and worn; their innocence gives way to greed, their hopes
become faded memories. Clicking in and out of sight upon an imaginary screen, they play their assigned roles with lines from an unwritten script, before they disappear once again on the other side.
The wheel that holds and destroys them is New York's self-
perpetuating centrifugal force.

Some come to the city from faraway lands or towns, some are
born here, either pushed by events into the alien world whose
strength they could not measure or unconsciously lying in wait in
hospital baskets where chance has brought them to life. From the
beginning the reader knows that there is little hope for those in the
city, for either they come "like apples fed down a chute into a
press," dismayed by the country that is to be their home, or they
were born there, in bilious hospital lights, and stand squirming "in
the cottonwool feebly like a knot of earthworms." One by one the
heroes of the story are introduced, their names undistinguished,
and quite forgettable, Bud Korpenning, Ed Thatcher, Joe Harland,
Nellie McNiel, George Baldwin; they all hold or have held a dream
and a hope, a desire to become somebody. Incapable of assertion
against the forces of the city, they capitulate in loneliness, poverty,
or sterile success.

The characters considered unforgettable in literature are those
whose problems and tensions, while not being necessarily unique,
present a challenge to the reader. Anna Karenina, Emma Bovary,
Captain Ahab, and Père Goriot are beings who reached out beyond
their frailties and human limitations; they wanted more, or better,
or something different from what was allotted to them; they had a
dream or a vision, a passion that reshaped and changed the meaning of their lives. Could a Karamazov ever disappear with his
search for redemption and leave no trace? Could the struggle with
his conscience ever completely blend with that of his times and his
country and assume the mask of anonymity? The questions are
rhetorical, for what makes Dostoevski's or Flaubert's protagonists
memorable is precisely their personal vision, which transforms the
world into a channel for individual expression. With Dos Passos's
novel the problem is the reverse. The author must refrain from
allowing his characters to have individual stories that could not be

seen as standard behavior; each of them can make only a brief entrance, to be seen as a mere intrusion in the general vision of the city. One meets them, or runs into them quite accidentally, it would seem, as when boarding a train or walking along the streets; one hears them talk, or watches their faces; one is struck by their expressions. But there is always a wall of resistance separating the reader and the characters, a wall made of social conventions and the natural distance between strangers; the reader's impressions are not allowed to become opinions, or his sympathies to develop into sentiments, nor can he deepen his psychological understanding of the protagonists. And this is as it should be. It is a tribute to the author to say that at each rereading the reader has to be reintroduced anew to all of his characters, having only a vague memory of familiarity, of a face probably met across a counter or a table, in a restaurant or a shop. Each time the reader comes in contact with them, he listens with a degree of interest to the vicissitudes of their lives; but their lives remain unrecorded histories of a humanity in motion such as one may see every day in New York. Each person has a distinct silhouette that is soon lost along the shadowy streets. There are no visible heroes or heroines in bars, taxicabs, or rooming houses, but only fleeting images devoid of reflexive moods or tragic dimension.

Bud Korpenning is the first name the reader encounters. He is first seen on the rail by the ferry, tired and hungry but with a song in his heart, or at least a "tingling" in his blood. New York is his destination: he has arrived. The reader keeps running into him as the book progresses—looking for a job, bartering work and the strength of his arms for a bowl of soup, being cheated at every turn, gradually more disheartened and worn, until he surrenders and acknowledges defeat. The first to appear, he is the first to make his exit. His is a banal story that could be editorialized in a few lines in the back pages of a local newspaper: "Brought up in the country, brutalized by father, kills same. Goes to the big city for new start but ends on dead-end road and a plunge into the river." In telegraphic style, his life is fed with others into the mass disposal of New York. What is left of him is only a link in the chain of man's defeat, of dreams of love and freedom that keep running into the city's tangle of decay. His role is unimportant and brief. After a few appearances and a meaningless struggle for assertion, he disappears leaving no marks, not even a memory.

> When he got to the tangle of girders of the elevated railroads
> of the Brooklyn side, he turned back along the southern drive-
> way. Dont matter where I go, can't go nowhere now. An edge of
> the blue night had started to glow behind him the way iron starts
> to glow in a forge. Beyond black chimneys and lines of roofs
> faint rosy contours of the downtown buildings were brightening.
> All the darkness was growing pearly, warming. They're all of em
> detectives chaisin me, all of em, men in derbies, bums on the
> Bowery, old women in kitchens, barkeeps, streetcar conductors,
> bulls, hookers, sailors, longshoremen, stiffs in employment
> agencies....He thought I'd tell him where the ole man's roll
> was, the lousy bum....One on him. One on all them goddam
> detectives. The river was smooth, sleek as a bluesteel gunbarrel.
> Dont matter where I go; cant go nowhere now. [Pp. 124-25]

Bud Korpenning has run out of space. He has covered all the
sidewalks of the city, the dirty streets in the Bowery, and the piers
along the river, chased by fear and betrayal, before finally coming
to the last refuge by the metal girders of the Brooklyn Bridge. His
Odyssey is now over; the last images of life he sees are those which
symbolize his defeat: the powerful iron masses under the night sky,
the cold water below, and the misty light behind the phantom
shadows of towering buildings. A caught man, insignificant, Bud
stands as a mere speck in the meanders of an endless night. "Dont
matter where I go," he says, and his voice is lost amid the rattling
metal of the bridge. His last satisfaction, "one on him," his
triumph over those who have cheated him of his wish to live, is
death. Away now from all the "bulls, hookers, sailors,
longshoremen" who crossed his path briefly only to deprive him of
hope and vitality, he senses in them the corrupt facets of an identical
picture, the components of an indistinguishable mass soiled by contact with the city. Bud's life is over, unmourned, a mere annoyance
to a passing boat, as his body plunges in the squalid waters below.

Ed Thatcher's entry into the story is that of a timid man who ex-
pects little from life and whose wishes are modest and hesitant. He
is a little man with an uneven smile who never acquires full dimension in the novel, for his life is monotonous and insignificant; it is
also indistinguishable from that of the many thousands in the city
bringing up their small families uneventfully, one pale day after the

other. His main role is that of being the father of a beautiful girl whose search for an elusive happiness he does not understand, but who becomes the symbol of his own unexpressed desires and lost hopes. The impersonality of the reader's encounter with Ed Thatcher is never mitigated by an inkling of psychological struggle. He remains to the end an unobtrusive presence within the general image of the city, a man whose life will soon be worn like the steaming asphalt and the torn newspapers of the streets. He first appears by the hospital steps, a little man lost along the marble pavement; he has come to greet life amid the smell of drugs. His wife is somewhere inside the large building, and next to her there will be his little daughter, just born. The new father advances holding his offering of roses, but what he meets in the ward is a "bilious" light and the close smell of decay. The view from the window is "like looking down into water," misty and unclear as the future that lies in wait and is tangled in the "cobwebs" of the trees and the smoke from the chimneys; the present, far from being a promise, has the anguishing presence of a nightmare. As he approaches the long line of beds in the ward and the sickly faces within, he offers an image of dismay and helplessness, clasping his hands by his screaming young wife whose only weapon against the inimical world of New York takes the form of hysteria.

The little daughter who has just come into the world—the dazzling china doll who will become Ellen Oglethorpe, then Ellen Herf, and finally Ellen Baldwin—seems to affirm with her presence the miraculous perseverance of life amid the sickly pallor of city lights ("Look she's breathing," marvels the father); and yet already she seems cast away and lost in the labyrinthine city as her mother screams, "Take it away." One wonders here about the strength and the endurance of this city in which she is born; was it ever different, was it conceived in love and hopes by all the Ed Thatchers trudging its ground; did it ever cherish a touch of poetry and beauty; how did its breath become contaminated? Only silence answers these questions, then as now, in Dos Passos's world and in ours. A sociological study could attempt to explain the inhumanity of a city too concerned with progress to notice the millions who are sacrificed to its cause; it could also investigate what has made some of the most articulate American writers look with diffidence at the ideals of their country and detect a sort of inner cancer at the very core of the structure in which they live. If Dos Passos sees decadence rather than misconception in the design of New York, he gives no indication of this. What seems evident in *Manhattan Transfer* is a kind of historical Nemesis holding the city to its appointed fate.

> They build their Plaza Hotels and their millionaire's clubs and their million dollar theaters and their battleships and what do they leave us? They leave us shopsickness and the rickets and a lot of dirty streets full of garbage cans....You look pale you fellers....You need blood....Why dont you get some blood in your veins? ... Back in Russia the poor people ... not so much poorer'n we are ... believe in wampires, things come suck your blood at night....That's what Capitalism is, a wampire that sucks your blood... day... and...night. [P. 255]

"They" build at the expense of the poor, and "they" live in luxury while those who toil and struggle are only exploited. The "they" of the quotation is the Kafkaesque god manipulating lives from somewhere in the background, the mysterious force against which man is powerless. It is also the strength of an abstract idea taking hold of man like fire sweeping through timber land; the original spark was perhaps beautiful and reached for the sky, but it ends in rubble and a pile of cinders. The "us" of the quotation refers ostensibly to the little people who have no entry into the millionaires' hotels and clubs; and yet it is a larger "us" than those caught in poverty and hunger. The author's tentatively simple answer of "Capitalism" does not explain the totally negative view, the bleak vision of life that leaves no room for hope not only to the have-nots, but to those who have climbed the ephemeral ladder of success. They are all caught, rich and poor, in a world that, like that of the bilious hospital room, only opens out onto "blue cobwebs." The dilemma here is perhaps none other than that of loss of faith, and implicitly of surrender to those forces of evil embedded in the structure of the city.

As Ellen arrives into the world her destiny seems already sealed; to be born in the city and to be raised there only means to be exposed to a constant grating force that will gradually absorb all joy and vigor and channel them into the narrow path of sheer survival. To follow her life is to contemplate the endless display of wasted efforts and the poignant vision of the might-have-been. Defeated at the end, she joins the ranks of all those who, in compromising with basic values, no longer discern the difference between peace and the monotonous evenness of wealth. Ellen's enigmatic personality is never explained, and she thus becomes confused with the shapeless crowd of the city where faces come into focus only briefly. Each of them in retreating behind the walls of private lives, leaves, more than an individual mark, the impression of continuity among those who remain in view. The suggestion here is not of individuality but of a large number of people seen through individuals, each suggesting different modes of life and backgrounds. The characters in the story are not denied a uniqueness of life and of experience, but they are simultaneously symbols of the amorphous masses along the sidewalks and the streets of the city. Ellen Thatcher is thus on the one hand a unique being, the only child of a consumptive mother and a loving father; on the other, she is one of the many beautiful girls who set out to conquer the world and are conquered instead. She is also, among all the protagonists of the story, the only one who is born in New York and whose arrival the reader witnesses in the sad wards of the hospital. Tainted, perhaps, and hardened from the very first, her beginnings symbolically illustrate the necessity to sheathe innocence with the mantle of emancipation and with an inured heart, in order to survive amid inimical elements. Ostensibly, she will succeed; one brilliant career after the other will lead her finally to a profitable marriage with an important man. But along the way she will have renounced love and retreated into a world of sterility and loneliness.

Rather than Ellen's story as such, what the reader is offered are little vignettes, snapshots of her life, which do not add up to continuity and development. Each encounter with her seems to underline the same basic problem—that of self-centeredness in a world that reduces sentiment to defeat. From beginning to end, from her dancing as a child, with tiny feet whirling on the sunny carpet, and her tearing the unread Sunday paper unmindful of her mother's entreaties, to her packing her second husband away in order to make room for further developments in her career, Ellen's life has a certain naive callousness, dominated by indifference to all that does not bear directly upon success. For one brief moment her rush toward life's ephemeral triumphs is interrupted by sentiment, by the yearning to give and to protect; after Stanley's casual betrayal and tragic end, all semblance of beauty disappears from her existence. Her surrender at the end is only indirect; her beautiful exterior, like the soaring skyscrapers of the city, hides a soul that has been contaminated by fear, ambition, and greed. "I'm a terrible sort of person. It's no use talking about it," she says to the sensitive young husband she has decided to cast aside. Quietly she accepts another man whose life is barren but who absurdly clings to a hope of happiness by the side of her fragile beauty.

> "Elaine," he said shakily, "life's going to mean something to me now....God if you knew how empty life had been for so many years. I've been like a tin mechanical toy, all hollow inside."
> "Let's not talk about mechanical toys," she said in a strangled voice.
> "No let's talk about our happiness," he shouted.
> Inexorably his lips closed on to hers. Beyond the shaking glass window of the taxi, like someone drowning, she saw out of a corner of an eye whirling faces, streetlights, zooming nickle-glinting wheels. [Pp. 375—76]

It is Ellen's last round before her surrender to the claims of the city. She has completed her short cycle full of hopes and illusions and now joins New York's destiny; she quietly accepts a reality that she cannot fight. She knows that she is nothing more than "a mechanical toy," without will or even desire; and she catches a reflection of her own image within the lifeless faces whirling by.

George Baldwin, the man Ellen marries at the end, is himself a victim of the city while appearing a conqueror. Having climbed to the pinnacle of success, he now claims, as a middle-aged man, the gift of love neglected in his youth. But love will elude him this time, too, for it is too late to cherish a sentiment that rests on beauty and a measure of surrender. He does not know that love is not simply another object to conquer, that it requires a degree of feelings he has never cultivated. Could George Baldwin have discovered a "truer" love elsewhere? Perhaps; but his story would have been completely different. His whole personality is one molded by New York's peculiar force, one that exacts the Mephistophelian price of the soul in exchange for success.

When the reader first meets George Baldwin, the third husband in Ellen's life, he sits behind a desk offering no indication that he would ever attempt to defy the city's unwritten law of anonymity. The letters of his name—which show in reverse through the glass door of his office, NIWDLAB EGROEG, might be an indication, with their jumbled appearance, of the random play of chance. Read from the proper perspective, they spell a name, just as chance, discerned with flair, may spell opportunity. Instinct leads George Baldwin onto the trail of success. But one wonders if the effort is worth the prize. Rich and disillusioned at the end, he reaches out for love but is doomed to failure, for Ellen's surrender in his arms resembles death rather than the beginning of a new life ("like someone drowning"); her acquiescence is mere capitulation, without magic and without promise.

There is nothing extraordinary in Baldwin's story; he is simply one of the "lucky" few to be emulated by those who struggle to assert themselves. What is sad in him is not simply the discovery that money and power do not stay the restlessness of the heart, a banal lesson in itself and one too often illustrated; what lends him a certain pathetic and almost appealing quality is rather the knowledge that he never had a chance, for he himself was walking on the footsteps of others, looking for a magical answer to the dubious quest for happiness. He believed, as others had before him, that chance lies in wait somewhere, that he must look for it and hold it in his two hands; he never knew that there was little point in looking for something that did not exist, and that all roads would have led him to the same end—to emptiness and to defeat.

The point underscored time and again in this novel that refuses heroic dimension to its protagonists is that the weight of the city is too crushing to allow any individual to measure his strength and perhaps perish, but perish on his own terms. They all move about, waving their arms, standing or falling; they retain their human shape, but they are all puppets at the end of a string, destitute of will and desire. There are no heroes. But there is, perhaps, an antihero, one who emerges from the shapeless mass of the city and walks on, past the line of demarcation like an escaped convict stealing away into the heart of the night. He is Jimmy Herf.

When young Herf arrives in New York with his dying mother, there is no promise for him "behind yonder bank of fog." It is the Fourth of July and the tall lady with the torch stands sentinel by the city proclaiming "liberty enlightening the world." Confusion, noise, glitter, and dirt come to greet the boy who returns as a stranger to the land of his birth. His eyes rest upon the murky waters by the pier, the shaky gangplank, the smelly cab, and the grimy children in the streets. He makes no comment, asks few questions, and finally the day is over, his first day in New York.

> Tucked into bed in a tall unfriendly room with hot eyes and aching legs....He lay there hemmed by tall nudging wardrobes and dressers. From outside came the sound of wheels and shouting, and once in a while a band of music in the distance. His legs ached as if they'd fall off, and when he closed his eyes he was speeding through flaring blackness on a red fire engine that shot fire and sparks and colored balls out of its sizzling tail. [P. 71]

Unfriendliness is evident from the beginning, not in any remote or abstract way, but tangible, visible, and in this regard Jimmy Herf is different from the other protagonists. He seems to know already, on his first night in New York, that there can be no peace here, and no rest. His eyes are "hot," feverishly looking for respite from the senseless movement of the day, his legs ache from aimless wandering. All lies ahead for him, but there are no surprises in store, for the future seems to unfold magically upon the oppressive screen enveloping the present; the wardrobes and dressers stand tall and narrow announcing the stifling presence of skyscrapers that hinder the sun. Jimmy lies paralyzed by darkness, "legless" and incapable of movement. He watches the "fire and sparks" of invisible machines at work and already feels their burning force.

It is too easy, perhaps, to talk of identification between the author and Jimmy Herf. The portrait does not emerge clearly enough to capture the reader's imagination, or to stand for the complexities of a life, for dreams, ideals, and hopes. Jimmy is, rather, a fluctuating image weaving its way through the pages of the book, a kind of "hero of our time," never fully held by the city or completely free from it. He is the stranger whose presence is fortuitous and who will remain, at least to a degree, an outsider to the end, for his role as a citizen of the city is taken only half-heartedly. Yet there is a continuous and sympathetic current enveloping him, as if the author had wanted to spare him not only the fate of the others but also their contamination. By endowing him with a certain bohemian heritage and the spirit of the wanderer, Dos Passos has preserved Jimmy Herf from too close an identification with the evil forces of the city, from wealth, ambition, or despair.

When the reader again meets Jimmy sometime later, he is in a hotel room, watching the street down below and the antlike crowd in the rain. Divining perhaps the tragedy of surrender in the pale features of his dying mother, he asks, "Mother who d'you want to be Mary Queen of Scots or Lady Jane Grey?" Thinking of seals, space, and freedom, he adds later, "it would be such fun to swim around in the sea whenever you wanted to." His desire to escape the constricting life of New York, its pale sky and phantom shapes, is not unconscious or ill-defined but a knowing effort of the will. "Gee I wish we were in the wilds of Africa," he says wistfully, and his tear-stained pillow at night is witness to the anguish of a child who feels trapped. Later, he will not allow the sterile world of the Merivale to intrude upon his simple dreams; he will not surrender, bow, or conform to the unwritten laws of the city and the god Money that rules over them. Jimmy is not a rebel like Stan Emery, bargaining his life against the whim of the moment, not one to destroy what he loves most; he does not dare the city, fight it, or try to reform it either. He simply faces it "squarely" and opposes to its coercive materialism the strength of his individual being.

> Jim Herf turns and stares long up the deep gash of Broadway, facing the wind squarely. Uncle Jeff and his office can go plumb to hell [P. 121]

He has decided here to go to Columbia University, in the heart of New York, and symbolically face the city in a rational manner, through its cultural institution; "uncle Jeff" would like him to go to Yale or Princeton, in keeping with the tradition of all those who seem to rise above the city, only to capitulate more fully in their eagerness to reach the top. Jimmy will test the resources of the city and its intellectual wealth, and, when he comes out of Columbia, he is a young newspaper reporter. His profession will thus entitle him to be in close contact with all aspects of the city, along the streets and river banks, an impassioned witness of crime and suffering. No ivory towers, then, and no climbing along rewarding business ladders for him. He has chosen a lonely road amid the crowd, one that will preserve the integrity of his private existence, however, while allowing him to observe the random play and struggle of city life. "Too innocent to live," comments his friend Ruth (p. 156). And still he lives, never losing his innocence perhaps, and yet with awareness, in close quarters with poverty and vice, but removed from squalor. One wonders how he can withstand the corroding force of the city and not capitulate to that most pervasive of all evils, which appeals to man's need to survive and to his very natural ambitions; but he does, in his own modest way, triumph over the city, for he does not lose sight, among cement rails, macadam streets, and oppressing buildings, of the "glory of the sun and another glory of the moon and another glory of the stars..." (p. 113). Jimmy Herf soon will have lost, on the one hand, all battles with the city, which will have sapped his mother's remaining forces and his wife's courage. He will have been deprived of the love and presence of those he cherished most, of hope too, perhaps, and of faith. But, on the other hand, something will have been left him, a mysterious force that refuses to surrender to the city in which the sun, the moon, and the stars are too far removed to throw light upon man's path. "Why did we come back to this rotten town anyway?" he had cried in anguish (p. 301). It is too late even to expect an answer to an absurd question, but he has still time to leave. Jimmy's departure at the end is not a triumph. But what is important is that the city relinquishes him, and in this it accepts defeat in the face of human dignity.

> The golden legend of the man who would wear a straw hat out of season. Jimmy Herf is walking west along Twenty-third Street, laughing to himself. Give me liberty, said Patrick Henry putting on his straw hat on the first of May, or give me death. And he got it. [P. 402]

Figuratively, Jimmy Herf too, like the Patrick Henry of the past, puts on his straw hat and affirms his right to freedom; he preserves his liberty as he retraces his steps to the ferry, which had deposited him on these shores, a ferry that now offers "a black mouth with a throat of light" (p. 403). He walks away from the sneering city that holds man prisoner of "the opinion of mankind, money, success, hotel lobbies," from all that has turned dreams into bitterness for the Ellens, the Emerys, the McNiels, the Oglethorpes, and the

Harlands who trudge the pavements of New York. Hope resides away from the contaminated city corrupted through man's greed.

The title of Dos Passos's novel, *Manhattan Transfer*, refers to the station exchange in which the old-fashioned steam-cars used to be switched to electric power. The transfer is the symbol of technical progress and the point where a demonic force begins to absorb man's command over his movements. Here the presence of the city is first felt, a presence that gradually transforms a promise into tyrannical domination. Manhattan begins beyond the tunnel, where dark outlines of buildings are swathed in fog. Before the crossing there is still light, but on the other side there is gloom and the rattle of metal. The warning, implicit and yet strong, is not to allow the din beyond the tunnel to sway man's yearnings and his dreams. That warning through the presence of Dos Passos' work, is still heard symbolically fifty years later, unheeded in real life perhaps, but forcefully true through the pages of the book and eminently valid, one might add, for New York still holds a promise amid the rotting pavements of its streets.

Notes to Chapter 8

1. This chapter, in a shorter version, appeared as an article in the Spring 1975 issue of *Centerpoint.*
2. John Dos Passos, *Manhattan Transfer* (Boston: Houghton Mifflin, 1925), p. 12. All quotations are taken from this edition.

9
Durrell's *Alexandria Quartet:* "A Whore among Cities"

If Dos Passos was a rebel in his own times and a champion of unpopular causes, Lawrence Durrell (b. 1912) can be considered an outright iconoclast. But where Dos Passos portrayed the city as a force at odds with humanity, Durrell's almost lascivious presentation of Alexandria is more a challenge to traditional mores and accepted ethical principles. D'Annunzio, too, and Zola before him had described cities whose alluring power alienated man from his moral world. Their heroes or heroines were invariably defeated at the end and surrendered, prey to their own weakness and the temptations of the city. Durrell's Alexandria is also an enticing mistress, or "a whore," as he prefers to call her; but her supremacy is singularly in harmony with the aspirations of her inhabitants. There is a suitable relation between the people's yearnings and the breath of the city, a mutual acceptance and synchronization of desires, from which only the outsider is perhaps excluded. There are neither vanquished nor victors there, but only a complex palette of unrequited cravings and sensuous longings within an ever-renewing—if corrupted—city.

"Who is Lawrence Durrell?" asks Harry T. Moore in his introduction to *The World of Lawrence Durrell* (Carbondale, Ill.: Southern Illinois University Press, 1962), p. x. "A small mischievously lively man with a round blond head," is the answer. The unprepossessing figure thus described is, however, also an exuberant writer, whose melodious and rich prose was acclaimed as a literary revelation when *Justine* was first published in 1957. He is an Englishman who has spent very little time in his country and has preferred instead to travel to exotic lands, from Greece, France, India, Yugoslavia, and Argentina to Corfu and Alexandria. He has written some dramas (*Sappho, Acte*) and poems (*Collected Poems*), aside from the by now noted *Quartet*, composed of *Justine, Balthazar, Mountolive* and *Clea*.

Fielding, Dickens, and Balzac himself had not put the names of London or Paris in the titles of their city novels. Eugène Sue, in the best-seller of the nineteenth century *Les mystères de Paris*, had claimed to depict only the more lurid aspects of the metropolis infected with crime. Zola had delineated, geographically and socially, only a few facets of the French capital in the novel of his latter years, *Paris*. Bely, more tantalizingly, had given the name of the Russian city to his strange story of son against father in *Saint Petersburg*. Each of those novelists was laying the scene of his fiction in the country he knew best, his own. With greater boldness, the expatriate Anglo-Irish Durrell became both fascinated and repelled by one of the most un-British cities of the Mediterranean world. He composed an ambitious quartet of novels revolving around Alexandria. Durrell set his narrative under the aegis of the Marquis de Sade and won immediate fame through presenting it as an exploration of diverse, and at time unorthodox, forms of love. He called upon other impressive sponsors—Bergson, Einstein, and Proust—and boasted that he was adding a new scientific and metaphysical dimension to the art of fiction. The word *quartet* suggested that the long and meandering story, with its recurring motives, was not unlike a musical composition. Bely was also a master of the dangerous and seductive genre of poetic prose (traditionally more warmly received in Russia or in France than in sober Britain), who had entitled his early dramatic and narrative works "symphonies". He had been a close student of poetic rhythm in prose, as became a scion of the Symbolists. But Durrell enjoyed displaying his virtuoso mastery of English prose almost as if he were a foreigner discovering with wonderment all its potentialities. He was hailed abroad as a flamboyant renovator of the anemic British fiction of the 1950s. France in particular, acclaimed his long-winded tales of eroticism and sensuality with the same rapture that had once greeted Byron or Wilde or Charles Morgan across the Channel. In gratitude, the author, ever critical of English cant, disabused with the Mediterranean shores along Alexandria, Corfu, and Cyprus, where he had once set his fiction, settled in the French countryside. His fame has since undergone an eclipse from which it may not recover easily. Still, his *Quartet* remains one of the most impressive attempts at capturing the complex and lurid swarming life of a southern city. The characters are at times weird and hardly credible. The devices to which the narrator resorts can be awkward. There are interminable letters of self-analysis or of sarcastic observation of others, interlinear comments inserted by one character into the diary or the narrative of another, quotes from an earlier novel supposedly composed by one of the main characters' first husband. An air of unreality hovers around those episodes of sexual life in its more sordid forms. In the midst of much fantasy and strangeness, "only the city is real," as the author himself states.

The four volumes of the *Alexandria Quartet*[1] appeared, at the rate of one yearly, in rapid succession, between 1957 and 1960. The first one, *Justine*, is the freshest and perhaps the strangest in its delineation both of elusive love affairs of the protagonists and of the natural and urban setting in which they chase or deceive each other. The narrator, going over his papers in the solitude of a Greek island where he now lives, conjures up the memories of his days in Alexandria, where he was a few years earlier. He is an English schoolteacher and author by the name of Darley. He is not content with reporting events and describing the behavior of people whom he confesses never having really understood. He had loved with protective tenderness a poor Greek girl, Melissa (whom he shared with quite a few other men) and Justine, the wife of a wealthy and cultured Copt, Nessim. The former, who was a professional dancer in a shabby cabaret, was submissive and gentle and, in her own fashion, virtuous and pitiful. She will, later on, have a child by Nessim. It will fall to the lot of the narrator to take care of that child, a girl, in his Greek refuge and, eventually, at the end of World War II, to return her to Nessim. There are few secrets in the meek and honey-sweet Melissa (her Greek name means "bee"). There are many contradictions in Justine.

Justine is a woman with a dark and enigmatic past. She is, in a way, a typical Alexandrian Jewess—or she is at least meant to represent one—with a mastery of French, English, and modern

Greek. She is torn between several facets of her self-tormenting personality, sensuous and forever unsatisfied in love by husband and lover alike. She is also prone to falling in love with the very men, and perhaps women, who spurn her advances in their dread of her unpredictable behavior. Previous to the events in the story as they are recounted by Darley, Justine had been married to a French writer of Albanian and probably Jewish descent, Arnauti, who had analyzed her idiosyncracies in a *roman a clef, Moeurs*. Darley and his friends will often quote from the novel when attempting to elucidate Justine's character. From that husband, whom she divorced, Justine had had a daughter who had been kidnapped, probably taken to a child brothel that, in her desperation, the distraught mother will visit one evening in her vain effort to recover the child. Much later, the reader learns that the little girl had died. All of Nessim's wealth and devotion to his wife had proved of no avail in the frantic search for the child.

Justine' sex life had been conditioned along strange lines by an incident that is only nebulously alluded to in the course of the saga novel—but in which Freudian scholars would have little difficulty detecting the root of her contradictory and restless behavior. She had, as a girl, been raped by a coarse, egocentric local Don Juan, who turns out to have been one of the Alexandrians who fleetingly recur through the story, Capodistria. Justine yearns for that brutal man, while at the same time detesting him. She offers herself to the narrator, who had impressed her when she heard him lecture on the Greek poet of Alexandria, Cavafy. Throughout the four volumes and until her lamentable decline toward the end, Justine seems both fascinated and repelled by every character. To none of them does she give herself unreservedly. She consented to marry Nessim without really loving him, in part because he, as a Copt traditionally irked by the Moslem predominance in Egypt, was willing to assist the Zionist cause in what was then British governed Palestine. Copts and Jews are presented as united in their dislike of the British rule in Egypt, which traditionally favored the Moslems.

A woman of superior intellectual gifts, Justine was prey to hysterical impulses and to contradictions that appear to symbolize the very soul of the city of Alexandria. The most cynical observer of the Alexandrian scene, whom Darley holds in rather naive admiration, is another English writer and diplomat, Pursewarden. He is fond of coining maxims and clever quips. He is disinterested enough to look upon Justine coolly and scornfully enought to call her "a vulpine Alexandrian Venus" (*Balthazar*, p. 105). She is hardly a pagan Venus, however, unlike the colder and untormented professional courtesan whom Pierre Louys presented in his Alexandrian novel, *Aphrodite*, and, if anything, closer to another venal Alexandrian beauty visited by mystical longings, Anatole France's *Thais*. Even more brutally, the same Pursewarden compares Justine, in *Balthazar*, the second novel of the *Quartet*, to "a tiresome old sexual turnstile through which presumably we must all pass." Justine seeks in her pursuit of love something that might increase her spiritual yearnings, satisfy her intellectual interests, explain the past of her city to her, and interpret its complex poetry. Mysticism and sexual promiscuity strangely and conflictingly blend in her as in most inhabitants of the baffling city.

Clea, after whom the fourth volume is entitled, is a less mysterious heroine. For her too, sexual love, in the city of facile liaisons and deviates, implied a surrender of the self and the necessity to subdue mental inhibitions. The task proves difficult for her. She is an artist, and her portrait of Justine betrays a mutual Lesbian attraction between the two women. She preserved her virginity throughout the years and in the midst of the Alexandrian paneroticism. After Pursewarden refuses her as a mistress, she finds a more accommodating and liberating lover in Syria. When Darley returns to Alexandria from his Greek retreat to find Melissa dead and Justine aged and soured, he engages in a liaison with Clea—for once, an almost sane and joyful liaison. But novels cannot long thrive on the dullness of love placidly shared. There is a touch of professorial pomposity in Durrell's "alter ego," Darley, painstakingly analyzing his fellow Alexandrians and mocking his British compatriots, ill adapted to the labyrinthine complexities of Alexandrian life. A rather heavy-handed satire of the British Foreign Office is inserted among the episodes of the story.

Darley senses a growing irritability in Clea. She herself hesitates about whether she should prefer the placid contentement of mutual love to the anxiety of her painter's calling. Just as Darley prepares to return for some solitude to his Greek island while Clea would go to France and paint, the poor woman, while swimming under water in the harbor, has her hand enmeshed in the coils of a harpoon.

Symbolically perhaps, the harpoon had once been given to her by Nessim's brother, Narouz, whose love she had rejected. Darley dives and rescues Clea from imminent death, but her hand is lost. She now wears a steel hook in replacement, built by the very same man, Dr. Amaril, who had unburdened her of the weight of her virginity. It is suggested that some day perhaps she and Darley will live together. But both are now weary with Alexandria, as the reader gets to be, inevitably, drawn by the author's own fatigue with the garish city. As melodramatic surprises multiply in the fourth and last volume of the *Quartet*, the characters themselves begin to appear displaced and without direction. There are several attempts made at disposing of them through death or otherwise, as one reads more passages of purple prose on the beauty of the Mediterranean harbor and of the inland lakes, more suggestions of the remote age of Cleopatra being relived, more glimpses of Alexandria, "princess and whore." But the morbid fascination with the city that gripped the reader through romantic and disturbed Justine has given way, with Clea's dominion over the narrator's imagination, to a quieter acceptance of things as they appear to his sobered gaze. In one of the moralizing remarks of which Durrell is fond, he prosaically declares, "When you are in love with one of its inhabitants, a city can become a world. A whole new geography of Alexandria was born through Clea" (*Clea*, p. 221).

There are sensuous descriptions of the city in the second and third volumes of the *Quartet, Balthazar* and *Mountolive*. But they are few and far between, and somewhat sketchy. Balthazar, a doctor, a Jew who delves into the Cabala and attempts to reinterpret it for the modern Alexandrians, is curious of all that is hermetic. He is a homosexual, accepted in the confidence, if not the intimacy, of both males and females. He is more thoroughly familiar with the past and present Alexandria than Darley, and he corrects and supplements his manuscript on the city. Much as he maligns the city with its intrigues and sordid love affairs, with idle pastimes of bored rich snobs, he well knows that he could never be happy anywhere but in "the impossible city of love and obscenity" (*Balthazar*, p. 19). Balthazar, the most philosophical and most benevolent of the men in the *Quartet*, reflectively ponders over the symbolic significance of the city for its history-conscious cosmopolitan inhabitants. His remarks are not tainted with the tone of superiority and of cynical persiflage, which spoils, for some readers, the long winded pronouncements of Pursewarden. They provide the reader with a different point of view on the city and its multifaceted people from the simpler perspective that had been Darley's.

Pursewarden and another Englishman, Mountolive, a young diplomat who later returns to Cairo as British ambassador, are the least colorful of the male characters, and the least entranced by the mysteries of Alexandrian life. The former suffers from the handicap that customarily afflicts fictional characters who are glowingly presented as writers of unusual talent: the samples of their letters and poems fail to come up to what the author had grandiosely led the reader to expect. Pursewarden wanders about, flinging his sarcasms here and there, scornful of his British compatriots. He gets involved into a foolish conspiracy of Copts and Jews plotting against the British rule in Egypt and in Palestine. He has had a long incestuous love affair with his blind sister, Liza, who, touchingly depicted at first, ends up as a maudlin and unconvincing woman. She eventually, after her brother-lover's suicide (one is reminded here of Cleopatra's brother-husband and even of earlier Egyptian queens who were their brother's wives), marries Mountolive. The latter, as a shy young diplomat, inexpert in matters of the heart, had discovered passion through a love affair with Nessim's mother, a refined Coptic lady older than himself who, like others in the *Quartet*, soon ages into pitiful decay and ends up by being grotesque and rejected.

There are occasionally skillful vignettes of Alexandrian landscapes in the third volume, *Mountolive*. Durrell is original among the successors of Hardy and Conrad in English fiction as a sensitive painter of scenery: lakes, harbors, sunsets, rainbows, palm trees. Occasionally, he is too lavish with jewels and with evocations with the garish effects of colored postcards. But one of his purposes, and perhaps most felicitously achieved (certainly far better than are Durrell's turgid metaphysical claims to having introduced relativity into fiction), was, in the *Quartet*, to seize and convey the "genius loci" of "the capital of Asiatic Europe," as he calls the city of Alexandria in *Mountolive* (p. 130).

Durrell is a strong believer in "the spirit of the place." In an article he wrote for the *New York Times Magazine* dated Sunday, June 12, 1960 (reproduced in his *Spirit of Place: Letters and Essays on Travel*),[2] he confessed that to him, characters, in life and in fiction alike, appeared "almost as functions of lanscape." The spirit of place, a mysterious entity—yet one to which man seems always to gravitate, even if he fails to define it to his own satisfaction—is "the important determinant of any culture." As one who mixed with diplomats and served as press attaché in Alexandria before being assigned to Argentina, Cyprus, and Yugoslavia, Durrell even ventures to assert that "half the political decisions in the world are based on what we call national character" (*Spirit of Place*, p. 158). That character molds and is in turn molded by the peculiar way the cultural heritage from Greece and Rome, the Catholic religion, and the attitudes to love, money, and food assume in Italy or France or Spain or Ireland. Rather than attempting a dry analysis of the sociopsychology of a group or of a city, which would immediately be opposed, the observer who is endowed with some imaginative talent will try to re-create the atmosphere of a country and the reactions of its inhabitants in a work of fiction.

Durrell is too cosmopolitan and too restless to have been content with depicting a closed and minuscule, static world in a small town, a "little old world" (*Piccolo Mondo antico*) as that of the Italian Fogazzaro, or an isolated and passionately fierce island such as the one Elsa Morante chose as a setting for an adolescent's obstinate dreams in *Arturo's Island*. He had first thought, he conceded, of composing a book about Athens. He is indeed far more drawn to, and more in sympathy with, the Greeks than the Egyptians. But Athens in those years (around 1935-45) was still too provincial a capital for him, its people not diverse and corrupt enough. "When it came to choose my city," he revealed, "I (being a romantic) chose the most various and colorful I could remember. . . .I had to have enough *color* to support four long novels without boring."[3] He had, moreover, been strongly impressed by the Greek poems about love in Alexandria written by Cavafy, in which homosexual love is treated with classical restraint, set in the humbler quarters of the city and against the memories of the glorious past. Two of the most evocative and resignedly mournful poems by Cavafy are quoted in full at the end of *Justine*. They had presumably presided

over the meeting of minds, and soon of bodies, of Justine and
Darley. The second conjures up Anthony, a more mysterious
character perhaps than either Cleopatra or Caesar who, since
Shakespeare's drama, seems to have been ignored or
misunderstood by writers. The first, "The City," a short poem of
boredom and unhappiness, as moving as might be Leopardi's
lyrical verse, was Cavafy's own favorite. The poet, like the
characters in the *Quartet*, vainly deludes himself with the dream
that he could ever be free from the noose tied around his neck and
his heart by the city. However, he will not succeed in shaking
himself free from it. "There is no new land,. . .no new sea; for the
city will follow you; in the same streets you will ever roam. The city
is a cage" (p. 227).

Egypt itself, especially the Moslem and the Pharaonic Egypt of
the Nile valley, had scant appeal for Darley and, presumably, for
Durrell himself. The narrator of *Justine*, at the end of the first
volume, has spent some time teaching at a school in Upper Egypt.
But he remained totally insensitive to its grandeur and to its past.
Nor does he evince the slightest admiration for Cairo, its mosques,
and its desert fringed with ruins. If one can trust the letters he wrote
during 1942 to female correspondents (published in the volume
Spirit of Place, mentioned earlier), his reaction to the Egyptian
capital was that of an Anglo-Saxon fond of hygiene and
cleanliness, disgusted with the sordidness of the East. "Cripples,
deformities, opthalmia, goitre, amputations, lice, flies. . . .Dust in
the air carrying everything miasmic, fevers, virus, toxins," he
writes (*Spirit of Place*, p. 75). Letters, to be sure, especially written
by a would-be novelist aiming at impressing his women correspondents with the lurid and repulsive environment where he is
seeking his subject matter, are hardly records of factual and banal
truth. In March 1944, when he had been assigned to Alexandria and
had married his second wife, he vented his angry reaction against
Alexandria itself in terms that betray a love-hate relationship, in a
letter to Diana Gould Menuhin:

> The thin exhausted lusts of the Alexandrians running out like
> sawdust out of dummies; the shrill ululations of the black
> women, the rending of hair and clothes in mourning—a skilled
> occupation—outside the white-washed hospital. [*Spirit of Place*,
> p. 76]

A final invective is flung at the city that he was to depict through four volumes, twelve years later, wistfully, as "this flesh-pot, sink-pot, melting-pot of dullness." It proved to be creative dullness for the novelist (see *Spirit of Place*, p. 76).

Durrell called his book "a big city poem." Poetical, indeed, is the author's vision. Nowhere does he undertake to trace a topographical or geographical map of the city, as Balzac or Robbe-Grillet might have attempted, or as Butor does for his imaginary Bleston. Although he fails to mention it, Durrell enjoyed the advantage of being able to make use of two literary as well as accurate and practical guidebooks of Alexandria by one of his predecessors among the important English writers, E. M. Forster's *Pharos and Pharillon*. This work, which was first published by the Hogarth Press of Leonard and Virginia Woolf in 1923, and *Alexandria: A History and a Guide*, which had appeared in Alexandria in 1922, were reprinted just before Durrell's discovery of the Mediterranean port, in 1938. Forster had been stationed in Alexandria as a Red Cross volunteer in World War I. He had fallen in love with the city, in part through his enthusiasm for Cavafy, whom he soon praised to T. S. Eliot and to Arnold Toynbee. He treated its history and its legends lightly and was even more irreverent toward its fierce theological controversies, Jewish, Gnostic, Neoplatonic. His anticlerical sarcasms are as biting, even if more subtle, than those of Voltaire. But he afforded to modern visitors a lucid insight into the complexities of Plotinus, Porphyry, the Arian schismatics, the Coptic Monophysites, and the foe of the flesh, the self-castrated Origen. His most casual reader might, from his pages, gain an amused understanding of Cleopatra and of the intricate loves—incestuous, homosexual, and even normal—of her Plolemaic predecessors and successors. He could likewise be impressed by the evocation of the once-much wondered-at Pharos, of the Mouseion, of Theocritus and Euclid and the founders of geography and grammar, when visiting a city that has preserved none of its ancient monuments and works of art.

Durrell's characters are not unaware of the past and the pristine glory of their city. Dead Alexander carried in his glass coffin or, as Hamlet puts it, "stopping a bung-hole with his noble dust," Cleopatra skillfully winning Roman generals one after the other, granting the last one, Antony, divine honors before betraying him

when she fled with her sixty ships—are not far from the occasional
broodings of the modern Alexandrians of the *Quartet*. But Durrell
is no antiquarian seeking historical scenes. His portrayal of the city
stresses its ever changing hues through the seasons and according to
the whims of the sea and of the winds blowing from the desert.
Justine, Nessim, Mountolive, and the narrator are seen walking
along the Corniche, that "magnificent long sea-parade which
frames the modern city" (*Clea*, pp. 26-27). The air breathed there is
now "sweet-smelling brick-dust" (*Justine*, p. 4), purified by the
northern breeze and deliciously cool to the visitor who arrives from
inland. The sky and the water seem to blend as in a poem by Rim-
baud, whose problematic passing through the city during his
Abyssinian career is once or twice recalled. To Durrell, whose
fondness for flowers almost equals Proust's, the sky appears at
times to be one of hot lilac; its mauve or tenderly pink hues over the
Mediterranean contrast occasionally with the crimson color of the
lake in the southeast: gardens of anemones, cyclamens, and frail
roses seem to want to dispel the stench emanating from the squalid
quarters of the city.

On each side of the protruding peninsula that led to the ancient
lighthouse and to the Ras el Tin palace where first the Khedive,
then the king of Egypt, his successor, stayed during the summer
season, lie the two harbors, the eastern and the western ones. From
the harbor, furrowed by dinghies entering and leaving, Alexandria
appears "like some great crystal liner asleep there, anchored to the
horn of Africa" (*Balthazar*, p. 143). That harbor, later in the
novel, serves as the shelter for the French fleet, disarmed so that the
Vichy government would not be forced by blackmail to hand it over
to the Germans. In the last volume, *Clea*, once the warships have
been allowed to steam away, Clea nearly perishes, caught in her
submarine harpoon. There also, Fosca, the English mistress of the
French diplomat Pombal, drowns accidentally. Behind the harbor,
the Corniche, and the busy commercial streets and the modern
hotels, there spread the Greek, Arab, and Jewish districts. Further
inland still, the sand of the desert extends, over which, in the spring
months, blows the hot, parching wind called Khamsin, darkening
the sky for several days, sending clouds of sand upon the buildings,
as if the desert suddenly were intruding upon the maritime city.

The most entrancing beauty of the Mediterranean harbor appears at night, when the squalor ceases to be obtrusive and the idle rich among the inhabitants, as in a poem from Baudelaire's *Parisian Scenes*, rush to their pleasures. Occasionally, they cast a glance at the nocturnal splendor: "the sea-gleaming ablutions of water and moonlight." The arteries of the city are then "splashed with silver and deckle-edged with shadow" (*Justine*, p. 122). At times also, the night-club habitués, the perambulating prostitutes, the procurers, and the begging children offer lurid scenes, worthy of Hogarth or Goya, a striking contrast to the splendor of the surrounding natural beauty. The most elaborate descriptions, in colorful and euphonic prose, inserted by Durrell into the novels, are those of the Lake Mareotis, on the southeastern fringe of the city. The annual shooting party that Nessim gives on the lake is described at length and obviously with relish by the novelist, at the end of *Justine*. Earlier in the same novel, Justine and the narrator had first felt the thrill of mutual desire when taking a walk along the lake and then swimming together in the shallow waters:

> In autumn the female bays turn to uneasy phosphorus and after the long chafing days of dust one feels the first palpitations of the autumn, like the wings of a butterfly fluttering to unwrap themselves. Mareotis turns lemon-mauve and its muddy flanks are starred by sheets of radiant anemones, growing through the quickened plaster-mud of the shore. . . .We had tea together and then, on a sudden impulse took our bathing things and drove out through the rusty slag-heaps of Mex toward the sand-beaches of Bourg El Arab, glittering in the mauve-lemon light of the fast-fading afternoon. Here the open sea boomed upon the carpets of fresh sand the color of oxidized mercury; its deep melodious percussion was the background to such conversation as we had. We walked ankle deep in the spurge of those shallow dimpled pools, choked here and there with sponges torn up by the roots and flung ashore. [Pp. 34-35]

The exotic loveliness of the watery landscape is colorfully rendered by Durrell, in contrast with the painters and writers from England and France who, in the nineteenth century, from Fromentin on down, had been fascinated by the sights of the Nile and the delicate hues of the sky over the parched desert.[4] The notations are precise and selected for the force of their sensuous evocation. The descriptions are seldom obtrusive, as they were with some Romantics who vied with painters' palettes, but neglected to imply any correspondence or contrast between the scenery and the characters. Throughout the *Quartet*, on the contrary, the artificiality of the city is stressed, built, as it were, "like a dyke to hold back. . .African darkness" (*Justine*, p. 52). We are all its children, Justine repeatedly hints, and its victims also: devitalized by its climate, unable to shake off the fatality that chains them to its decadent life, to its cosmopolitanism and to the myth that the past has erected over it.

With all the sordid aspects that are presented, the heavy sensuality, the decay and vice of which walls and streets seem to be imbued, the true subject of the four novels is the "spiritual city." From the outset, Alexander, "the soldier god in his glass coffin," haunts the Alexandrians of today after twenty-three centuries. He had intended, by an act of will and with a keen vision of the future, to transport to that harbor and to perpetuate there the very best of Hellenic civilization. He then departed to wage war against the Persians and there met an early death. His body was returned, but the high priest at Memphis refused to receive within a Greek temple a conqueror whom another priest at Siwa had declared to be a god: for, E. M. Forster recalls in his learned guidebook, "wherever his body lies, the city wil be unquiet, torn with feuds and battles."[5] The glass coffin sailed down the Nile back toward the city newly built on the conqueror's orders. It was laid to rest in the center of the city, the "Soma," where the mosque of Nebi Daniel now stands over the tomb.

Cleopatra, a less legendary figure, is an even more haunting presence in the city. A queen at seventeen, with a brother-husband seven years younger, she seduced Caesar, after his victory over Pompey, having wrapped herself up in oriental carpets. Through him, she got rid of her husband, married her younger brother, gave Caesar a son, and followed him to Rome. In 44 B.C. Caesar was murdered. She lost no time in seducing Caesar's heir, Antony, coming to him in her famed gilded barge. She taught him the refinements of voluptuous love and of delicate living, bore him several children, and, when her city, the capital of the Eastern world, affronted Rome and Caesar's nephew, betrayed him in the naval battle of Actium. Still he followed her to Alexandria, made a suicide pact with the queen, and when Octavian landed in the harbor, he threw himself upon his sword. She was then thirty-nine, assured of her place in history, and was buried in Antony's tomb in 30 B.C..

The Moslem history of the city appears to leave the population of the *Quartet* indifferent. Except for a few servants, superstitious exorcizers of jinns, and the gullible crowd that worships, at the end of the last volume, at the shrine where Scobie, most ironically, is sanctified, Moslems hardly appear in the novel. If they do, they are crudely caricatured, like the corrupt prime minister who distrusts the Copts and the foreign residents of Egypt, extorts priceless gifts from Nessim, and ends up being a fascinated adorer of Clea. Durrell, it is obvious, made little attempt to penetrate into the soul of Islam. He was only sensitive to the picturesque poetry of the minarets and of the muezzins calling the time for prayer. The historical and legendary characters whose memory has remained imprinted upon the city are the Ptolemaic kings from whom Cleopatra descended. At the very beginning of *Justine*, Darley, catching his first glimpse of the heroine, identifies her at once with "that race of terrific queens which left behind them the ammoniac smell of their incestuous loves to hover like a cloud over the Alexandrian subconscious." He conjures up "the giant man eating cats like Arsinoe" whose relative or heir she was symbolically, or "poor Sophia of Valentinus who died for a love as perfect as it was wrong headed" (*Justine*, p. 10).

The heritage to which the composition of the *Quartet* is truest is that of Jewish and Christian Alexandria. Allusions are frequent to its passionate theological quarrels, its ascetics and cenobites in the nearby desert, its fierce and implacable fights between Arius and Athanasius in the fourth century, its riots opposing Greeks and Jews, and Bishop Cyril's persecution of the Platonic philosopher Hypatia, stoned by an enraged Christian mob. An inveterate bent toward self-analysis and intellectual torment acting as a condiment to their sensuality marks many of the characters. Pombal, the French "jouisseur," and Pursewarden the mocker, alone are immune from that mental torment and attempt to live like cynical Epicureans. But they yield to sentimentality in the end. The others are far removed, however, from pagan attitudes. They take their pleasures gloomily, and they wallow in psychologicl complications. The proportion of incest-haunted persons, of homosexuals, of women afraid of frigidity, and of men dreading impotence is high among the characters. The city, it is repeatedly remarked, is one both "of extreme sensuality and of intellectual asceticism" (*Justine*, p. 84). The Jews are especially attracted to mysticism: a number of them have formed a group for the interpretation of the Cabala, surrounded with an aura of conspiracy. In that city of sects and gospels, Balthazar, the Jewish homosexual doctor who is typically adept at blending "Alexandrian scepticism" with speculations on the Gnosis, remarks, "We are all hunting for rational reasons for believing in the absurd" (*Justine*, p. 78). As in much of its past history, that conglomerate of Europeans, Levantines, Copts, and Hellenes makes Alexandria the ideal home of syncretism. They are for the most part uprooted characters—even the truest descendants of the Egyptians of old, the Copts—steeped in French culture, striving to endow with a soul a city that has created little art and hardly any literature, erected no original monuments, but loves to play with ideas as it also does with money and with sex.

Durrell, an admirer of D. H. Lawrence and of Henry Miller, a devotee of the author of an earlier *Justine*, that divine Marquis whose name has remained affixed to sadism, declared more than once that his saga amounted to nothing less than an exploration of modern love. He never matches the intensity of the obsession with sex to which Miller gave poetical expression in his more scandalous volumes. In fact, Durrell, whose love of Greece and of flamboyant style was celebrated by Miller in his *Colossus of Maroussis* (1941), almost turned against the American writer when, disgusted with Miller's *Sexus* (published in 1949), he sent a cable pronouncing the new book "disgracefully bad."[6] Nor does Durrell ever match the depth and the mystery of Lawrence's finest analyses of love or the latter's final poetical message that "sex is a state of grace."[7] The uses to which the theme is put in the *Quartet* are varied and often border on an attempt at titillating the reader somewhat cheaply. Child brothels such as the one where Justine catches a glimpse of her dead daughter, other establishments for voyeurs such as that where the narrator observes the performing of a sex act, carnivals in which a woman lies with a lover over a pile of dominos under which lies the body of a man just murdered are all described or alluded to by the author with a morbid zest. Incest is no less recurrent a theme, as becomes the city of Serapis (*Justine*, p. 82), and Byronic Pursewarden, who had a wife at home in England (as did

Antony when he was Cleopatra's lover) justifies his liaison with his sister Liza through presenting incestuous love as "the attempt to possess oneself as a member of the opposite sex."[8] The number of gloomy and sordid homosexuals and of sexual deviants is also disproportionately high. Durrell spared no effort to present Alexandria as "a whore among cities" and to show, through the perversion of its inhabitants, the city's corrupting power.

Why such a predominance of promiscuous love in the *Quartet*? Obviously, it helps the popularity and the sales of a novel, and it lends a note of exotic quaintness to the fiction. Sex is a condiment to be added to conspiracies, plots, and counterplots, and it passes for the favored topic of conversation in the cafés of any Mediterranean harbor. The number of people who make up the "upper crust" in a city where the mass of Arab, Sudanese, and other workers is systematically ignored by the Europeanized rich is limited. They constantly meet each other at parties given by the foreign consuls and by the wealthy Moslems, who do not allow their wives to go out. They read the same new books, applaud the same musical performers and dancers from abroad, learn every secret about each other's amorous affairs. It is a perpetual dance in front of a mirror. The originality of the Alexandrians' sex life lies in its narcissism. Durrell, somewhat heavy-handedly, has woven the theme of the mirrors ubiquitously through his four volumes. No character escapes self-contemplation in his and her mirror. And the mirrors are often multifaceted, reflecting the inner and outer contradictions of the persons. Like many other people, but far more than most, Durrell's characters are in love with themselves in their sex affairs, even while they hate themselves.

Nowhere does Durrell reach the profundity in the analysis or in the philosophy of love that has made one of his predecessors and masters, Proust, the supreme delineator of passion in this age. The English novelist repeatedly nods his approval of the French who see in love "a form of metaphysical inquiry." The characters are deliberately lacking in consistency; they are devoid of any fixed personality. Not unlike the Proustian ones, they are first presented under one of their appearances—usually a superficial and deceptive one that waylays the reader. Subsequently, not just the gullible reader, but the narrator, Darley, stands to be corrected by another commentator, Balthazar or Pursewarden; they both treat the first

narrator with condescension and show him to have been taken in by
the complex and tortuous women of Alexandria who refuse to be
summed up in one formula. Even Justine's advances to him are exposed as the caprice of a woman attracted to literature and to an
eloquent discourse on Cavafy's poems, or as the mere gesture of a
woman with sex on her mind who had just been spurned by
Pursewarden and fell back upon a weaker individual who sensed
some mystery in her. All of Durrell's grandiloquent claims to having attempted a four-dimensional type of fiction amount to little
more than a manipulation of time, no longer irreversible in modern
fiction, and to an attempt to baffle the reader, who is never made
fully acquainted with what has taken place earlier in the story. It is
not to those rather naive and too neatly contrived complexities that
the *Alexandria Quartet* might owe its survival.

   The important merit of Durrell's work is to have depicted the city
of Alexandria and to have made it live through the pages of the
four volumes as a chaotic and contradictory metropolis. The vitality of that most unusual of all capitals lies in the force that emanates
from its past and becomes inseparable from the present. The
characters sense upon them the working of a spell that pushes them
to relive that past and come to terms with it, before they can free
themselves from it. With less theorizing didacticism than Jules Romains in his *Men of Good Will* or than Waldo Frank in *City Block*,
or even than Michel Butor in his conscientious study of one small
Parisian street in *Passage de Milan*, Durrell has proved the most
skillful practitioner of a poetical form of Unanimism in the evocation of a city. There is not the drab and squalid misery of a
naturalistic novel here, nor the pervading gloom of Manhattan as
seen through the eyes of Dos Passos. Those men and women pursuing their pleasures sadly, indulging their sex urges away from the
path of orthodoxy as in a mysterious ritual, are all afflicted with an
obstinate "world weariness." This phrase occurs in *Balthazar* (p.
230) and is supplemented on the next page by Durrell's conclusion
about love, more romantic and even puritanical than pagan: "Love
joins and then divides. How else would we be growing?" All the
agents in the *Quartet* are in fact acted upon rather than active. They
are but pawns in a big, perfidious game that the city plays with
them as if it were bent upon experimenting on human beings. In
Justine, at the very beginning, the sad, fatalistic remark is made by

the narrator that all those Alexandrians over whom Justine holds her sway are merely creatures "trapped. . .in the gravitational field which Alexandria threw down about those it had chosen as its exemplars" (*Justine*, p. 8).

Notes to Chapter 9

1. The references to the *Alexandria Quartet* are all to the current paperback edition brought out by E. P. Dutton (New York, 1961). The original edition of *Justine*, also published by Dutton, appeared in 1957 (Copyright © 1957 by Lawrence Durrell; reprinted by permission of the publishers, E. P. Dutton); *Balthazar* in 1958 (Copyright © 1958 by Lawrence Durrell; reprinted by permission of the publishers, E. P. Dutton); *Mountolive* in 1959; and *Clea* in 1960 (Copyright © 1960 by Lawrence Durrell; reprinted by permission of the publishers, E. P. Dutton).
2. All quotations from Durrell's *Spirit of Place* are from this same edition. (*Spirit of Place: Letters and Essays on Travel*, ed. Alan G. Thomas [London: Faber and Faber, 1969]). In this same edition is found the *New York Times Magazine Section* article of June 12, 1960
3. Harry T. Moore, ed., *The World of Lawrence Durrell* (Carbondale, Ill.: Southern Illinois University Press, 1962), p. 159, from "Durrell Answers a Few Questions."
4. The allusion here is to Fromentin, Gautier, Loti, and the many artists and writers studied in Jean-Marie Carré's *Voyageurs et Ecrivains frncais en Egypte* (Le Caire; Institut français d'Archéologie, 1932).
5. E. M. Forster, *Alexandria: A History and a Guide* (Alexandria: Whitehead Morris Limited, 1938), p. 8.
6. John A. Weigel, *Lawrence Durrell*(New York: E. P. Dutton, 1966), p. 26.
7. "Sex is a state of grace" appears in the opening line of an untitled poem by Lawrence published posthumously in the collection called *Pansies* (New York: Knopf, 1930), p. 71.
8. Weigel, *Lawrence Durrell*, p. 100.
9. Moore, ed., *The World of Lawrence Durrell*, p. 157 n. 3.

10
Butor's *Passing Time:*
The Equivocal Reality of a City

In literature, the reality of the city, in spite of all attempts at documentation of sociological and geographical facts, resides primarily in the realm of the imagination. Even Zola's effort to depict realistically a circumscribed area and the lives of the people within is imbued with fantasy; his Père Colombe's spirit machine in the dingy quarters of *L'Assommoir*, for instance, is a monster of diabolical faculty, and the tenement building where the story takes place gradually appears more like an ant-heap swayed by the moods of the city than a building of unvarying size and consistency. D'Annunzio's Rome, the Paris of Rilke or Balzac, Bely's St. Petersburg, and Durrell's Alexandria are all unique portrayals embellished or damned through romantic, inspired, or dejected personal visions. Proust's Venice hardly even attempts an objective portrait of the city. There are no outer dimensions that could symbolize inner virtues or decay there, as might be found in Thomas Mann's vision of the same city. Proust's presentation is unabashedly a personal dream, adorned with old longings and singular hopes, unreal but true, eminently valid and strangely convincing. It is along these lines that I shall place Butor's *Passing Time*. The Bleston that emerges from its pages resembles, however, a nightmare more than a dream. The author's preoccupation with the geographical-temporal relations of the city gives it a dimension that simultaneously asserts and denies the reality of both time and space.

Michel Butor (born 1926) was identified at the beginning of his literary career with the postwar vogue of "the new novel." Similarities between him and Robbe-Grillet or Nathalie Sarraute are not very evident, however. Trained in philosophy, he is in fact much more concerned with the psychic dimensions of words and thoughts than with geometrical patterns and designs traced by a hypothetical observing eye. His works mirror, in their varied and innovating ways, the tentacular realities of space and time, and man's metaphysical relation to the elements around him—from his first novel, *Passage to Milan* (1954), to *Passing Time* (1955), *A Change of Heart* (1957), which was much praised by critics, *Degrees* (1960), *The Genius of Place* (1958), *Extraordinary Study* (1961) and, *Words and Painting* (1969). Michel Butor does not try to develop characters or to endow individual cities with life; rather, he shows the oscillating perception of places in conformity with an always personal and anguished search, in a constantly changing vision and mutable grasp of reality.

The title of *Passing Time*[1] points to the novel's central interest, time. But the element of time is intricately woven with that of imagination and creation, a time that embraces both the flight of months and hours, and the ticking seconds of an inner dimension. Time is a presence here, with images conjured through the constant awareness of its passing, through fear or the ominous sense of waiting. The images are dictated by a feverish imagination and find an echo, a coincidence in exterior shapes; together, the real and the imagined shapes assume the outlines of a city. Time itself then takes a form; but it is an elusive form, one that yearns for an entity and an identity within a city that denies both. It becomes a quest for a city and the city itself, for the city only exists within the confines assigned to it in time.

The city is Bleston, somewhere in England. The fact that Butor spent two years in Manchester, and that Manchester might indeed have inspired the book, has little if any bearing upon the reality of Bleston. Bleston only exists within the pages of *Passing Time*, which denies its reality in the very act of giving it shape. In a very Proustian sense, to hold eventually means to destroy, and by seizing the elusive shape of a mysterious city within the pages of the book (which is in the form of a diary) the protagonist, Jacques Revel, creates Bleston and conquers it at the same time. Bleston is a memory of unreality, and as such it continues to hover within the confines of the real and the imaginary, perpetuated within the truth of the work of art.[2]

How much time, strictly, is involved is easy to define. Revel, a Frenchman with a halting knowledge of English, is sent to Bleston for one year, twelve months to the day. But here clarity stops. Seven months have already passed when the journal is started, and five remain; the entries aim at recapturing the time lapsed, while moving within a present forever in flight toward the future. That future has an end, which is the last day of the twelfth month of his stay; that end must coincide with the beginning, in order to form a circle, a whole, containing the city of Bleston. The ticking clock rushing toward the completion of this circle reshapes each day in the line already traced and in the light of the one being traced. Each new day, intricately enmeshed in the reality of the English city shrouded in fog, superimposes a new interpretation upon the past entries of the diary. But each new understanding increases rather than diminishes the mystery, for the city of Bleston—like all dreams and nightmares—is a reality that resides in the imagination.

If in Proust's work each day reshapes the consciousness of the past, here each day is an attempt to *give* a consciousness to the past. Jacques Revel's past days and months in the city of Bleston, begun on the foggy day of his arrival in the late hours of an October evening, lack the clarity of commitment and the passion of purpose of young Marcel. His days are caught from the very beginning in the unreality of the mist in the air and the blurred vision through the opaque glass of the train. As the months go by, time is marked off from the haunting dates of an invisible calendar, fog thickens, persistent, dismaying, with only a rare glimmer of sun to draw a miragelike streak on the pavement. Revel's effort in his diary is to seize the shapeless opacity of the past seven months and to measure it in the light of the time that remains. He wants, in a way, to break the misty mirror of unreality, to blot away the darkness encompassing the past and replace it with form and content. But shape is forever elusive, and the clouded train window streaked with dirt and lingering drops of rain, is symbolically interposed at the end between him and the city of Bleston. Introduced in the uncertain light filtered through a "black window," Bleston recedes finally behind the same dark glass and undefined consciousness. What remains is a pile of pages, a journal, bound in book form; it is called

Passing Time. The book depicts the image of the city it wanted to capture, its reflection, its soul, its pervasive and haunting quality. The portrait that emerges at the end is more real than the bricks of the city, for it holds their essence and it bears the impression of their shape. Perhaps this image, as all reflections are, is distorted, but Butor has caught in it precisely the reality of truth, forever changing, contemplated through the misty eye of a personal vision.

The city of Bleston is a composite of reality and imagination, in which imagination creates reality, and in which reality spurs the imagination. The layout of the city is both its plan and its heart, with the labyrinthine roads bearing direct relevance to the people who inhabit them.[3] The legend of Theseus, Ariadne, and Phoedra depicted in the tapestries of the City Museum, beckons to life to partake of the past, to blend indissolubly with it, and to create new myths out of the old. Ann and Rose are thus seen through the screening power of the fables that mark the walls of the museum. The two English sisters the reader meets in the city of Bleston embody at once the charm of youthful beauty that is their own and the fascination of images caught beyond the spectrum of time past. They, too, hover between the real and the imagined. Their tender beauty kindles sentiment and at least the contemplation of lasting love; they also suggest the force of fate shaping life, the same force that pulled Theseus in its snare. As the two heroines of the past, they are not separable from the ties that link them to the labyrinth, as the mythical structure gradually emerges from the walls of their city. Ann and Rose are not only middle-class and possibly simple girls of modern England, who live uneventful lives leading, in all probability, to uneventful marriages. They are simultaneously images of another world and other times, part of the mysterious shape of Bleston, as their counterparts were to the horrors of Daedalus's work.

Butor's use of mythology has been amply discussed by eminent critics such as Leon Roudiez, Vivian Mercier, René-Marill Albérès. I shall limit my comments to those features in the heroes of the past which focus on the role of the city. The three legendary figures appearing in *Passing Time* are Cain, Theseus, and Oedipus. Their imprints upon the events taking place (real and imaginary) are interchangeable; they appear both fixed in their traditionally assigned roles, and fluid, one running into the other, until the lines of demarcation separating them become uncertain and indistinguishable. The important link between them is that all three were rulers of a city: Cain built the first town, Enochia, after the murder of his brother Abel; Theseus became king of Athens after slaying the Minotaur and involuntarily causing the death of his own father; and Oedipus is crowned king of Thebes after killing its rightful master and his own father. Each of them is not only a founder of a city, but a betrayer and a murderer; and each of them is a ruler and is ruled in turn: the first by jealousy, the second by lust and ambition, the third by blindness. Their images now stare from the dark recesses of the Cathedral or from the walls of the City Museum in the English town. Their valiant, desperate, heroic stances present a choice or a warning to the citizens of Bleston. The paths toward which they lead are divergent and yet the same, all ending in death and horror. It is, on the one hand, only in the Old Cathedral that the image of Cain's fratricide is depicted; but, on the other hand, the theme of murder is injected anew in the New Cathedral through *The Bleston Murder*, the novel within the novel, discussed later in this chapter. The two cathedrals, with the modern one theoretically replacing the old, are the visible symbols of repetitiveness and circularity in man's aims and the fate ruling him within the confines of Bleston. The tall pilasters in the New Cathedral, with the whole of the animal kingdom clustered along their sides, only interject an element of banality in the old myths. Conservatism is indeed emphasized through the link of Mrs. Jenkins with the New Cathedral and her eye meekly turned toward the past and the imprisoned fly in her ring.

Vivian Mercier speculates that Butor's use of myths is purposely directed to "erroneous" and ironic ends.[4] This interpretation is tenable and persuasive. After all, Revel, the self-cast Theseus, turns out to be not quite the conqueror of feminine charm he had envisaged, and the Minotaur, symbolized by Bleston itself, is not exactly slain and threatens, in fact, to devour the would-be hero instead. All this is true, but it is perhaps not the whole truth, for ambiguity plays a role here too. Jacques Revel does not leave the labyrinth (Bleston) with the seductive Phaedra (Rose) at his arm. Ariadne (Ann) is not abandoned weeping in loneliness. The monstrous city, far from being destroyed, lives on. And yet the modern Theseus is, in a way, the conqueror of the pretty sisters and of their squalid residence. Ann and Rose are both seduced by his charm, each smiling and holding a promise in her eyes; and the city is vanquished by the only possible weapon available to civilized man. If one looks at the mythic characters Cain, Theseus, and Oedipus as the symbolic choices offered by the town of Bleston, one knows that in a way they constitute no choice at all. Since they all point the way to death, the only exit to life must be out of the city itself. Revel does indeed leave, resisting the lures of love and the temptation of surrender.

Just as the Minotaur and the labyrinth became identified with the whole Cretan civilization, Bleston is presented as a microcosm of modern civilization. Its urbanity and systematized pattern of existence are offered as a reflection of modern life, with the attraction of facile comfort and the lulling conformity that preys upon individuality. The weblike pattern of the city holds the same perils of complacency and escape from inner truth found in the Minotaur's residence, the same threat of annihilation in sleep. To leave, to resist the insidious lure of this town, is in itself a triumph. But in order to be faithful to the legend of Theseus, triumph is not enough: Jacques Revel must conquer. He will thus hold the nefarious city with the only binding force granted by his times: he will encapsule it in the pages of his journal and hold it within the pervasive strength of art.

Much has been written already about the technical divisions and subdivisions of Butor's work.[5] There are five main parts in *Passing Time*, covering the remaining five months of Revel's stay from the day the journal is started, and stretching simultaneously backward toward the seven months already lapsed from the day of arrival in the city. Each entry is a unity of both time and space presented during a five-day writing week, but each encompasses the remaining two days, Saturday and Sunday. These mathematics are not merely devices of a puzzle with a cleverly disguised mechanism; they are symbolic unities of a circular occurrence encompassing the city of Bleston. The repetitiveness of days within weeks, within the months of a year, stands for the unraveling of the eternally known and the forever new. It represents also the laying down of a structure, brick by brick, and the unfolding of a mysterious monument that is the life of a city.

The opening chapter is called "First Steps." (The French title,

"L'Entrée," conveys "coming in," the act of entering, which is slightly lost in translation.) This chapter introduces the hero's arrival into the city of Bleston. After the title page for chapter 1, the reader is in fact ushered into the city. The map of Bleston appears after the title page. That it is placed at the beginning, before the story even opens, points to the fact that the town dictates the story as much as the story contains the town. The first impression, renewed each time one looks at the map, is that of a maze. As one follows the intricate lines toward the northern top, along the longest and widest street, one gets to the station or, rather, to the stations. There are three of them, Hamilton, New, and Dudley, forming a ring around Alexandra Place, which is both point of arrival and point of departure. Black lines spread out of it like webs embracing all directions at once; they are the railroads which seem to have no destination other than the city itself. The importance of the map is both real and symbolic. Real, for it points out that *Passing Time* is indeed about Bleston, and that the town lies at the foundation of the work just as much as the element of "time" appearing in the title. The symbolic value is more complex. First of all, it represents a labyrinth, reminiscent immediately, if vaguely, of Daedalus's construction. This modern labyrinth, which is the city of Bleston, holds its own key in the pattern that reveals the way in and out of the maze itself. The labyrinth is thus both the prison and the means to freedom. The map is also the first page in Jacques Revel's journal—a journal that is written in defiance of the enslaving forces of the city, and in a quest for clarity. The numerous pages that follow are an extension of that first one. They also represent the unraveling of Ariadne's thread contained in that shapeless, original mass. They are, every one of them, symbolic bricks resting upon the initial one, the map, rising gradually until they become a fortress of resistance to the sordid city. Just as that first page shows both the labyrinth and the thread leading the way out of it, the map is both the image of Bleston and the start of the monument that will conquer the city, in the very act of placing it within the lasting hold of the written word.

The first chapter recaptures the early impressions received upon arrival—the suffocating atmosphere that meets Jacques Revel, the panic seizing him suddenly at the station of Bleston.

I remember I was seized with sudden panic, ... for an endless second I was overwhelmed by an absurd wish to draw back, to give it all up, to escape; but a huge gulf now separated me from the events of that morning and the faces I knew best, a gulf that had grown inordinately wide while I was crossing it, so that now I could not plumb its depths, and its other bank, incredibly far away, appeared to me only faintly, a jagged skyline on which no detail could be discerned. [P. 10]

The station is nothing else than the entrance into the labyrinth, with gates closing behind and nowhere to go but forward, into the lurking night and the oppressive squalor of Bleston. From the very beginning the city is introduced as a strangling force, a mold shaping and containing the helpless shadows of the people within. The past, the sun, the lights, the hopes themselves—all are suddenly obliterated to give way to the anguish of entrapment and a new sense of loss. But a challenge is also born at this moment, dictated by the need for survival, by the urge to retain an identity and a personal direction. The next entry, following immediately the passage just quoted, begins: "I grabbed my suitcase and I began to walk on that new soil." There is strength, or at least resolution, in that "grabbed," and if the road ahead is full of peril and inspires the dread of the unknown, its power will have to be measured against the resolution of this latter-day yet unnamed Theseus. He begins his walk along the misty path ("I began to walk") and, in the very act of telling his story, he begins also his conquest of the city.

Horace Buck is introduced in this first chapter recapturing the early stay in Bleston. The personality of this strange man is explored no more than that of any other character in the story. Yet he comes out of the diary's entries curiously alive, with his bent gait and a bitter smile hovering on his sad lips. What is important about him is his one-sided relation with Bleston, his pitiful struggle in a place that obstinately refuses to acknowledge his existence. His thwarted need to elicit some kind of response turns into unreserved hate for this city of white people plunged into grayness. For Horace Buck is a black man, a total stranger in Bleston—not only to the city, the people, and the country, but to the race itself. His blackness is the symbol of alienation and of the impossibility of blending with the world around. Horace Buck embodies man's inability to communicate with man, his ferocious impotence and empty revolt against society. He represents, finally, man's frustration and his refusal to submit, his pride and humble pathos. This black man, so different from those around him, is a curious mixture of anarchy and conformity. Perhaps he is a symbol of humanity itself, caught in the vicious cycle of its compounded mistakes and inherited tragedy. Through him one learns that man's search for warmth is an ephemeral quest, that "home" is a chimera dictated by inner thirst and the passionate desire to satisfy that thirst. There is no home possible for Horace Buck, not even within the mythic schemes of old legends, not in the stained-glass windows of the old cathedral, not in the tapestries on the museum's walls. Nowhere can he capture an echo of his own being in this opaque city of glimmering reflections. Horace Buck is the "invisible man" whose only mirror is the hidden fabric of the city itself, made up of hatred and a vindictive grinding of all energy.

That Horace Buck may be an echo of the intricate aspects of Bleston is both clearly alluded to and subtly disguised. The more obvious or "visible" link between this unfortunate man and the wretched city is precisely their respective "invisibility." The black man from faraway Africa and Bleston, the northern town of England, are both wrapped in shadows—the first through his black skin, the second through endless fog. For both, darkness is a barrier of impenetrability and mystery, hiding a strange mixture of passivity and ravaging force. The strangling, suffocating violence of the city becomes, in the black man, an urge to ignite and to destroy; and both the power of Bleston and the rage of Horace Buck hold the suggestive quality of an invented tale inspired by truth. For the city and Horace are the feverish creation and the startling reality in Jacques Revel's tormented imagination.

The ambiguity contained in the personality of Horace Buck cannot but lead to the center of the story and the equivocal vigor of Bleston. This city is characterized as a bleak, soot-laden repository of human destinies. Yet it is well arranged on the surface, with a wide main street and the relative elegance of its center. Here, at the heart of Bleston, life seems smoothly contained, with the comfort of continuity conferred by the presence of old monuments, and the bustling activity of modern commercial buildings. In Horace Buck, too, what one sees mostly is the kindness of his manner, his generosity and apparent openness. But the black man and the black city are both composed of two layers, very different from one another and yet coinciding.

On the other side of Bleston's center, beyond the murky river, lies an amorphous zone, wide and encircling, rambling and with vague boundaries lost in spectral fog. This gray area, larger by far than the center that it envelops, is both the body of the city containing a minute heart—which is the city itself—and the main bloodline leading to that heart. Very different on the one hand from its more elegant core, it has the self-same qualities of torpor and energy. Also, the vague confines it represents are as illusory as those of the dark river in the center of the city, with Hades stretching out beyond it in perpetual and sinister shadows. In the periphery, continuity is suggested precisely by that vagueness of the boundaries, and movement is caught in the cyclical changes of the fair's location. What is interesting is that both continuity and movement are only tantalizing forces within their respective contexts, both in the center and on the outskirts of town. The Old Cathedral's naves are in fact deserted now, banished to total oblivion. This symbol of duration and history is thus plunged in lifeless silence. And the periphery with its boundless spaces beyond the city is merely a shadowy path leading nowhere, as Revel discovers on his one outing in search of a change. The impression of dissimilarity between the outer and inner cores of the city is thus one that contains both the image of truth and its mask.

It may appear irrelevant to establish a complete relationship between the deceptively double aspect of Bleston and the personality of Horace Buck. Yet *Passing Time* is, in a way, patterned along the lines of the detective novel, and it makes the same demands of perception and apprehended associations. What in a different work would be considered merely symbolic is here to be seen as a clue to the mysteries therein. The black man and the black city are, in fact, separate manifestations of the same principle of duality and indivisibility. If the city's periphery and its heart are basically one and the same in spite of obvious differences, Horace Buck's quiet demeanor on the surface is an expression of the rebellion contained within, and his heart in revolt yearns for the peace and the kindness that show on his face.

When Revel first meets the black man during his early stay in Bleston he is received with friendliness and generosity. But these two qualities represent only one side of the bonds that unite the two foreigners. Deeper, yet immediately recognizable, is the current of resentment and fear, which draws them together and makes them brothers in hate. For Horace Buck is as calmly passive and acquiescing on the surface as is the city of Bleston, and equally ravaged by the furious desire to hold and to destroy. If the sad smile on his face suggests easy acceptance, his words on the very first day belie this demeanor. "Are you ashamed because a colored man has paid for your lunch?" he asks, and one senses here all the challenge the question contains. The mysterious inner life of Horace Buck is caught in the reverberation of the successive fires he has perhaps ignited; yet that same heart in revolt holds a dream, a longing, a need for love. He wanders along the streets of the despicable city with his love and his hate, the kindness and the vindictiveness that are extensions of his indomitable spirit and his perishability. Like the cathedrals in the center of town or the shapeless area surrounding that center, he has the endurance of stone and the limitations assigned to it. Like Bleston, which holds them all, he is a part of that same city, a microcosm of its uniformity and the insidious power of hatred.

The first section, written between May 1 and May 30 and covering the events of October when Revel first arrived in Bleston, comes to a close with his acquisition of a detective novel, *The Bleston Murder*. The title, both in its English translation and in the original French (*Le Meurtre de Bleston*) contains an obvious double meaning. Here, too, ambiguity takes the reader, and the narrator himself, to a false lead. They both fail to perceive until much later that the murder *in* Bleston is only as real or as illusory as the murder *of* Bleston. The complicated story within the story—the killing of a brother in the book by Hamilton, whose real name is not Hamilton but Burton, the likelihood of its being patterned after a possible fratricide in the city, the betrayal of the author's identity through Revel's revelation of his name, and the possibility that the author Burton becomes through this the victim of a murderous trap—reinforces the impression of labyrinthine paths full of mock answers and unreliable trails. The ancient murder of Cain depicted in the stained-glass window of the Old Cathedral throws a shadow upon the more recent past and the events in Hamilton's book. The brother's killing is caught here within that shadow and projects its enlarged shape into the present and the life of Bleston. And here humanity is finally held, in helplessness, ignorance and fratricidal blood. The myth becomes reality, and truth is encapsuled in the fable. Jacques Revel, imprisoned in the red glow cast from Cain's window and mesmerized by the oscillations of his own conscience, gradually slips within the trap of old evils. Vanity triumphs, and, in his unconscious game of seduction with the two Bailey sisters, he reveals the name of the author of *The Bleston Murder*. The betrayal, the revelation that Hamilton is only a pen name and that the real name is Burton, becomes, symbolically, the "murder of his brother" and the obsessive focus of Revel's quest. He wants to see more clearly, to understand fully, his role and the events around him; but the threads he holds are slippery and soon become a tangled mass.

If Revel's quest for truth is not successful, his failure is due to his insistence upon the totality of truth. More ambitious than Proust's hero Marcel, who made no claim upon objectivity, he is as unwilling to renounce factual reality as he is unable to disentangle his emotions from it. It is as if he wanted to walk all paths at the same time and to leave no stone unturned, and as if each stone were to be firmly held in shape, color and impression. Determined to embrace the elusive truth of Bleston, he turns to the written word. Through his diaries he wants to relive his experiences as they appeared in the past, and to them he means to add his knowledge of the present. The result, however, is a series of images reflected through changing mirrors, and in which reality becomes fused with the dream. The failure of Jacques Revel to come to terms with his past could be seen here as an indictment of literature, for it is through his journal (which is the book one finally reads, *Passing Time*) that he endeavors to succeed. This could amount to what Leo Spitzer calls "the annihilation of the novel."[6] But the novel does exist and its reality is unchallengeable, even if it makes no claim upon truth. The narrator's quest may well end in a confused mass in which intuition, facts, warning signs, dreams, and impressions are inextricably mingled; but that mass is composed of impressionistic blotches of colors from which slowly emerge design and shape. It is here that "truth" is caught, within the incantatory presence of a city delineated in man's longing and fear.

The second chapter, "Portents," explores the possible ties between the novel bought in October and the events that followed. It is here that the chronological presentation begins to get tangled and truth becomes more elusive. The first entry, dated June 2, rather than picking up what followed the day of October 27 (to which the previous entry of May 30 had led) refers directly to the events of the night before, or of June 1. The link between the two dates is not clear yet, either to the reader or to Revel himself; only instinct pushes two separate days across the distance of seven months and draws them together.[7] The memorable event on October 27 was the acquisition of *The Bleston Murder*, the detective novel that contains the story of brotherly betrayal and murder. Here the title, ambiguously echoing the wickedness of the town, finds a sympathetic response in Revel's embittered soul.

> What I hoped to find in the author, this J. C. Hamilton, was not merely an entertainer but, on the strength of the title of his book, an accomplice against the town, a magician familiar with its peculiar perils, who would arm me with spells potent enough to enable me to defy these and survive undefeated my year's ordeal in this place, of whose powers of subtle corruption and patient erosion I was not yet fully aware. [P. 56]

From the first, Revel feels kinship with the yet unknown author, the same instinctive kinship that had led him to befriend Horace Buck, dictated by the hatred for Bleston and the hope of finding an accomplice in the unavowed desire to destroy the city. He eventually meets Hamilton, befriends him, and discovers his true identity and his name, Burton. This identity, which has been confided in secret, is revealed to the Bailey sisters on June 1. The pervasive hatred for the city that had led to the purchase of the book now brings about the act of betrayal. Revel's search for an accomplice and his readiness to use charm or "spells" against the city has ironically already plunged him into those very evils he wanted to oppose. The corrupting force of Bleston that made him select one book among so many on display in the window of Barron's bookstore is thus at the root of his betrayal seven months later. That betrayal is unwittingly also an act of "charm" intended to gain the sympathy of the sisters.

The impression made by my words was far greater than I had ex-

pected. ...Ann and Rose started simultaneously... "Do you
know the author of *The Bleston Murder*?" [P. 62]

Both Ann and Rose are full of admiring surprise, smiling, ap-
preciative; they are, in a way, conquered. But from this conquest
will slowly rise obsessive questions, linked to a tormented conscience and the act of betrayal. Thus the need to crystallize events,
impressions, and all the deluded hopes springing within the city will
inspire Jacques Revel to write his diaries. Page after page, the diary
will capture the stay in Bleston. Like accumulating bricks, on the
left corner of the desk and resting upon the map full of intricate
lines, they will form the visible structure opposing the forces of the
hallucinating city. And so it is that the purchase of the book and
the revelation to the sisters are linked with the confrontation with the
city, and with the city's final surrender within the pages of the journal.

The third chapter is called "The Accident." The word *accident*
on the title page appears in quotation marks, suggesting some ambiguity, or at least uncertainty—a warning, to the reader, that the
word must not be taken at face value. As the journal progresses,
that ambiguity remains unclear and is even compounded with new
doubts and intricacies. There may or may not have been an accident, or perhaps it was an attempted murder. George William Burton, whose pen name is J. C. Hamilton, may have been the chosen
victim of a hit-and-run incident, or merely a fortuitous one. What
is interesting, in fact, is not really the hidden truth, whatever that
happens to be; the reader hardly cares if there was an act of
vengeance and fear involved, or if the whole mishap was an error
and only incidentally bloody. What seems more important is that
the spell of Bleston so molds the events that the resulting confusion
is itself permeated with the haunting quality of the city.

The city never lets go, it seems. It could be argued here that it is
the vision of the narrator that is unclear and hence distorts every
object around him. But mine is not a psychological study of Jacques Revel, and I accept what he "reveals" quite literally, as if the
reader were borrowing his sight. What the reader sees is equally
haunting, with the eerie quality of a nightmare, the unreality of
endless bleak roads and human shadows gripped with fear:

Even at midday the few passers-by, hugging the walls, humming
to themselves with lowered heads as if it were black night. [P. 94]

Revel knows, in effect, that the phantoms surrounding him are
conjured by his feverish eye. But his powerlessness to lift the
obscuring curtain comes from the endless rain and the sooty vapors
of the streets.

When at last I tear myself away from Bleston, from that Circe
and her sinister spells, when, set free at last, I shall find it possible to recover my human shape, to wash my eyes clear. [P. 119]

Revel knows that it is not so much his own vision that is naturally
deformed, as it is the city that distorts its focus. Bleston, with its
hidden torrents of passions and the calm display of uniformity, is
the key to its own movement and civilization, just as the labyrinth
became the symbol of decay in Minoan culture.

As the pages of the journal accumulate, an increasing sense of
fatigue is introduced, the exhaustion from pushing, day after day,
deeper into the dark maze of the city. The end is hidden
somewhere, within a date that spells September 30. But "hatred
destroys time"[8] remarks Leo Spitzer, and that date is a mere
abstraction with little or no relevance to the struggles of the present. Time, circumvented by the ticking of the clock and the span
of a year, stands still. In endless repetition the struggle continues,
halted, resumed, oscillating between the ensnaring appeal of abandon and the urge to endure. Pushed by the mysterious designs of
the city, Revel advances along the circular paths, finding himself
over and over again in the same spots—the same events, the same
recurring dates haunting his memory. And more and more the intricate pattern of Bleston introduced from the very first acquires
through repetition the maleficent image of decay. To be able to
escape from all this, at any price—to give up all, even love—is all
that matters. Jacques Revel wavers between the temptations to
keep on fighting to the end and that of surrender. He burns the city
in effigy, but the flames that destroy the map of Bleston leave the
city itself unscathed, while symbolically they demolish the secret to
its exit. It is the mere fumbling of youthful vigor wielding a weapon

with an inexpert hand. Only time will show the way and measure Revel's strength against that of the monstrous city. Only in the journal will he find the right weapon and a lasting conquest.

The last two chapters, "The Two Sisters" and "The Adieu," explore the temptation of surrender to the city and the will to resist. The attraction of love—a love that is rebutted by the two girls on the one hand, and on the other remains basically unexpressed—is not different from the lull of sleep in Theseus's legend and the fight against it. Jacques Revel would like to let himself go, to blend with the amorphous city and accept perhaps the easy bliss of family life. He thus allows his imagination to roam the gardens of sentiment. But restraint and the urge not to bow to conformity instinctively prevent him from confessing his love and asking to be loved in return. Thus the battle against this type of surrender unconsciously waged is easily won.

The more difficult trial is that waged against the supreme symbol of resistance in opposition to the city: the journal itself. To burn and destroy this last bastion of strength would amount to a cry of impotence before total defeat.

> ...and when on Saturday I came back here and saw all these pages piled up, scored with line after line of writing ...I was overcome with a wild longing to burn them one after the other completely, meticulously, without leaving one scrap....It was the number, the time, the weight, which kept me from obeying that insidious, persistent counselor, permitted me to wait for the voice to grow weary or to change. [Pp. 268—69]

While the burning of the map of Bleston had symbolically made it more difficult to escape from the city, the destruction of the journal could only have amounted to a total surrender to the city and a renunciation of independence in the outside world. But the "insidious" voice is stilled and temptation is resisted. When the danger is over and strength regained, the city still looms behind, larger than life. But tall before it stands a pile of sheets, painful reminder of a city conceived in hatred and yet a bulwark, too, the monument holding that city in bondage. Within those sheets—the diaries, Revel's journal—reside the perilous avenues, the shadows and misty lights of Bleston, the treacherous refuge, the labyrinth of deceptive hopes and stultifying slumber. On the actual city, built of stones and roads and encompassed in geographical measurements and factual reality, are thus superimposed the magic transparency of the written word and the echoes that are hence thrust into a new artistic truth.

Notes to Chapter 10

1. The quotations in this chapter are taken from Michel Butor, *Passing Time*, trans. Jean Stewart (New York: Simon and Schuster, 1960).

2. Lucien Dällenbach sees a strong contrast between the unidimensional quality in Butor's work and Proust's concept of space. He calls Butor's relation to place and time "epidermic," a purely personal, undefined but geometrically constructed, irrational but functional, reality of space (in *Le Nouveau Roman* [Paris: Garnier, 1972], pp. 148-50).

3. J. H. Matthews, in his interesting article on Butor (in *La Revue des Lettres Modernès*, nos. 94-99 [1964], Pp. 51-66), discusses the "alchemy" of Revel's search and the symbolism of events, which cannot be detected before the events take place, but only retrospectively—flexibly, changeably—reveals their tenuous presence.

4. Vivian Mercier, *The New Novel* (New York: Farrar, Straus and Giroux, 1971), p. 246.

5. For a complete breakdown of the time system employed by Butor, see Mercier, *The New Novel*, Pp. 242—44.

6. See Leo Spitzer, *Etudes de Style* (Paris: Gallimard, 1970), p. 487.

7. The sequence of dates in the novel points to an obsessive quest for truth, and, while it can be mathematically traced, its jumbled appearance reflects the confusion in the hero's perception and, perhaps, the impossibility of ever coming fully to terms with the flight of time. John Sturrock points to the *limitation* and the circularity imposed on time in the novel: "Ultimately, of course, he has to admit that these researches will never be complete; he quite literally does not have the time. In fact there is a somewhat skittish lacuna in Revel's timetable: at the end of *L'Emploi du Temps* he explains that he has no time left to record the events of one particular day during his year in Bleston—the previous February the twenty-ninth. But it would be misleading to assume that because of this he was only foiled by a leap-year—Revel's stay in Bleston is arbitrarily limited, and if it continued he would have to return over and over again to what he had already written in order to amplify or correct it" (John Sturrock, *The French New Novel* [London: Oxford University Press, 1969], p. 167).

8. Spitzer, *Etudes de Style* p. 494.

Conclusion

The only fitting conclusion to a study of the city in modern novels is, possibly, that there is none available. Cities vary in time and location, and so does the artistic eye that captures them within the pages of a book. Yet the problems presented by cities—or by their beauty, one might add—appear unchanged even from distant perspectives. In his chapter "Fourth-Century urban Inventory," Lewis Mumford (*The City in History* [New York: Harcourt, Brace and World, 1961], p. 237) discusses the ills of ancient Rome, or what he calls "megalopolitan elephantiasis." Those ills are the same today, he concludes, and Rome "remains, in its vastness and confusion, the complete embodiment of purposeless materialism."

Literary appraisal of city life cannot be based on empirical evidence, however. The city is a poetical source of inspiration for novelists, and from it images emerge that both resemble the shapes of cities and transcend them. The individuality of a city rests more on personal selections and views than on historical vouchers. Yet this is not to say that literature is of negligible sociological value. We know that sociology itself does not rely merely on cumulative data, and that it does not shun personal interpretations or psychological analysis altogether. It is precisely in these areas that literature can come to the aid of sociology, just as observations of social dealings may initially have inspired, and are eventually found at the core of, the work of art. That a city such as Paris, for instance, could be seen in so many different ways by so many writers, does not mean that the reality of Paris resides outside their individual optics and must therefore be sought beyond the world of letters. Art is a purified, unemcumbered form of truth, as valid in its restricted presentations of the city as any individual's laboratory research might be.

Are ten novels sufficient to draw the portrait of the city in all of its vast elements? Of course not, the answer must be—and yes, at the same time. These do not present merely ten individual points of view. They are more like condensed surveys and microcosmic worlds. Singly, they draw powerful paintings, each encapsuled in its own frame and yet thrusting their illuminations well beyond their respective limitations. Together, they offer a kaleidoscopic image in which colors and shapes change in prismatic effect. Each new image catches the compounded lights and apprehensions that are reflected upon it. This is to say that the values caught in the work of art rely to a great extent upon sensitivity and the discerning eye, before they can assume their rightful dimension and cast echoes into the distance.

What is the essential difference, one might wonder, between a purely sociological study of the city and a literary one? Would the inferences differ between a statistical presentation of a slum area and, say, Zola's portrait of Rue Neuve de la Goutte d'Or, where Gervaise of *L'Assommoir* watches the disintegration of all her dreams? Most likely the conclusions about the destructive power of poverty and rootlessness would be the same in both instances. It would emerge from both types of work that overcrowding and unemployment undermine not merely the individuals affected but also the moral fabric of a society. Still, what computerized results would probably neglect is the dimension and the pathos of human suffering.

"Art should not only be the concentrated filth at the bottom," wrote Theodore Dreiser, "but the wonder and the mystery of the ideals at the top" (from the Sunday, September 28, 1912, issue of the *New York Evening Post*). Studies of behavioral patterns such as those devised by Durkheim could on the one hand bring attention to the frightful recurrence of the same problems presented by city life; but on the other, the shape of the individual and the dimentions of his will might not receive their due. Literature is more prone to project through the individual the macrocosmic world of cities that stretches beyond his reach. That world is composed of small crannies and immense expanses simultaneously, all of them imbued with the magnitude of the dream. "O yes," wrote Hart Crane to Gorham Munson[1] on March 2, 1923, "the 'background of life' and all that is still there, but that is only three-dimensional. It is to the pulse of a greater dynamism that my work must revolve. Something terribly fierce and yet gentle." That is, in essence, the shape of the city as I hope it has emerged from a study of ten novels, "something terribly fierce and yet gentle."

NOTE TO CONCLUSION

1. *The Letters of Hart Crane*, ed. Brom Weber (New York: Heritage House, 1952), p. 129.

Selected Bibliography

Introduction: The City

Bourdin, Alain. "La Ville, dans le miroir de l'Ancien. Le Cas Tours." *Stanford French Review*, Spring 1977, pp. 107-21.

Caillois, Roger. "Paris, mythe moderne." *Nouvelle Revue Fra caise*, May 1937, pp. 682-99.

Chevalier, Louis. *Classes laborieuses et classes dangereuses à Pa pendant la Ire moitié du XIXe siècle*. Paris: Plon, 1958. Trai lated as *Labouring Classes and Dangerous Classes*. New Yor Howard Fertig, 1973.

Churchill, Henry S. *The City is the People*. 1945. New ed. N York: Norton, 1962.

Citron, Pierre. *La Poésie de Paris dans la Littérature française Rousseau à Baudelaire*. 2 vols. Paris: Edition de Minuit, 196

Dyos, H. L. *Urban History Yearbook 1974*. Leicester: The Univ sity Press, 1974.

Gelfant, Blanche. *The American City Novel*. 1954. New ed. N man, Olka.: University of Oklahoma Press, 1970.

Granet, Paul. *Changer la Ville*. Paris: Grasset, 1975.

Gravier, Jean-François. *Paris et le Désert français*. 1947. Pai Flammarion, 1958.

Hoffet, Frédéric. *Psychanalyse de Paris*. Paris: Grasset, 1973.

Howe, Irving. "The City in Literature." In *The Critical Point: Literature and Culture*. New York: Horizon Press, 1973.

Le Corbusier. *The City of Tomorrow*. Cambridge, Mass.: T MIT Press, 1971.

Ledrut, Raymond. *Les Images de la Ville*. Paris: Anthropos, 19

Lynch, Kevin. *The Images of the City*. Cambridge, Mass.: M Press, 1962.

Maurice, Arthur Bartlett. *The New York of the Novelists*. N York: Dodd, Mead and Co., 1916.

————. *The Paris of the Novelists*. New York: Doubleday, Page and Co., 1919.

Mumford, Lewis. *The City in History: Its Origins, its Transformations and its Prospects*. New York: Harcourt, Brace and World, 1961.

————. *From the Ground Up*. 1949. New York: Harcourt, Brace, 1956.

Schlesinger, Arthur. *The Rise of the City 1878-1898*. New York: MacMillan, 1933.

Steffens, Lincoln. *The Shame of the Cities*. New York: McClure, Phillips & Co., 1904.

Welsh, Alex. *The City of Dickens*. Oxford: Clarendon Press, 1971.

Wright, Frank Lloyd. *An Autobiography*. New York: Dell, Sloan and Pearce, 1943.

Chapter 1: Balzac's *Girl with the Golden Eyes*

Balzac, Honoré de. *The Thirteen and Other Stories*. Translated by Ernest Dowson. New York: Groscup and Sterling Company, 1901.

Barbéris, Pierre. *Balzac et le Mal du Siècle*. 2 vol. Paris: Gallimard, 1970.

Bardèche, Maurice. *Une Lecture de Balzac*. Paris: Les Sept Couleurs, 1964.

Béguin, Albert. "La Fille aux Yeux d'Or." *Fontaine* 52 (May 1946): 729-38.

————. *Balzac Visionnaire*. Geneva: Edition Albert Skira, 1946.

Bellos, David. *Balzac Criticism in France, 1850-1900*. Oxford: Clarendon Press, 1976.

Bersani, Leo. *Balzac to Beckett*. New York: Oxford University Press, 1970.

Bilodeau, François. *Balzac et le Jeu des Mots*. Montreal: Presses de l'Université, 1971.

Bolster, Richard. *Stendhal, Balzac et le Féminisme romantique*. Paris: Minard, 1970.

Bonard, Olivier. *La Peinture dans la Création balzacienne. Inventions et Visions picturales de La Maison du Chat qui pelote au Père Goriot*. Geneva: Droz, 1969.

Butor, Michel. "Balzac et la Réalité." *Nouvelle Revue Française*, August 1959, pp. 228-47. Also in Butor. *Répertoire I*. Paris: Editions de Minuit, 1960. Pp. 79-93.

Chevalier, Louis. *Classes laborieuses et Classes dangereuses à Paris pendant la lre Moitié du XIXe Siècle*. Paris: Plon, 1958. (On "The Girl with the Golden Eyes," pp. 487-88.)

Conner, Wayne. "La Composition de *La Fille aux Yeux d'Or*." *Revue des Sciences Humaines*, Oct.-Dec.- 1956, pp. 81-84.

Curtius, Ernst Robert. "Balzac et l'Amour." *Revue de Paris*, no. 20, Oct. 1933, pp. 815-34.

————. *Balzac*. Paris: Grasset, 1933.

Delattre, Geneviève. "De Séraphita à la Fille aux Yeux d'Or." *L'Année Balzacienne* (1970), pp. 183-226.

Drent, Janke. "Balzac et le Nom de Paquita Valdes." *L'Anneê Balzacienne (1974), pp. 325-26.*

Gheude, Michel. *"La Vision colorée dans La Fille aux Yeux d'Or."* *Synthèses*, July-August 1970, pp. 44-49.

Hemmings, F. W. J. *Balzac. An Interpretation of La Comédie Humaine*. New York: Random House, 1967.

Kanes, Martin. *Balzac's Comedy of Words*. Princeton, N. J.: Princeton University Press, 1975.

Laubriet, Pierre. *L'Intelligence de l'Art chez Balzac*. Paris: Didier, 1961.

Mozet, Nicole. "Les Prolétaires dans La Fille aux Yeux d'Or." *L'Année Balzacienne* (1974), pp. 91-120.

Philip, Michel. "Balzac's Heaven and Hell." *Yale French Studies* 32 (1964): 79-83.

Poncin-Bar, Geneviève. "Aspects fantastiques de Paris dans les Romans de Balzac." *L'Année Balzacienne* (1974), pp. 227-44.

Stevenson, Norah. *Paris dans la Comédie Humaine de Balzac*. Paris: Georges Courville, 1938.

Chapter 2: Zola's *L'Assommoir*

Albérès, René Marill. *"Que revèle L'Assommoir* en 1967:" *Revue de Paris* 74 Feb. 1967): 51-59.

Block, Haskell M. *Naturalistic Triptych*. New York: Random House, 1970.

Bédé, Jean-Albert. *Emile Zola*. New York: Columbia University Press, 1974.

Brown, Calvin S. *Repetition in Zola's Novels*. Athens, Ga.: University of Georgia Press, 1952.

Gauthier, Guy. "Zola et les Images." *Europe* 468-69 (April-May 1968): 400-415.

Grant, Elliot M. *Zola*. New York: Twayne, 1966.

Hemmings, F. W. J. *Emile Zola*. 1966. Oxford: Clarendon Press, 1953.

―――. "The present Position in Zola's Studies." *French Studies* (Oxford) 10 (1956): 97-122.

Kranowski, Nathan. *Paris dans les Romans de Zola*. Paris: Presses Universitaires, 1968.

Leroy, Maxime. "Le Prolétariat vu par Zola dans *L'Assommoir*." *Preuves* 20 (October 1952): 72-75.

Levin, Harry. *The Gates of Horn: A Study of Five French Realists*. New York: Oxford University Press, 1963. Pp. 305-71.

Matthews, J. M. *Les deux Zola*. Geneva: Droz, 1957.

Max, Stephan. *Les Métamophoses de la grande Ville dans les Rougon-Macquart*. Paris: Nizet, 1966.

Mitterand, Henri. Edition of *Les Rougon-Macquart*. Vol. 2. Paris: Gallimard, 1961. Pp. 1532-1566, notice on *L'Assommoir*.

Robert, Guy. *Emile Zola*. Paris: Les Belles Lettres, 1952.

Schorr, Naomi. "Zola: from Window to Window." *Yale French Studies 42 (1969): 38-51.*

Wilson, Angus. *Emile Zola. An Introductory Study of his Novels*. New York: William Morrow and Co., 1952.

Zola, Emile. *L'Assommoir*. Translated by Leonard Tancock. Baltimore, Md.: Penguin, 1974.

―――. *Une Page d'Amour*. Paris: Garnier-Flammarion, 1973.

Chapter 3: D'Annunzio's *Child of Pleasure*

D'Annunzio, Gabriele. *The Child of Pleasure*. Translated by Georgina Harding. Boston: Page and Company, 1906.

Gullace, Giovanni. *Gabriele D'Annunzio in France*. Syracuse, N. Y.: Syracuse University Press, 1966. Chap. 2, on the reception of the "novels of the rose" in France.

Meozzi, Antero. *Significato della Vita e dell'Opera de D'Annunzio*. 2 vols. Pisa: Vallerini, 1929.

Pasini, Ferdinando. *Gabriele D'Annunzio*. Rome: Stock, 1925. On "the cycle of the rose," pp. 205-30.

Schiliró, Vincenzo. *L'Arte di Gabriele D'Annunzio*. Rome: Societá editrice internazionale, 1948. Chap. 3, pp. 21-32, on the psychological novels.

Stauble, Antonio. "D'Annunzio Poète de Rome" (inaugural lecture at Lausanne, August 23, 1970). In *Etudes de Lettres* 4, no. 3 (July-September 1971).

Chapter 4: Rilke's *Notebooks*

Angelloz, J. F. *Rilke*. Paris: Hartmann, 1936.

Batterby, Kenneth A. J. *Rilke and France: A Study in Poetic De velopment*. London: Oxford University Press, 1966.

Bauer, Marga. *Rainer Maria Rilke und Frankreich*. Bern: Haupt, 1931.

Betz, Maurice. *Rilke à Paris et les Cahiers de Malte Laurids Brigge*. Paris: Emile-Paul, 1941.

Butler, Eliza Marian. *Rainer Maria Rilke*. Cambridge: At the University Press, 1941.

Goertz, Hartmann. *Frankreich und das Erlebnis der Form im Werke R. M. Rilkes*. Stuttgart: Metzler, 1932.

Holthusen, Hans Egon. *Rainer Maria Rilke: A Study of His Later Poetry*. Translated by J. P. Stern. New Haven, Conn.: Yale University Press, 1952.

Jaccottet, Philippe. *Rilke par lui-même*. Paris: Seuil, 1970.

Peters, H. F. *Rainer Maria Rilke: Masks and the Man*. Seattle, Wash.: University of Washington Press, 1960. Chapter 4, "Hamlet in Paris," pp. 69-95.

Rilke, Rainer Maria. *Letters. 1892-1910*. Translated by Jane B. Greene and M. D. Herter Norton. New York: W. W. Norton and Co., 1945.

———. *The Notebooks of Malte Laurids Brigge*. Translated by M. D. Herter Norton. New York: W. W. Norton and Co., 1949.

Chapter 5: Proust's *Remembrance of Things Past*

Note: No bibliography relating to Proust's work can long remain up to date. The most useful ones—in works by Alden, Bonnet, and de Chantal—are listed herein.

Albouy, Pierre. "Quelques Images et Structures mythiques dans *La Recherche du Temps perdu*." *Revue d' Histoire littéraire de la France* 71, nos 5-6 (Sept.-Dec. 1971): 972-87.

Alden, Douglas. *Marcel Proust and his French Critics*. Los Angeles, Calif.: Lymanhouse, 1940.

Alley, John. "Proust and Art. The Anglo-American critical View." *Revue de Littérature Comparée* 29e (Sept. 1963): 410-30.

Bardèche, Maurice. *Marcel Proust romancier*. Vol. 1 Paris: Les Sept Couleurs, 1971.

Barker, Richard. *Proust, a Biography*. New York: Criterion, 1958.

Bailey, Ninette. "Le Rôle des Couleurs dans la Genèse de l'Univers proustien." *Modern Language Review* 60, no. 2 (April 1965): 188-96.

Bell, William Stewart. *Proust's Nocturnal Muse.* New York: Columbia University Press, 1962.

Bersani, Leo. *Marcel Proust: The Fictions of Life and of Art.* New York: Oxford University Press, 1965.

Bonnet, Henri. *Le Progrès spirituel dans l'Oeuvre de M. Proust.* 2 Vols. Paris: Vrin, 1946.

———. *Marcel Proust de 1907 à 1914.* Paris: Nizet, 1959.

Brée, Germaine. *Proust and Deliverance from Time.* New Brunswick, N.J.: Rutgers University Press, 1950.

———. "La Conception proustienne de l'Esprit." *Cahiers de l'Association internationale des Etudes françaises,* no. 12, June 1960, pp. 199-210.

Bucknall, Barbara J. *The Religion of Art in Proust.* Urbana, Ill.: University of Illinois Press, 1969.

Busson, T. W. "Proust and Painting." *Romantic Review* 34 (Febr. 1943): 54-70.

Butor, Michel. *Les Oeuvres d'Art imaginaires chez Proust.* London: Athlone Press, 1963. Also in *Répertoires II.* Paris: Edition de Minuit, 1964. Pp. 252-92.

———. "Entre les 'Mille et une Nuits' et 'Barbebleue.'" *Le Monde,* July 9, 1971, p. 15. (The Proust-Ruskin relationship is seen here as having the same importance as the Baudelaire-Poe relationship.)

Chernowitz, Maurice. *Proust and Painting.* New York: International University Press, 1945.

Cocking, J. M. *Proust.* London: Bowes and Bowes; New Haven, Conn.: Yale University Press, 1956.

———. "Proust and Painting." In *French XIXth Century Painting and Literature.* Edited by Ulrich Finke. Manchester: Manchester University Press; New York: Harper and Row, 1972. Pp. 305-24.

Coleman, Elliott. *The Golden Angel.* New York: Corey Taylor, 1954.

De Chantal, René. *Marcel Proust Critique littéraire.* 2 vols. Montreal: Presses de l'Université, 1967.

Deleuze, Gilees. *Proust et les Signes.* Paris: P.U.F., 1964.

Doubrovsky, Serge. *La Place de la Madeleine. Ecriture et fantasme chez Proust.* Paris: Mercure de France, 1974.

Ferré, André. *Geographie de Marcel Proust*. Paris: Sagittaire, 1939.

Graham, Victor. *The Imagery of Proust*. New York: Columbia University Press, 1954.

———. "Proust's Alchemy." *Modern Language Review* 60, no. 2 (April 1965): 188-96.

Kadi, Simone. *Proust et Baudelaire. Influences et Affinités électives*. Paris: La Pensée Universelle, 1976.

Kolb, Philip. "Proust et Ruskin: nouvelles Perspectives." *Cahiers des Etudes françaises*, no. 12, June 1960, pp. 256-74.

La Sizeranne, Robert de. *Proust et la Religion de la Beauté*. Paris: Hachette, 1897.

Matoré, Georges et Mecz, Irène. *Musique et Structure romanesque dans La Recherche du Temps perdu*. Paris: Klincksieck, 1972.

Megay, Joyce N. *Bergson et Proust. Essai de Mise au Point*. Paris: Uron, 1976.

Milly, Jean. *Les Pastiches de Proust*. Paris: A. Colin, 1970.

———. *Proust et le Style*. Paris: Minard, 1970.

Monnin-Hartung, Juliette. *Proust et la Peinture*. Geneva: Droz, 1961.

Painter, George D. *Marcel Proust: a Biography*. 2 Vols. London: Chatto and Windus, 1959-65.

Picon, Gaetan. *Lecture de Proust*. Paris: Gallimard, 1963.

Piroué, Georges. *Proust et la Musique du Devenir*. Paris: Denoël, 1960.

Poulet, Georges. *L'Espace proustien*. Paris: Gallimard, 1963.

Price, Larkin B. *Marcel Proust. A Critical Panorama*. Urbana, Ill.: University of Illinois Press, 1973.

Proust, Marcel. *Pastiches et Mélanges*. Paris: N.R.F., 1921. On Ruskin, pp. 148-97.

———. *Remembrance of Things Past*. Translated by C. K. Scott Moncrieff. 2 vols. New York: Random House, 1934.

Shattuck, Roger. *Proust's Binoculars*. New York: Random House, 1963.

Souza, Sybil de. *L'Influence de Ruskin sur Proust*. Montpellier: La Charité, 1932.

Stambolian, George. *Marcel Proust and the Creative Encounter*. Chicago: University of Chicago Press, 1972.

Tadié, Jean-Yves. *Proust et le Roman*. Paris: Gallimard, 1971.

———. *Lectures de Proust*. Paris: A. Colin, 1971.

Terdiman, Richard. *The Dialectics of Isolation*. New Haven, Conn.: Yale University Press, 1976.

Ullmann, Stephen, "Transposition of Sensations in Proust's Imagery." *French Studies* 8, no. 1 (January 1954): 28-41.

Vogely, Maxime Arnold. *Italy in the Life and Works of Marcel Proust*. Ph.D. dissertation, University of Illinois, 1969.

Wolitz, Seth. *The Proustian Community*. New York: New York University Press, 1971.

Zima. P. V. *Le Désir du Mythe. Une Lecture sociologique de Proust*. Paris: Nizet, 1974.

Chapter 6: Bely's *Saint Petersburg*

Bater, James H. *St. Peterburg, Industrialization and Change*. London: Edwin Arnold, 1976.

Bely, Andrei. *Saint Petersburg*. Translated by John Cournos. New York, Grove Press, 1959.

Cioran, Samuel D. *The Apocalyptic Symbolism of Andrej Belyj*. The Hague: Mouton, 1975.

Elsworth, J. D. *Andrey Bely*. Letchworth, England: Bradda Books, 1972.

Poggioli, Renato. *The Poets of Russia. 1890-1930*. Cambridge, Mass.: Harvard University Press, 1960.

Steveni, William Barnes. *Petrograd Past and Present*. London: Grant Richards, 1915.

Chapter 7: Romain's *Death of a Nobody*

Boak, Denis. *Jules Romains*. New York: Twayne Press, 1974.

Bourin, André. *Connaissance de Jules Romains: Essai de Géographie littéraire*. Paris: Flammarion, 1961.

Cuisenier, André. 3 vols.: *Jules Romains et l'Unanimisme, L'Art de Jules Romains, Jules Romains et les Hommes de bonne Volonté*. Paris: Flammarion, 1935-54.

Ehrenfels, W. *Das unanimistische Bewusstsein im Werke J. Romains*. Greifswald: University Press, 1940.

Romains, Jules. *Death of a Nobody*. Translated by Desmond MacCarthy and Sidney Waterlow. New York: Boni and Liveright, 1925.

Chapter 8: Dos Passos's *Manhattan Transfer*

Astre, Georges Albert. *Thèmes et Structures dans l'Oeuvre de J. Dos Passos*. Paris: Minard, 1956.

Blake, N. M. *Novelists' America: Fiction as History, 1920-1940.* Syracuse, N.Y.: Syracuse University Press, 1969. See the chap. entitled "The Rebels."

Dos Passos, John. *Manhattan Transfer.* Boston: Houghton Mifflin, 1925.

Gelfant, Blanche. *The American City Novel.* Norman, Okla.: University of Oklahoma Press, 1954. Gelfant's "The Synoptic Novel" appears in Hook, ed., *Dos Passos* (see below), pp. 36-52.

Hook, Andrew, ed. *Dos Passos: A Collection of Critical Essays.* Englewood Cliffs, N.J.: Prentice-Hall, 1974.

Kazin, Alfred. *On Native Grounds.* New York: Harcourt, Brace, 1942. See "All the Lost Generations," pp. 341-59.

Krause, S. J. *Essays on Determinism in American Literature.* Kent, Ohio: Kent State University Press, 1969. See John Lydenberg's "Dos Passos: *U.S.A.*"

Lowry, E. D. "*Manhattan Transfer:* Dos Passos' Wasteland." In Hook, ed., *Dos Passos* (see above), pp. 53-69. Reprinted from *The University Review* (Mo., 1963).

Magny, Claude Edmonde. "La Trilogie de Dos Passos ou le Roman impersonnel" and "Le Temps chez Dos Passos." *L'Age du Roman américain.* Paris: Seuil, 1948. Pp. 117-58.

Millgate, Michael. *American Social Fiction.* New York: Barnes & Noble, 1964.

Sartre, J. P. "A Propos de J. Dos Passos et de '1919.'" *Situations I.* Paris: Gallimard, 1947. Pp. 14-25. Translated as "John Dos Passos and *1919*" in Hook, ed., *Dos Passos* (see above), pp. 61-69.

Whipple, T. K. "Dos Passos and the U.S.A." *The Nation*, February 19, 1930. In Hook, ed., *Dos Passos* (see above), pp. 87-92.

Wren, John H. *John Dos Passos.* New York: Twayne, 1961.

Chapter 9: Durrell's *Alexandria Quartet*

Alyn, Marc. *Lawrence Durrell: The Big Supposer.* Translated by Francine Barker. New York: Grove Press, 1974.

Cavafy, Constantine. *Poems.* Translated by Rae Dalven. Introduction by W. H. Auden. New York: Harcourt, Brace and World, 1961.

———. *Collected Poems.* Translated by Edmund Keeley and Philip Sherrard. Princeton, N.J.: Princeton University Press, 1975.

Corke, Hilary. "Mr. Durrell and Brother Criticus." *Encounter* 14 (May 1960): 65-70.

Durrell, Lawrence. *Alexandria Quartet*. New York: E. P. Dutton, 1961.

————. *Spirit of Place: Letters and Essays on Travel*. London: Faber and Faber, 1969.

————. *Tung*. New York: E. P. Dutton and Co., 1968.

Forster, S. M. *Pharos and Pharillon*. New York: A. Knopf, 1962; London: The Hogarth Press, 1923.

————. *Alexandria: A History and a Guide*. 1922. Alexandria: Whitehead Morris Limited, 1938; New York: Anchor Books, 1961.

Fraser, G. S. *Lawrence Durrell: A Critical Study*. New York: E. P. Dutton, 1968.

Golffing, Francis. "The Alexandrian Mind: Notes toward a Definition." *The Partisan Review* 22 (Winter 1955): 73-82.

Hamard, J. P. "L'Espace et le Temps chez Durrell." *Critique* (Paris) 16 (May and December 1960): 387-413, 1025-33.

Highet, Gilbert. "The Alexandrians of Durrell." *Horizon* (London) 2 (March 1960):113-18.

Keeley, Edmund. *Alexandria: Study of a Myth in Progress*. Cambridge, Mass.: Harvard University Press, 1976.

————. "Cavafy's Mythical Alexandria." *Boston University' Journal* 23, no. 1 (Winter 1975):42-58.

Lund, Mary Graham. "Submerge for Reality: The New Novel Form of Lawrence Durrell." *The Southwest Review* 44 (Summer 1959):229-35.

Moore, Harry T., ed. *The World of Lawrence Durrell*. Carbondale, Ill.: Southern Illinois University Press, 1962.

Unterecker, John. *Lawrence Durrell*. New York: Columbia University Press, 1964.

Weigel, John A. *Lawrence Durrell*. New York: E. P. Dutton and Co., 1966.

Chapter 10: Butor's *Passing Time*

Albérès, René Marill. *Michel Butor*. Paris: Editions Universitaires, 1964.

Alter, Robert. *Partial Magic: The Novel as a Self-Conscious Genre*. Berkeley, Calif.: University of California press, 1976.

Barthes, Roland. "Littérature et Discontinu." *Le Nouveau Roman*. Paris: Garnier, 1972. Pp. 140-43.

Butor, Michel. *Passing Time*. Translated by Jean Stewart. New York: Simon and Schuster, 1960.

Dällenbach, Lucien. *Le Livre et ses Miroirs dans l'Oeuvre romanesque de Butor*. Paris: Minard, 1972.

Deguise, Pierre. "M. Butor et le 'nouveau Roman.'" *The French Review* 35, no. 2 (December 1961): 155-62.

Grant, Marian. "The Function of Myth in the Novels of Butor." In *Australian Universities Modern Language Association*, no. 32, November 1969, pp. 214-22.

Janvier, Ludovic. *Une Parole exigeante*. Paris: Editions de Minuit, 1964.

Leiris, Michel. "Le Réalisme mythologique de Michel Butor." *Le Nouveau Roman*. Paris: Garnier, 1972. Pp. 129-36.

Matthews, J. H. "Michel Butor: l'Alchimie et le Roman." *La Revue des Lettres Modernes*, nos. 94-99 (1964), pp. 50-73.

Mercier, Vivian. *The New Novel*. New York: Farrar, Straus and Giroux, 1971. Pp. 215-65.

Morrissette, Bruce. "Narrative 'You' in Contemporary Literature." *Comparative Literature Studies* 2, no. 1 (1965: 1-24.

Raillard, Georges. *Butor*. Paris: Gallimard, 1968.

Ricardou, Jean. *Le Nouveau Roman*. Paris: Seuil, 1974.

Ricardou, Jean, and Rossum-Guyon, Françoise Van, eds. *Nouveau Roman: Hier, Aujourd'hui*. 2 vols. Paris: Union Générale d'Editions, 1972.

Rossum-Guyon, Françoise Van. "L'Emergence du JE." *Le Nouveau Roman*. Paris: Garnier, 1972. Pp. 136-39.

Roudaut, Jean. *Michel Butor ou le Livre futur*. Paris: Gallimard, 1964.

Roudiez, Leon S. *Michel Butor*. New York: Columbia University Press, 1965.

St. Aubyn, F. C. "Michel Butor and Phenomenological Realism." *Studi Francesi* 6 (1962): 51-62.

Sellier, Philippe. "La Ville maudite chez Michel Butor." *Mosaic* 7, no. 2 (Winter 1975): 115-30.

Seylaz, Jean-Luc. "La Tentative romanesque de Michel Butor de *L'Emploi du Temps* à *Degrés*." *Etudes de Lettres* 2, t. 3, no. 4 (October—December 1960): 209-21.

Spencer, M. C. "The Unfinished Cathedral: Michel Butor's *L'Emploi du Temps*." *Essays in French Literature* (University of Western Australia Press), no. 6, November 1969, pp. 81-99.

Spitzer, Leo. "Quelques Aspects de la Technique des Romans de

Michel Butor." *Archivum Linguisticum* 13, facs. 2 (1961): 171-195; 14, facs. 1 (1962): 49-76.

Sturrock, John. *The French New Novel*. London: Oxford University Press, 1969. Pp. 104-69.

Walters, Jennifer R. "Butor's Juxtaposed Selves." *Essays in French Literature* (University of Western Australia Press), no. 9, Nov. 1972.

Index